EUROPEAN ART CINEMA

European art cinema includes some of the most famous films in cinema history. It is elite filmmaking that stands in direct opposition to popular cinema, and yet, it also has an intimate relationship with Hollywood.

This guidebook sketches successive phases of art cinema in Europe from its early beginnings of putting Shakespeare's plays on the screen, through movements such as Expressionism and Surrealism, to the New Waves of the 1960s and more recent incarnations like Dogme 95. Using film examples, John White examines basic critical approaches to art cinema such as semiotics and auteur theory, as well as addressing recurring themes and ideas such as existentialism and Christian belief. The different levels of political commitment and social criticism which appear in many of these films are also discussed.

The book includes case studies of eight representative films:

- *The Cabinet of Dr Caligari* (Wiene, 1920)
- *Earth* (Dovzhenko, 1930)
- *A Man Escaped* (Bresson, 1956)
- *Hiroshima mon amour* (Resnais, 1959)
- *Aguirre, Wrath of God* (Herzog, 1972)
- *Comrades* (Douglas, 1986)
- *Le Quattro Volte* (Frammartino, 2010)
- *Silence* (Collins, 2012).

John White is Senior Lecturer in Film and Media at Anglia Ruskin University, UK. He is co-editor of *The Routledge Encyclopedia of Films* (2015) and author of *Westerns* (2011).

Routledge Film Guidebooks

The Routledge Film Guidebooks offer a clear introduction to and overview of the work of key filmmakers, movements or genres. Each guidebook contains an introduction, including a brief history; defining characteristics and major films; a chronology; key debates surrounding the filmmaker, movement or genre; and pivotal scenes, focusing on narrative structure, camera work and production quality.

James Cameron
Alexandra Keller

Jane Campion
Deb Verhoeven

Horror
Brigid Cherry

Film Noir
Justus Nieland and Jennifer Fay

Documentary
Dave Saunders

Romantic Comedy
Claire Mortimer

Westerns
John White

Fantasy
Jacqueline Furby and Claire Hines

Crime
Sarah Casey Benyahia

Science Fiction
Mark Bould

Bollywood: a Guidebook to Popular Hindi Cinema, 2nd Edition
Tejaswini Ganti

European Art Cinema
John White

EUROPEAN ART CINEMA

JOHN WHITE

Routledge
Taylor & Francis Group
LONDON AND NEW YORK

First published 2017
by Routledge
2 Park Square, Milton Park, Abingdon, Oxon OX14 4RN

and by Routledge
711 Third Avenue, New York, NY 10017

Routledge is an imprint of the Taylor & Francis Group, an informa business

British Library Cataloguing in Publication Data
A catalogue record for this book is available from the British Library

Library of Congress Cataloguing in Publication Data
Names: White, John, 1956– author.
Title: European art cinema / John White.
Description: London; New York : Routledge, 2017. |
Series: Routledge film guidebooks |
Includes bibliographical references and index.
Identifiers: LCCN 2016019409| ISBN 9781138829176 (hardback : alk. paper) | ISBN 9781138829183 (pbk. : alk. paper) | ISBN 9781315737898 (ebook)
Subjects: LCSH: Motion pictures–Europe–History.
Classification: LCC PN1993.5.E8 W48 2017 | DDC 791.43094–dc23
LC record available at https://lccn.loc.gov/2016019409

ISBN: 978-1-138-82917-6 (hbk)
ISBN: 978-1-138-82918-3 (pbk)
ISBN: 978-1-315-73789-8 (ebk)

Typeset in Joanna
by Out of House Publishing

CONTENTS

LIST OF FIGURES

1

INTRODUCTION

There was a period around the 1970s when the term 'European art cinema' was generally understood to refer to the films of a pretty definite group of Continental filmmaking auteurs working at the time. In his essay, 'The Art Cinema as a Mode of Practice', published at the end of that decade, David Bordwell argued that you could consider this body of work, what he called 'the "art cinema"',

> as a distinct mode of film practice, possessing a definite historical existence, a set of formal conventions, and implicit viewing procedures.
> (1979, 56)

The aim of this book is to consider the same term, 'European art cinema', but within a much wider historical context, to argue in fact that there has always been in some guise or other the very definite presence within European cinema of filmmakers who have seen their work as offering, or whose work has been seen by others to offer, an enhanced artistic experience when set against mainstream cinema of the time. The exact relationship of these various 'art cinemas' to mainstream cinema has been defined differently by different groups of filmmakers at different historical moments according to their agreed and, just as often argued over, aims.

Much of what will be considered as 'European art cinema', in addition to being part of a somewhat vague catch-all grouping, could perfectly justifiably be seen as elitist and complicit in a rather Eurocentric perspective on cinema. Even so, it remains the case that awareness of the body of work seen to fall beneath the umbrella concept employed here is important to anyone who may wish to study film. So, while it does not seek to underplay any negative features of the term, this book, nevertheless, argues for the importance of having an awareness of 'art cinema' made in Europe over the past 100 years or so. Failing to explore the concept of 'art cinema', and the body of work that has in various senses been seen as 'art cinema', denies us the opportunity of engaging with some of the most profound insights and challenging questions raised by film texts.

Following Bordwell's approach to art cinema of the 1970s, given above, Janet Staiger has argued that both 'independent' cinema and mainstream Hollywood have:

> - a definite historical existence
> - a set of conventions
> - implicit viewing procedures.
>
> (2013, 22)

This book will consider the films under discussion here in relation to this same tripartite perspective. Staiger, we should note, is not under any illusion that some simple ideological split exists between the two forms of cinema she is discussing. Both independent films and Hollywood movies, she says:

> exude fairly conservative ideologies as well as occasionally progressive ones. An alternative film practice, as with art cinema, does not guarantee better representation of women, or minorities, or social

> justice. In fact, often indie films reinforce sexism and racism, and revel in elitist viewing practices for the initiated cinephile.
>
> (2013, 25)

Again, this is a line of argument that should be seen as underpinning everything found in this book.

Much of the historical record currently on offer dealing with the development of film in Europe depends on a conceptualization of European cinema as an 'art cinema' that came and went as a succession of cultural waves throughout the twentieth century. This may be a questionable historical record that can be interrogated on various levels, but it is the ideologically in-place history and needs to be understood as such before it can be questioned. The 'waves' highlighted in this historical record are usually each seen in relation to the production of a body of related work made in a specific time and place but may, on occasion, also be viewed as related to the exhibition and promotion of particular bodies of work. So, for example, a range of significant films in the late 1950s and early 1960s that challenged what had gone before are undeniably linked to a group of filmmakers connected to the magazine *Cahiers du Cinéma* based in Paris. Equally, various bodies of 'cutting edge' European film work need to be seen from an Anglocentric perspective as linked to the founding of the Film Society in London in 1925. This was the organization that ensured works such as *Battleship Potemkin* (Sergei Eisenstein, 1928) from the Soviet Union were shown in a conservative, class-structured Britain. Of course, within both of these particular contexts – *Cahiers du Cinéma* in Paris and the elite intellectual club of the original Film Society – we might see the making, screening and promotion of films as existing (and being contained) within very 'safe' middle-class enclaves.

It is not possible to study filmmaking in Europe, nor assess received cinema history, without investigating the ascribed 'art' dimension given to much European film. As part of this enquiry we should expect to question both the validity and the usefulness of the term 'art cinema'.

However, we should also expect to acquire an enhanced understanding of the insights that critical analysis of 'art cinema' can continue to offer. It is possible to be too keen to reject any use of the term 'art' as elitist and divorced from the mainstream experiences of making and watching film. In order to reject anything it is important to know what you are rejecting. It is also possible that, unless care is taken, that which is rejected may be something that actually carries useful understandings of the human condition that can be, and should be, developed and carried forward. When preparing their book, *Global Art Cinema: New Theories and Histories*, Rosalind Galt and Karl Schoonover found that:

> The sense of art cinema as elitist and conservative remains in such force that many scholars to whom we spoke about this volume responded with perplexity that we would endorse such a retrograde category.
>
> (2010, 5)

Galt and Schoonover, however, felt that the category continued to be useful in helping to define a certain area of 'cultural, economic and aesthetic meaning' (5).

The working hypothesis here will be the suggestion that it is possible to view 'art cinema' as a genre, seeing it as 'art film' produced specifically for cinema exhibition. One element of this approach will be to interpret this type of film in relation to various concepts of 'art'; and this will involve some exploration of the use of the term 'art' within Western cultural history. At the same time, these films will be categorized as strongly related to, but distinct from, 'art film' made to be exhibited in a gallery space or constructed as installation art. Here our interest is with film which manages to continue to find a niche within the arena of cinema exhibition. This is, therefore, film which depends on the commercial market but has an ambiguous relationship with the concept of being seen as 'commercial'. Part of its definition of itself is to see itself as eschewing popularity, the mass market, and, therefore, a mass audience. Its self-proclaimed aim is usually to achieve something over and above entertainment, and its proponents tend to view themselves as driven by something beyond the desire to 'turn a profit'.

This book will consider the term 'art cinema' solely in relation to European films. It would be fair to say that the implication here is that 'art cinema' has been predominantly defined by, and critically evaluated in relation to, '*European* art cinema'. Whether this elevation of European film has validity and can be sustained, either historically or within a contemporary context, should be carefully considered by the reader. Beyond this, the introduction of such a geographical space brings additional difficulties. Put simply, what do we mean by 'Europe'? How are we to define this spatially, politically and culturally shape-shifting space? Certainly, in a book of this size it will be impossible to do justice to the full extent of the body of work we might, like a Victorian taxonomist, classify beneath the overarching term of 'European art cinema'. All that can be hoped is that an introduction to some of the key parameters can be put in place and that the reader will be able to apply these structures of thought to further films.

Following a short introductory chapter, Chapter 2 briefly considers how we might map out the problematic parameters of European art cinema. Chapter 3 then offers a historical overview of the development of European art cinema, which the reader should understand as a version of a history that could be re-evaluated in many ways and from many alternative perspectives. Chapter 4 considers two important theoretical approaches to art cinema. Chapter 5 investigates some key themes found in European art cinema. Chapter 6 looks at the socio-political outlook of certain European art films. Chapter 7 briefly reviews experimental filmmaking within European art cinema. Chapter 8 offers some reflection on European art cinema in relation to Hollywood. Chapter 9 considers eight short case studies, before Chapter 10 gives a few concluding thoughts.

2

OUTLINING THE THEORETICAL LANDSCAPE

DEFINING 'ART'

The whole notion of 'art cinema' as some different and distinctive realm of film should be seen as highly contentious. Necessarily, the implication is that some works made for cinema do not attain the status of 'art' while others do; that, while some filmmakers manage to elevate their work to the level of 'art', others merely 'craft' products that, while they may be perfectly functional, fail to move beyond this level of serviceability. Such distinctions between 'art' and 'craft' depend on 'a notion of aesthetic experience that sharply distinguishes between practical, physical activities on the one hand and contemplative ones on the other' (Markowitz 1994, 69). Applying the term 'normative dualism' (Jaggar 1983, 27–47), Sally J. Markowitz argues in our society 'we not only distinguish the mental from the physical but we value things mental over things physical' (1994, 68). She contends this dualism 'has a powerful effect on how most Westerners view the world' and 'is so well entrenched (in our culture) that we take its validity – and its innocence – for granted' (68). Markowitz suggests the work of 'marginalized groups' is often seen as 'craft' rather than 'art' but says there is more to this culturally ingrained distinction than simply the fact that 'art' tends to be made by upper-class white men. We do need to find 'the lost or misclassified artworks of women and non-Western peoples' and appreciate more fully 'the (different) values of craft traditions' (67), she argues, but this is not enough. Beyond this, we should ask what is behind our tendency to value the sorts of qualities we take art to have; a tendency, she says, which occurs alongside an 'enshrining' of 'the act of interpretation' (68).

Jean Renoir would presumably have had no truck with this sort of debate. In *My Life and My Films*, he said:

> You can make films or you can cultivate a garden. Both have as much claim to be called art as a poem by Verlaine or a painting by Delacroix … The pastry-cook who makes a good cake is an artist. The ploughman with an old-fashioned plough creates a work of art when he ploughs a furrow.
>
> (1974, 99)

The obvious questions, of course, are what constitutes a 'good' cake and what if the furrow is all over the place? To which there are a range of responses, such as: the quality of a cake is determined not by any immutable culinary laws but by the thinking of the person consuming it, and, has the furrow been deliberately created in a non-conventional way and does this deliberation, or the contemplative act behind its construction, elevate it to the status of work of art. All of which, probably, only takes us back to Markowitz's dilemma of why we in the West might value such deliberative thought, whether relating to the creation of the object or the interpretation of the meaning seen to reside within the object. Those who see themselves as artists might at this point question what is meant by a 'deliberative thought' that results in a 'deliberative act' of creating a non-linear furrow. While they might agree a lot of contemplation goes on during the creative process they might be far from happy with the notion of this as a deliberate, calculated, rational pattern of thought and might be more likely to view creative acts as of much less certain origin.[1]

Earlier in his book, Renoir does not seem to have been thinking about cakes and furrows when he offers a much more elevated definition of art, suggesting that:

> A work of art is only worthy of the name if it offers the beholder the chance of uniting with the creator. To gaze at *The Raft of the Medusa* is like having a conversation with Géricault.[2]
>
> (1974, 55)

How we define 'art' is intensely problematic, as is, by extension, the definition of 'art cinema'. A person could use the term 'art' in a closed and exclusive fashion at one moment and then shortly afterwards employ apparently the same term in an open and inclusive manner.

Frequently, art is associated with beauty, but that does not help much because it just means we have to define 'beauty'. Often, art is associated with creativity, but that does not help because it simply means we have to define 'creativity'. One person's art, one person's beauty, one person's creativity, is another person's avocation, crudeness, or arbitrary act. It may be all we can finally agree on is that there is no single definition of art but only a series of definitions that by their multiplicity, if nothing else, testify to the importance of this area of activity to human society. However, this does not mean that having the discussion has been pointless. In 'Is It Reasonable to Attempt to Define Art?' Robert Stecker suggests:

> What we can reasonably hope to do is suggest ways of making sense of a practice which is not so uniform as to yield an essence of art and not so shot through with inconsistency as to resist any attempt at sense making.
>
> (2000, 61)

This seems a very reasonable position to take.

FILM AS ART

In 1911, in *The Birth of the Sixth Art*, Ricciotto Canudo argued the cinematograph was pointing the way towards a new art form which would eventually come to be added to the list of arts, which he saw as currently comprising architecture, sculpture, painting, music and poetry.[3]

> The new manifestation of Art should really be more precisely *a Painting and a Sculpture developing in Time*, as in music and poetry, which realize themselves by transforming air into rhythm for the duration of their execution.
>
> (Canudo 1993 [1911], 59)

This concept of film bears some further consideration. Canudo was seeing film as somewhat analogous to painting (*and* sculpture) but painting (*and* sculpture) that, rather than being fixed, could 'develop' as we watch it, as a poem 'develops' as we read our way through it, or as a symphony 'develops' as we listen to it. Poetry and music are seen here as arts that come into 'realization' over time; that is, they involve a dimension that is that of time. Now, it might be argued that paintings and sculptures also develop through time the longer we stand before them in contemplation; but, nevertheless, Canudo is offering an interesting perspective on film, because his focus is not on the narrative but what might be seen as the aesthetics of film. Paintings like *The Raft of the Medusa* (and sculptures, let us say, Auguste Rodin's *The Burghers of Calais*, for example) do rely to some extent for meaning (or for their relationship with the viewer) on the story behind them, but Canudo seems to be looking for art to have some further, more vital, qualities.

Rudolf Arnheim, writing originally in 1933, picked up something of Canudo's thought, suggesting: 'Film resembles painting, music, literature, and the dance in this respect – it is a medium that may, but need not, be used to produce artistic results' (2006, 8). In 1948, arguing for film to be accepted as an art, Ernest Lindgren highlighted the fact that film depended on the same thing as any other art 'ordering and arranging elements taken from life' (1970 [1948], 287). In 1955, Roger Manvell asserted that what he outlined in *The Film and the Public* was 'the story of the phenomenal and exciting growth of a new art' (14). His struggle he felt lay in convincing 'critics of the older, fully-established arts' (286) of the worth of film. But by 1972, Stanley J. Solomon felt film was accepted by 'a significant portion of the public' as 'a major – perhaps the major – art form of the age' (223). The difficulty for these critics, as they saw it, was to establish the right of film to sit alongside other art forms. Subsequently, the effort for scholars has largely revolved (quite rightly) around attempting to move beyond the narrow boundaries of the 'film as art' position, to challenge the accompanying elitism, patriarchy and Eurocentrism, as well as the associated devaluing of film as popular culture.

DEFINING 'ART CINEMA'

To return to the central question: what do we mean by 'art cinema'? We might say, quite simply, art cinema demands thoughtful, questioning engagement that ponders and reflects on meaning. In this sense, art cinema requires a very particular form of creative involvement on the part of the spectator.[4] In 1974, Roy Armes proposed 'a triadic model' to enable us to 'see clearly the range of the cinema as an art form' (10–11). He suggested there were 'three major cinematic approaches to reality':

- 'the uncovering of reality' aiming 'quite simply to show the world as it is';
- 'the imitating of the real' focusing on 'the narrative function';
- 'the questioning of the real' involving 'using film not to convey surface reality or to sustain a make-believe but to explore an inner reality beneath the surface'.

Armes associates all three cinematic approaches with 'art' but the focus here will be to see 'art cinema' as very much concerned with the third of his possibilities.

These films may at moments be expressionistic, experimental, or surreal, but may not sit wholly within any of these sub-genres. They will be likely to have a sense of a narrative structure involving developing relationships between characters, but there will be something about them that will challenge both Hollywood norms and the expectations of a mainstream audience.[5] They will tend to be character-driven rather than plot-led and usually will not present the audience with a protagonist who could be defined as a hero fulfilling the classical narrative trajectory. But how do we finally define what it is that marks out these films as in some way different to mainstream fare, and how does this difference come about? Is it as a result of the people who have worked on these films, or as a consequence of the socio-historical contexts in which these films have been made? Is it a real difference that can be sustained, or is it ultimately a false demarcation? These films will generally reach only a niche audience, but when is a niche no longer a niche? Can an 'art film' reach a wider audience and still be seen as 'art cinema'?

Under pressure to clarify what we mean by art films, we might suggest they could be defined by the way in which:

- they aim not at 'entertainment' but at interrogation of the self, and/or cultural exploration, and/or social examination;
- they view themselves as representing a 'serious' artistic endeavor to examine the human experience;
- they employ a style which is often slower than mainstream cinema, allowing the viewer room for contemplation;
- they express an interest in advancing social criticism and offering their own critiques of societies;
- they explore personal struggle and angst relating to the nature of the human condition;
- they present the spectator with layers of potential meaning, whether the content is socio-political or more psychological.

We might add that art films could also be defined in relation to the expectations of the audience that come to see these films; but also, maybe, in relation to the class and/or income/socio-economic status of the audience.

ART CINEMA AND GENRE

A further issue would be whether 'art cinema' could be defined as a genre. According to David Andrews, film scholars have 'never fully thought out the term "art cinema"' and yet it is a phrase in common usage (2013, x). This combination, he suggests, makes the term 'seem both "fuzzy" and ordinary at the same time'. But what is seen here as a problem is in fact the norm: any genre is both 'fuzzy and ordinary' at the same time. This is the nature of genres and what theorists have always felt uncomfortable with when using the term. We need to be content to exist within that space, identified above by Stecker in relation to the definition of art, where we are able to 'suggest ways of making sense of a practice which is not so uniform as to yield an essence', but which at the same time is 'not so shot through with inconsistency as to resist any attempt at sense making'. Finding that a genre is 'fuzzy' does not mean we, necessarily, have to expand the boundaries to take in yet more 'fuzzy' genres beneath our overarching starting term, as Andrews seems to want to do. We might note, explore and be excited by interesting correspondences between genres (as Andrews admirably does with traditional art films and cult films, for example) without feeling the term 'art cinema' in its original dimensions needs to be abandoned. All genres are to varying degrees subjective, all are loose in the parameters of their style, all are built around highly variable narrative structures, and all are certainly multifarious in their debated and debatable meanings.

Andrews suggests: 'A practical way of imagining art cinema is as an idea of cinematic high art', describing it as 'at most a value-orientated super-genre like "mainstream cinema" and "cult cinema"' (2013, 2).

'Art cinema' doesn't have a form, he says, but is built around high-art ideals such as anti-commercialism, the valuing of authorship, and a general supposed opposition to the values of Hollywood. According to Andrews:

> The standard history of art cinema pays lip-service to the avant-gardes that coalesced in Europe in the 1920s and 1930s but it mostly focuses on the achievements of the 'new waves' that formed at postwar film festivals between 1946 and 1970.
>
> (2013, 3)

His interest in the way that 'art cinema' centres on notions of 'art' and, in particular, 'high art' gives a useful focus to the investigations that will be taking place in this book. This book will see those concepts as sufficient in and of themselves and not wish to move beyond them.

The processing and experiencing of all films amounts to a matter of producers, product and audiences, or, if you wish, authors, texts and readers. Art cinema is no different. Art cinema can be defined in relation to audience, in relation to content and subject matter, in relation to film construction techniques, and in relation to the attitudes of filmmakers towards their subject and/or product. In *Global Art Cinema: New Theories and Histories*, Rosalind Galt and Karl Schoonover talk about films with 'overtly artistic textuality' produced for 'art-house theater exhibition' (2010, 4). As we approach 'European art cinema', we simply have to be clear that what we finally achieve, as with all genre definitions, is the outline of a territory with rather sketchy borders. It is what Galt and Schoonover describe as 'an elastically hybrid category' with a 'mongrel identity' (3). For Andrew Tudor, originally writing in the early 1970s, art films were no different to any other genre category. He suggested, 'there does not seem to me to be any crucial difference between the most commonly applied genre term – the western – and the art-movie … They are both conceptions held by certain groups about certain films' (2012, 10).

DEFINING 'EUROPE'

Galt and Schoonover also discuss 'art cinema's foundational Eurocentrism' (2010, 4). The aim here will be to begin tentatively, and without any possible claim to comprehensiveness, to introduce something of that European bedrock to the reader. Scholars tend to split European art cinema into a pre-war period built around avant-garde film and a postwar period founded on the new waves that emerged at that time, and we will largely follow that version of cinema history. The additional question that might be asked at this stage is what we might mean by 'Europe', and hence, 'European'. Shelves of books have been devoted to debating the definition of this 'continent'. According to the authors of *The European Culture Area: A Systematic Geography*: 'The belief that Europe possesses the characteristics of a continent can be traced to the civilizations of the ancient Mediterranean, in particular those centred on Greece and Rome' (Murphy, Jordan-Bychkov and Bychkova Jordan 2014, 2).[6] The problem is, although most people regard Europe as a continent, the reality on the ground is that Europe 'does not satisfy the most common definition of a continent since it is not a separate landmass … in the east, the notion of continentality flounders' (1). The authors go on to outline the difficulty:

> many different physical features could be – and have been – proposed as markers of the border between Europe and Asia. The Don, the Dnieper, and the Ural Rivers have all been advanced as demarcators of Europe's eastern edge; other scholars have proposed that only those lands drained by streams flowing into the Atlantic Ocean, Baltic, Mediterranean, and Black Seas should qualify.
>
> (2014, 4–5)

Leaving aside issues of geographical boundaries, we might ask whether films from such a vaguely delineated territory, originating from countries with divergent cultures and histories, can be successfully bracketed together in any meaningful way.

It is certainly the case that filmmakers from across Europe have felt themselves inspired and challenged by each other's work. One consistent theme of European art film might be the interplay, not only between filmmakers, but also between filmmakers and audiences, across the 'continent'. For Hans-åke Persson and Bo Stråth, looking not at films but at politics, this sort of perspective is crucial:

> Europe consists of various civilizational heritages and is not the expression of a single Western civilization. We must think of it rather as a constellation of civilizational traditions which have emerged from interaction with each other. The crucial dimension is the interaction and the relations rather than any imagined underlying foundation … A rewritten history underpinning a European culture must confront Europe as linear and affirmative progression and emphasize culture as an integration of tensions and oppositions.
>
> (2007, 23)

Looking at the contentious issue of European identity, Jeffrey T. Checkel and Peter J. Katzenstein concluded: 'There is no one European identity, just as there is no one Europe' (2009, 213). And yet, we are still able to use the term 'European', and people still know what we are talking about. Katzenstein and Checkel suggest 'identities flow through multiple networks and create new patterns of identification' (213), and this terminology may be useful in discussing European art films. What we see are 'flows' of films that pass through 'multiple networks' (industrial, commercial, cultural, national and international) and create not just 'new', but also reinforced, re-established, revived and re-imagined 'patterns of identification'.

In a variety of ways, categorizing films as belonging to European art cinema is intensely problematic, and yet, the notion of 'European art cinema' has underpinned much that has been written about film in academic, critical and fan-based spheres. Not only that, but the phrase would clearly seem to have real practical currency in denoting a type of film people are generally pretty well able to identify.

3

A BRIEF HISTORICAL OVERVIEW OF EUROPEAN ART CINEMA

This chapter will briefly contextualize 'art cinema' in relation to history and social change, and in relation to twentieth-century artistic and cultural developments. Given the fact that this is no more than an overview, it cannot be anything other than a glimpse of a few European films, film movements and filmmakers that have been linked to the concept of 'art cinema'. Nevertheless, it should provide something of a mental map from which further investigations can begin. Swathes of filmmaking practice, involving both lone filmmakers and groups of filmmakers, who have come together to express common concerns and experiment with similar approaches, will necessarily be overlooked. Critically recognized groupings, such as the Polish Film School, Czech New Wave and Yugoslav Black Wave from the 1960s, and the Berlin School and Romanian New Wave that have emerged since the collapse of the Soviet Union, will remain missing parts of the jigsaw. There will be no room to consider how cultural flows into and out of Europe intensified after the Second World War, or how the postwar Japanese and Indian New Waves, for example, could be viewed in relation to European cinema. Nor will there be the scope to assess the impact of European art cinema on Hollywood that has gone on since at least the

1920s, but which is often seen to be particularly strong after 1980. What is on offer is a starting point for the reader's own investigations.

Some reflection on the nature of the narrative of European art cinema that develops here will be necessary. If a story is told enough times from a certain well-defined position, it becomes established as 'history'. Something similar happens with genres: if the contours of a given 'genre' are outlined enough times, the genre becomes established as 'fact' when it is no more than a flag of convenience. Both 'history' and 'genre' offer convenient ways of being able to talk about our ongoing experience of film, but it is important to consider the ways in which 'history', in particular, needs to be seen as an arena of contesting views and perspectives, and not something that exists as a definitive version. This survey tells a story of an aspect of European cinema largely from an established Eurocentric perspective. It provides a framework of a certain sort for the understanding of some aspects of the multiplicity of films available year after year across Europe. Even the very boundaries of what we define as 'Europe', remember, are 'up for grabs', defined and re-defined both across time and from different positions during any given moment in time. And yet, we still do need to give shape and form to a body of films such as that provided by European cinema, and we do need to see that body of films within a series of cultural, social and historical perspectives that enable us to make sense of those films, otherwise we have no way of discussing the resultant films, neither in relation to each other, nor in relation to the audiences (or individual spectators) that watch them, nor in relation to the societies (or individual filmmakers) that produce them.

So, what we end up with here is a useful framework, and no more; a framework that you are able to take apart for yourself and re-construct in a myriad of ways according to the nature of the debate in which you wish to take part. It should be possible to use some of the main markers provided (whether dates, individual films, film movements, or ideas), reject others as unimportant for your purposes, re-shape still others, and put ideas back together in different ways. It should be possible to introduce new dimensions that remain unexplored (or underexplored) here, adopt new perspectives from which to view the resulting construction, and then move on to repeat the whole process time after time in a never-ending process of reframing and rethinking possibilities.

FILM ART IN EUROPE BEFORE THE FIRST WORLD WAR

The question as to what the term 'art cinema' means, or what it implies about any group of films under discussion, has been implicit in the phrase since it was first used in France before the First World War. Within a little over ten years of the Lumière brothers' first screening in Paris, 'film d'art' was being seen as one expression made possible by the new technology. The term was designed to suggest the films in question were related in some way to high culture rather than popular culture. It reflected the cultural aspirations of the filmmakers and producers for their products; but it was also a marketing device employed with the aim of attracting the high-brow market.

The company Le Société Film d'Art was formed in 1908 to bring high culture to the screen, and the most famous 'art film' from the period, *L'Assassinat du duc de Guise/The Assassination of the Duc de Guise*, directed by Charles Le Bargy and André Calmettes, was made in the same year. The film is a melodramatic stage production and amounts to little more than a play filmed by a static camera, although it does employ cuts on action that take us from one staged area to another, essentially from one room to another. As a character leaves through a curtain we cut to see him emerging into the new space on the other side of the curtain. Because it confines itself to a theatre-size stage space, there is no room to replicate the depth of action receding into the distance and the complexity of set design achieved in an earlier static-camera film like *La Naissance, la vie et la mort du Christ* (Alice Guy and Victorin Jasset, 1906).[1] What *The Assassination* does, however, is to create high-art references,[2] existing, for example, in relation to the opéra comique *Le duc de Guise, ou Les états de Blois/The Duke of Guise, or the Council of Blois* (1837) by George Onslow, which was based on an earlier play by François-Juste-Marie Raynouard.[3] With a film like *Le Retour d'Ulysse* (Calmettes and Le Bargy, 1909), made slightly later, there is some realization that cinema enables possibilities beyond staged theatre. Here, Penelope's dream of her husband is allowed to materialize, only to disappear on her waking.

What Le Société Film d'Art did achieve was to extend the concept of 'films d'art' beyond this organization and establish the possibility of employing the medium of film outside of the realm of popular culture. In the four years following the making of *L'Assassinat du duc de Guise*, Calmettes directed a stream of filmed versions of literary, theatrical and operatic classics such as *Macbeth* and *La Tosca* in 1909,[4] and *L'Avare/The Miser* and *Don Carlos* in 1910.[5] The management of Film d'Art, under Charles Delac from 1911, not only continued with literary and theatrical adaptations but tended to produce longer, near feature-length, films in keeping with their aim 'to seduce the middle classes into cinemas by elevating the aesthetic and intellectual content of the moving picture' (Parkinson 1995, 52). The policy was commercially successful for a time. According to Richard Abel, the company 'succeeded in turning out a consistent series of profitable films' (1998, 50). As a play, Emile Moreau's *La Reine Elisabeth* only ran for twelve performances in Paris but the filmed version, made not by Film d'Art but L'Histrionic Film, *Les Amours de la reine Élisabeth/Queen Elizabeth* (Louis Mercanton and Henri Desfontaines, 1912), took the concept of the European art film of the period to a wider Anglo-American audience.[6] At a little over 50 minutes in length it also further promoted the concept of the feature film.

Products that we might call 'art films' were being made in other countries in Europe during this period and by companies other than Film d'Art. For example, in 1908 when a version of *Hamlet*, directed by Henri Desfontaines, was released in France (and exported to the United States) a further two re-workings of the same Shakespeare play were made in Italy. Increased awareness of the cinematic possibilities offered by film is demonstrated in the version brought out by Società Italiana Cines. When the Ghost of Hamlet's father recounts the way in which he was poisoned, Hamlet stands in the foreground with his back to the camera while the Ghost stands to the left of the frame, directing us with his arm to look to the right of the frame where the poisoning in the orchard is being played out. The use of a complex shot composition allows the silent film to side-step the necessity for inter-titles and, instead, re-tell the story visually (Buchanan 2014, 51). Two years earlier the same company had filmed *Otello* (Mario Caserini and Gaston Velle, 1906), derived from Giuseppe Verdi's opera.

As a term, 'film d'art' may have a very specific reference to France in the pre-First World War period, but the impulse to bring established literary classics to the screen was not confined to that country. *Hamlet* was re-visited by filmmakers from Italy, Denmark and the United Kingdom as well as France, in total around a dozen times by 1914, and none of this is surprising. Stylistically, the films under discussion here may be very different from today's film products, but the commercial underpinnings of cinema have remained broadly similar: in general terms, a high-art cultural form has continued to exist alongside a popular cultural form throughout the 100 years plus under consideration and, for entrepreneurial and artistic reasons, filmmakers have looked to service those markets and pleasure those audiences. In Germany, just before the First World War, some of those associated with the Berlin theatre began to follow the lead of French film d'art and produced filmed stage productions, or autorenfilm (authors' films). According to Sabine Hake, 'a growing number of stage actors began to appear regularly in films, attracted by the high pay and the promise of instant celebrity' (2013, 23).

At isolated moments some of these films did begin to use the camera in slightly new ways. So, in *Der Andere* (Max Mack, 1913), for example, during a scene in a working-class café, from a shot with characters aligned in three layers of depth of field (foreground, middle-ground and background), we cut to a tight mid-shot of three characters in the middle-ground, effectively placing the camera where the foreground characters had been sitting. *Der Student von Prag/*

Fig 3.1 Expressionist sets (*Der Student von Prag/The Student of Prague*, 1913).

The Student of Prague (Stellan Rye, 1913) went beyond staged settings to film lengthy scenes on location and also employed expressionist sets at some points. This film picks up the interest found in *Der Andere* in split personalities (the central character has a dark other self who operates as a criminal) but moves beyond this towards stronger depths of expressionistic horror. The devilish character, Scapinelli, who persuades the student to enter into a Faustian pact, embodies this expressionism, looking somewhat like a slightly younger, less rotund Caligari, the mysterious character at the heart of *The Cabinet of Dr Caligari/Das Cabinet des Dr Caligari* (Robert Wiene, 1920). All of this reminds us that it may not only be French films that follow the film d'art pattern of attempting to bring literary works and the like to the new medium of film that should be classified for our purposes as 'art films'.

Returning to France, we could also consider the serials of Louis Feuillade, *Fantômas* (1913–1914), *Les Vampires* (1915) and *Judex* (1916) in order to explore the growing *art* of film during this pre-war period. David Bordwell argues:

> Louis Feuillade is probably the most prolific of the great filmmakers. Between 1906 and 1925 he made at least five hundred films for the Gaumont company – some only a few minutes long, others running more than seven hours. He worked in every genre – comedies, costume pictures, contemporary dramas, mystery films, sentimental melodramas, patriotic epics, even westerns shot in Parisian parks.
>
> (2005, 43)

Can such an output across such a range of genres be seen as related to 'art films'? Or, can work that was not originally seen in terms of 'art' come to be seen at a later date, and with hindsight, as 'art'? These films neither pushed the medium towards new ways of editing nor attempted to introduce a more mobile camera, and certainly the director himself was not aiming to produce 'art'. Bordwell says Feuillade professed to aim 'at the ticket punchers in the Métro, not the elite wooed by the avant-garde' (2005, 45). But could we argue, perhaps, that despite all of this he came closer to displaying the art of film than those in France who produced 'film d'art'? Feuillade was perfecting a form of cinema that neglected editing but instead relied on fully exploiting the depth of space available within the frame.

> Feuillade's films of the 1910s offer inexhaustible lessons in a craft nearly forgotten. They show us how the simple choreography of bodies in space can create a dynamic, intelligible presentation of a scene's action.
>
> (Bordwell 2005, 66)

SOVIET CINEMA AFTER THE RUSSIAN REVOLUTION

The quotation attributed to Vladimir Ilyich Lenin, head of government for the Soviet Union from 1917 until 1924, that 'Of all the arts, for us the cinema is the most important' (1971 [1922], 388–389) is, as Richard Taylor amongst others points out, a political rather than an aesthetic judgement. It 'reflected the desperate need for an efficient and effective medium of political communication between the new government and the masses' (Taylor 1988, 36). Mark Joyce sets the context:

> The transition to communism ... would have been a monumental task at the best of times, but the Bolsheviks had seized control of a country whose industry and agriculture were relatively underdeveloped. In addition, they had to confront internal and external opposition, civil war and famine. In such a situation, artists and filmmakers were perceived as having a special role as proponents of propaganda cinema.
>
> (2012, 449)

The Russian Revolution of 1917 encompasses two revolutionary moments: one in February, which effectively saw the overthrow of Tsar Nicholas II, and another in October, which brought Lenin to power. It is also strongly associated with the earlier Revolution of 1905 that was put down by Tsarist forces. There is a range of ideological interpretations of these events and the subsequent development of communism in the Soviet Union. Generally, it is suggested that 'within months of the October uprising, the revolution was in retreat from the aims of social liberation it had proclaimed' (Pirani 2008, 1). However, whatever historiographic trajectory we see as having occurred in Russia following 1917, what is undeniable is that sweeping social changes took place alongside an explosion of cultural creativity.

> Workers and peasants received increased access to higher education. A special institution for workers, the *rabfak*, provided an equivalent of secondary education; by 1928 *rabfak* graduates constituted a full third of entrants to institutions of higher learning.
>
> (Freeze 2009, 334)

There was the establishment of an eight-hour working day, abolition of all former Russian ranks and titles, the introduction of new courts administered by elected officials, the setting up of free education and healthcare, and in response to increasing demands from the workers themselves, increased nationalization of industry.

Alongside these changes, agitprop emerged as a socially engaged art form that aimed to politicize the audience. In photography Alexander Rodchenko, amongst others, began to employ extreme camera angles, powerful close-ups and superimpositions. Explaining his aim, he suggested that, 'in order to accustom people to seeing from new viewpoints, it is essential to take photographs of everyday, familiar subjects from completely unexpected vantage points' (Cohen 1995, 90). The aim for those involved in propagandizing the revolution was to encourage people to see things from new perspectives; to see themselves as capable of re-shaping their lives in new, previously unimaginable, ways. Alongside developments in photography, photomontage and poster art emerged as vibrant forms of image construction. Just as Berlin Dadaists used photomontage to respond to the horrors of the First World War, so Russian artists such as Rodchenko, El Lissitzky and Gustav Klutsis employed these forms to respond to the historical moment in which they found themselves. In turn, these artistic avenues influenced moving image making such as the documentary work of Dziga Vertov, but also the more narrative-based films of Sergei Eisenstein. In Vertov's series of over twenty newsreels made in the early 1920s, entitled *Kino-Pravda* ('film truth'), which each contained several filmed episodes generally of the everyday experiences of ordinary people, ever-increasing use is made of abstract images, close-ups of trains passing carriage after carriage, for example, or film taken from within a mesh of girders as a camera moves up within an iron tower, or shots of the shapes and forms of moving machine-parts. These are approaches to image-making that are taken up by Eisenstein, at the start of *Stachka/Strike* (1925) for example, but in his case with the introduction of fictional, rather than real-life, characters. Eisenstein also follows up the focus given by Vertov to the lives of ordinary people, showing for example a group of workers and their families taking part in country dances to the accompaniment of an accordion in *Strike*. To some extent it is true to suggest, as Betsy A. McLane does, that, 'Vertov confined himself, for the most part, to capturing what he could of undirected action as it was occurring' (2012, 45). But, in fact the images are, of course, as

Fig 3.2 Use of abstract images (*Stachka/Strike*, 1925).

McLane goes on to suggest, carefully chosen and subject to intensive editing: 'He edited extensively in order to make clear and emphatic the meanings he wished to communicate to his audience, often with rapid cuts' (46).

In this sense, Vertov's work is in line with Eisenstein's fiction films, which rely heavily on editing for the construction of meaning, and focus, often in a documentary-like style, on the lives of ordinary people. As McLane rightly suggests, the purpose of both Eisenstein's and Vertov's films was to educate the public about the need for the Revolution and to emphasize the necessity of moving forward in constructing a new society. According to the Russian journalist and screenwriter, Aleksandr Kurs, writing in 1927: 'The basic and shared thing in Vertov and Eisenstein is the organization of new material which the cinema has not made use of before, in creating "socio-influential constructions" (Eisenstein)' (quoted in Tsivian 2004, 149). However, Yuri Tsivian points out the fundamental divergence between Eisenstein and Vertov. 'For Eisenstein,' he argues, 'art was an essential condition of human society', whereas for Vertov, art 'becomes otiose in a society where everyone works, and will be banished from such a future republic, where the only form of art will be the art of the artisan' (8). For Vertov, adds Tsivian, art is like religion in that it is the opiate of the people.

A feature of the surge of activity in filmmaking in Soviet Russia in the mid-to-late 1920s was the accompanying explicit and implicit debate around the nature of the audience for film and the way in which that audience should be addressed. *The Extraordinary Adventures of Mr. West in the Land of the Bolsheviks* (Lev Kuleshov, 1924) made a particular knowing (even homage-like) use of dominant Hollywood cinema. Vsevolod Pudovkin's *Mother* (1926) depends in large part on a classic, emotionally moving, melodramatic form. In *Battleship Potemkin* (1925), Eisenstein uses a series of strategies relating to cinematography, performance and mise-en-scène, as well as editing, to make it clear exactly where our sympathies should, and should not, lie. Interestingly, it would be possible to accuse Vertov of elitism in his use of film form, as a result of the way in which he refused in the making of *Man with a Movie Camera* (1928) to accommodate perceived audience needs in 'his'[7] vision.[8] What is expressed here is a difficulty for the whole revolutionary movement: addressing committed revolutionaries is one thing, but speaking to those who need to be persuaded to move forward in the creation of a new society is quite another. Referring to this body of work as a whole, Nicholas Reeves points out that, while these 'avant-garde films':

> may have been the subject of almost universal critical acclaim and some commercial success, the dissenting critical voices were all to be found at home, and almost all the commercial success was achieved abroad – by and large, the films failed at the Soviet box-office, where they were invariably perceived as, at best, too serious and 'worthy', at worst, so difficult and innovative as to be all-but incomprehensible.
>
> (2003, 73)

The situation facing filmmakers in the 1920s in Soviet Russia was exhilarating in that both the nature of the medium and the role of film in society were open to debate, and it was exciting in that filmmaking existed in dynamic relationship to other cultural forms, such as theatre, literature, circus, painting, printmaking, photography and architecture; but, it was also challenging in that it existed in relation to a shifting and unpredictable political landscape. It is more complex than this, but fundamentally, the period saw the shift in power from Lenin to Stalin, a move from an essentially evolutionary interpretation of social change to one of heavily imposed social change from above.[9] The space that the Revolution opened up for a liberation of artistic expression quickly became closed down. Eisenstein's *Old and New* (1929), originally *The General Line*, directed with Grigori Aleksandrov, attempted to celebrate the move towards the establishment of agricultural collectives. However, even as it was being made and released, agrarian policies in Russia were shifting as Stalin, opposed by others in government, attempted to secure grain supplies by force. Furthermore, political perspectives on art were also closing down, with Stalin's emerging preferred 'socialist realism'[10] taking centre stage; and, in this atmosphere, Eisenstein's continued attempts to experiment with form in this film were rejected by the Party. Eisenstein himself was clear that:

> Positivist realism is by no means the correct form of perception. It is simply a function of a particular form of social structure, following on from an autocratic state that has propagated a state of uniformity of thought.
> (quoted in Goodwin 1993, 112)

GERMAN CINEMA AFTER THE FIRST WORLD WAR

As in Russia after 1917, in Germany after the First World War a dynamic cultural scene developed alongside massive social and political upheavals. The unsuccessful German Revolution (Die Novemberrevolution) began with rebellions by sailors in Wilhelmshaven and Kiel in late October into early November, 1918. This led to uprisings across the country and to the abdication of Kaiser Wilhelm II; but, although it looked possible that Germany might experience its own full-blown revolution, this never happened. The existing moderate political parties, in particular the Social Democratic Party, retained control of the situation and Germany became a republic – the Weimar Republic. According to Theo Balderston, 'The prospect of radical socialism was averted by the astute tactics of the MSPD[11] (which could still count on the overwhelming support of socialist voters)' (2002, 4).

Eberhard Kolb argues the phenomenon known as 'Weimar culture', which is seen as a high point for artistic experimentation, genuinely existed and is not 'the result of a posthumous glorification or a selective treatment of cultural history' (2008, 83). But Kolb also suggests that culture and politics in Germany in the period were kept separate from each other, and that those working in the arts failed to realize the cultural freedoms they enjoyed were only available via the liberal attitudes of the Republic. Avant-garde artists continued to push revolutionary interpretations of artistic freedom even though the political moment of revolution had passed. The Nazis, Kolb notes, 'branded the whole of modern art as degenerate "cultural Bolshevism"' (85), emphasizing a perceived link between challenging artistic experimentation and left-wing revolution. With a view to the impending Hitlerian right-wing backlash, Kolb counsels that:

> this prevalence of modern trends in literature, painting, architecture and stagecraft, along with manifestations of a freer attitude towards morals and lifestyle, was fiercely combated by strong conservative, anti-modernist forces that were rooted in broad sections of the population.
>
> (84)

Nevertheless, despite the thought-provoking proposal that politics and culture were in some way separate during Weimar, films made in the period clearly exist as not only artistic but also political statements. Siegfried Kracauer famously asserted in *From Caligari to Hitler: A Psychological History of the German Film* that, because they were not the product of any single individual and were designed to appeal to the masses: 'The films of a nation reflect its mentality in a more direct way than any other artistic media' (1966, 5). Films, he claimed, reflected 'deep layers of collective mentality' (6). But the politics with which we are concerned has nothing to do with mysterious 'deep layers' of a nation's mind. Films unavoidably represent on the screen the political nature of the society within which they are made because they, like the filmmakers themselves, are sutured into the very fabric of that society. The nature of these representations, and the ways in which they are created and read, will vary tremendously but each screen representation, each aspect of the creation of these representations, and each reading of these representations, cannot avoid existing in relation to the politics of the period.[12]

Metropolis (Fritz Lang, 1926) deals directly with Marxist issues such as class and the alienation of labour. However, although it contrasts the lives of a rich elite and an oppressed workforce, ultimately it attempts to bring under control any move towards revolutionary upheaval. It is heavily didactic in its promotion of the notion that, 'The mediator between head and hands must be the heart.' But this final message imposed on the material by the filmmakers may not be able cancel out images we have seen, such as Maria entering the elite pleasure garden with her arms around ragged children like some awakened image from a Käthe Kollwitz lithograph,[13] or the concentration camp-like hordes of doomed workers, heads bowed, shuffling forward. In this futuristic world, machines are not fascinating, shiny objects to be celebrated for the speed and dynamism with which they are taking us into another age, but are relentlessly demanding other-worldly things dictating the shape and pace of human life. The question of what exactly audiences take away from any film is always debatable, but it is certainly the case that the politics swirling around a film such as this are very much of the period in Germany. Beyond the German context, the politics at stake relate to a wider, pan-European contestation between fascism, communism and a posited liberal-democratic middle way (and to ongoing debates as to where we should position Lang, and his wife and scriptwriter, Thea von Harbou, on the

Fig 3.3 Maria enters the elite pleasure gardens (*Metropolis*, 1926).

political spectrum). Exactly the same type of issues are present in relation to other art films from Germany in this period, although maybe not always with the same immediate obviousness. Both the violent revolution seen as on offer from communism and the hedonistic self-indulgence seen as on offer from Weimar's cultural liberalism are presented in *Metropolis* as guaranteeing nothing but chaos and destruction.

Bruce Murray claims *The Cabinet of Dr Caligari/Das Cabinet des Dr Caligari* (Robert Wiene, 1919) promoted 'a conservative perspective' (2010, 26). In line with what others have suggested, he says the producer, Eric Pommer, and director, Robert Wiene, changed the script in a very specific way.

> In contrast to the original script, which portrayed Caligari as the tyrannical head of a mental institution, the film portrayed him as a benevolent

> authority to whom the healing of a mad and chaotic society could be entrusted.
>
> (26)

While this idea of Caligari as 'a benevolent authority' may be true in terms of the way issues are resolved in the final scenes, there is again the question of to what extent any resolution phase can dictate what is taken away from a film by the spectator. Is it not the previous manic images of Caligari that live on in the mind of the spectator? Certainly, Kracauer saw Caligari as a demonic tyrant, suggesting: 'he stands for an unlimited authority that idolizes power as such, and, to satisfy its lust for domination, ruthlessly violates all human rights and values' (1966, 65).

Faced with the expressionist set designs and performances found in *Caligari*, an alternative approach might suggest this film should be seen in relation to the interior (repressed) world of the individual rather than being set against the backdrop of the sweep of a collective national history. Certainly, Bert Cardullo proposed another Expressionist film from this period, *Nosferatu, eine Symphonie des Grauens/Nosferatu: A Symphony of Horror* (F.W. Murnau, 1922), could be seen as a drama exploring the self of the central character, Hutter, with his wife, Ellen, and the Dracula figure, Nosferatu, essentially depicting aspects of that self (1987, 136). In this reading, Hutter's journey towards and into Nosferatu's castle in the mountains is a journey 'into himself' (138). But Cardullo combines this psychoanalytical approach with his own confident recognition of 'the film's contemporary sociopolitical implications' (143) and even draws the two approaches into one:

> Despite the fact that Nosferatu would suck the life out of him and his wife, just as a tyrant would suck the life out of his people, Hutter can do nothing to oppose him. Hutter seems repulsed by yet drawn to an aspect of himself that he sees in Nosferatu.
>
> (143)

It has been suggested that *Der Golem, wie er in die Welt kam/The Golem: How He Came into the World* (Paul Wegener, 1920) is also predictive of impending German history through its approach to anti-Semitism.[14] Elizabeth R. Baer refers to 'scholars who find persuasive evidence of varying kinds that Wegener's film exemplifies the pervasive, "every day" anti-Semitism of Germany in the early days of the Weimar Republic' (2012, 52). But, while this may be true, it is important to place this in context: anti-Semitism was rife throughout Europe in the inter-war period.[15] What this reminds us is that, even as we quite correctly look to consider German film from the period in the light of German history, we need to continue to think beyond this and place this version of history within a still wider political context.

If the German films so far discussed tend to be associated with Expressionism in art film, others from the period, such as *Der letzte Mann/The Last Laugh* (F.W. Murnau, 1924) were seen as moving the art of cinematography forward. *Der letze Mann* is filmed by Karl Freund within the studio but employs shots that involve a more mobile use of the camera, known as entfesselte Kamera ('unfastened camera'). Using the camera in this way to give perspectives to the viewer that help to suggest the story means the film is able to almost totally dispense with inter-titles, moving towards what has been seen as a certain purity of film form. Noah Isenberg explains that, 'Elaborate tracking shots had become possible through dramatic advances in camera technology such as the introduction of smaller and lighter cameras, more light-sensitive lenses, and a motor-driven cranking device' (2009, 122). This film, in particular, has been credited with passing on 'a vastly extended and refined mode of handling the camera and lighting' (Scheunemann, 2003, 26).[16] Freund also worked with the director, E.A. Dupont, on *Varieté* (1925) where the circus subject matter allowed for cameras to swing through space as if part of the trapeze act. Allied to this, *Varieté* uses depth of shot to show not only characters in relation to the spaces around them but also characters in relation to each other, and employs editing to show action such as dancing in a party scene from a range of angles.

Direct recognition of the realities of poverty and class divisions in the inter-war period was given in Strassenfilme ('street films'), like *Die Straße/The Street* (Karl Grune, 1923). The storyline for *Die Straße* is weakly melodramatic, but the use of realistic interiors, noir street scenes and, above all, the way in which light and shade, canted camera angles and layers of superimposed shots are employed to show the vibrancy of the street in the opening to the film is genuinely inventive. Although there are tendencies towards Expressionism in *Die Straße*, these films generally moved away from Expressionism towards Neue Sachlichkeit, or New Objectivity, in their attempts to capture the world in a more straightforward realistic style. *Die Verrufenen/Slums of Berlin* (Gerhard Lamprecht, 1925) is in many ways a simple melodrama but has a strong edge of social criticism and genuine scenes of urban poverty shot on location (Jelavich 2006, 204). It concludes with lines that make its political perspective clear: 'Poverty and misery, vice and alcohol, turn people into what is called the Fifth Estate. People who cannot escape their fate. A world of its own, which we attack rather than fix.' G.W. Pabst's *Die freudlose Gasse/The Joyless Street* (1925) is generally seen as the key text to embody this approach, giving some sense of life as lived by the poor of Vienna.

AVANT-GARDE CINEMA IN FRANCE IN THE 1920s

Filmmaking in France during the inter-war period has been seen as dividing pretty clearly into the silent era of the 1920s and the sound era of the 1930s, with the 1920s being associated with what has been called French Impressionism and the 1930s with Poetic Realism. Yet both of these terms describe only very loose 'movements', and it is also the case that filmmakers were experimenting with specially written scores to accompany their films before the technological move to synchronized sound.[17] What is evident is that throughout this inter-war period in France a series of filmmakers was seeing film as an art, the fledgling form and style of which they were working to develop. Furthermore, the practical filmmaking that was being undertaken was intimately connected to increased theoretical exploration of the nature of the medium.

The term French Impressionism is a rather vague term covering the work of a range of filmmakers. The fundamental concept, championed by theorist and filmmaker, Louis Delluc, is that cinematography lends itself to the creation of images replete with suggestive possibilities of thought and emotion existing somewhere beyond any supposed objective reality. From this perspective, film's strength is the way in which it allows filmmakers to present ambiguous, impressionistic images that, somewhat like, for example, Claude Monet's series of paintings of Cathédrale Notre-Dame de Rouen,[18] challenge the existence of any final, singular certainty of reality. These filmmakers employed 'such devices as irises, masks, superimpositions, filters, distorting lenses, vertiginous camera movements, and rhythmic and point-of-view editing to reinforce the disturbing ambiguity of their images' (Parkinson 1995, 65). Ian Aitken has suggested what Delluc, and filmmakers associated with him, described as 'photogénie' amounted to 'the camera's ability to poeticize the ordinary' (2001, 82). According to Aitken, this quality, when employed by an auteur, 'aestheticizes external reality' (82). Delluc's *Fievre/Fever* (1921) is an interesting example of how this approach might work in practice and can usefully be viewed in order to clarify what is meant here.

Germaine Delac, an early feminist and filmmaker, also worked in this loosely aligned movement. Her film *La souriante Madame Beudet/The Smiling Madame Beudet* (1923) uses techniques of cinematography, editing and performance to capture the despondency of a wife locked in a marriage she finds unfulfilling. The acting has inflated melodramatic gesture sitting alongside a strong sense of everyday realism. The editing situates flights of escapist fantasy alongside humdrum, closely observed details of everyday life. Certainly on one level we are dealing with a trapped wife wishing to escape; but, perhaps, we should be careful not to treat her plight too seriously. She is a thoroughly

Fig 3.4 Poeticizing the ordinary (*Fievre/Fever*, 1921).

middle-class woman, a well-positioned member of the bourgeoisie; her fantasies of 'escape' include wishing a luxury automobile seen in a magazine advertisement, a Sizaire-Berwick, would whisk her away into fluffy clouds that are like something from a film by Georges Méliès. The one thing that is certain about Madame Beudet is that she is not 'smiling' but scowling and sullen. As Dulac suggests, the film has 'little action' but attempts to convey 'the life of a soul' (Williams 2014, 127). The importance for the film of the symbolist movement with its focus on the imagination and a spiritual dimension to life is suggested, not only through Madame Beudet's longings, but also through her playing of Claude Debussy's *Jardins sous la pluie* and her reading Charles Baudelaire's poem, *Le Mort des Amants/The Death of Lovers*. However, this notion of 'the life of a soul' is not the only level on which the film works. There is also irony and humor, as the shot of the resolution of a Punch and Judy show taking place behind Monsieur and Madame Beudet makes clear towards the end.

Dulac is, nevertheless, profoundly interested in ways in which film might be able to activate a deeper, more direct, more intense engagement with an artwork than is possible with other forms such as poetry, drama and the novel, and this lies at the heart of her collaboration with the writer Antonin Artaud on *La Coquille et le Clergyman/The Seashell and the Clergyman* (1928). Writer and director ultimately disagreed over what they were attempting to achieve with this film. Sandy Flitterman-Lewis argues Dulac saw 'the cinematic image as a site of a fusion', so that, 'the film was conceived as a condensation of associations whose gradual accretion of meaning allowed the story to proceed, image by image, in a chain of metaphors' (1996, 110–111). By contrast, Artaud was interested in the way in which film could offer a 'liberating assault on the continuity system of traditional narrative'. He wanted to see images brought alongside each other in order to clash with each other, so that 'a series of disruptive relations' was created for the spectator (111). What is clear is that both Dulac and Artaud, and those Surrealists working around them, were wrestling with the potential connections that were seen to exist between film and the world of dreams and the unconscious.

Marcel L'Herbier's work was more mainstream than this but was again interested to some extent in visual representations of inner worlds. *El Dorado* (1921), a melodrama without a happy ending, was particularly notable for the use of blurred and distorted images to suggest the mood and perspective of characters, as well as a score written specifically for the film.[19] With *L'Inhumaine* (1924) L'Herbier gave himself a wider remit, attempting to incorporate innovative artistic approaches from painting, architecture, fashion, choreography and music into the style of the film.[20] The film's science fiction base allowed for a series of abstract, Cubist-related images, culminating in a final scene in which these types of shots are linked through rapid editing as the central character is restored to life. In *L'Argent* (1928) L'Herbier updates Émile Zola's novel in order to offer an exposé of corruption amongst bankers. Technically, the film is particularly interesting for the mobile camera movements achieved by cinematographer, Jules

Kruger, within the huge spaces of massive set designs. Steve Higgins asserts: '*L'Argent* is now viewed by film critics and historians as perhaps the finest synthesis of the avant-garde and commercial cinema ever produced' (2006, 136).

One further filmmaker generally classified with the French Impressionists is Jean Epstein, best known for *La Chute de la maison Usher/The Fall of the House of Usher* (1928) based on an Edgar Allan Poe short story. This film has been described as 'a kind of dictionary of the language of the early French impressionist avant-garde' (Klinowski and Garbicz 2012, n.p.). In each of his films from the 1920s Epstein consistently focuses on what has been described as the heart of cinematic impressionism: 'the use of film to evoke extremes of subjective experience' (Aitken 2001, 75–76). Every opportunity is taken to create mobile camera movements, as in a single continuous shot in *La glace à trois faces/The Three-Panelled Mirror* (1927) in which a car negotiates a series of spiraling bends inside a multi-storey building with various-sized windows casting an ever-changing permutation of light and shade, or in the shots on a fairground carousel in *Cœur fidèle/Faithful Heart* (1923) which cut between a point-of-view perspective looking out at the world spinning past, to a young couple on the ride positioned as a still centre with the blurred, distorted world passing in the background. To further encourage audience engagement with the interior worlds of the characters, tight close-ups, superimpositions and a range of suggestive editing techniques are employed, as in the opening to *Cœur fidèle* in which the triangular relationship between Marie (Gina Manès), Jean (Léon Mathot) and Petit Paul (Edmond van Daële) is rapidly sketched. According to Viva Paci, 'for Epstein the cinema, thanks to the mechanical vision of the camera lens, is a true cognitive instrument which makes it possible to be aware of the constantly varying and elusive essence of the life of people and objects' (2006, 135). The range of Epstein's work is impressive while always trying to capture this 'elusive essence': the year after *La Chute de la maison Usher* he released a documentary-style fictional film using non-actors and looking at life on the Brittany coast, *Finis Terræ* (1929).[21]

All of these impressionistic explorations of silent (and sound) cinematic possibilities took place in France against the intense political backdrop of the inter-war period, but this context is most apparent in the work of Abel Gance, who began *J'Accuse*, a powerful look at the futility of war, in the final months of the First World War. This film could be seen as rather vague in terms of who is being accused and of what, but ultimately, it starkly and forcefully accuses us, the viewers. It moves towards a climax in which the war-dead rise as if in a Judgement Day scenario and was released less than a year after the end of the war. Later, with the possibility of conflict looming, Gance remade the same film one year before the start of the Second World War.

It was in response to Gance's *La Roue* (1923) that Dulac suggested films could be seen as 'symphonic poems' with images replacing notes, describing *La Roue* as: 'Movements of eyes, of wheels, of landscapes, black, white, eighth notes, sixteenth notes, combinations of orchestrated visuals; the cinema!' (Valcke 2008, 209). This film may originally have been as long as nine hours but now exists primarily in a four-and-a-half hour version released in 2008.[22] It may be rather too melodramatic for modern tastes but it is clear that the film had a considerable impact on critics and other filmmakers in the 1920s,[23] and it is equally clear that the film employs the full range of available filmmaking techniques. Gance followed *La Roue* with the equally epic *Napoléon* (1927). This was reconstructed by British film editor, Kevin Brownlow, with a five-hour running time and was first shown in this form in 1980 (Welsh, Phillips and Hill 2010, 1).

Naturally, filmmaking in any single country such as France does not occur in a vacuum. During this period a range of European filmmakers, particularly in France and Germany, saw themselves as attempting to move towards something described as cinéma pur, or 'pure cinema'. This involved ignoring narrative and, instead, focusing on the 'pure' elements of the medium: movement and light, composition of shot, and rhythms of editing. Short pieces of just a few minutes, like those of Hans Richter (*Rhythmus 21* (1921)), Walther Ruttmann (*Lichtspiel: Opus 1* (1921) and *Opus 2* (1923)), Viking Eggeling (*Symphonie Diagonal* (1924)) and Dulac (*Thème et variations* (1928), *Disque 957* (1928) and *Étude cinégraphique sur une arabesque* (1929)) attempted to distill the essence of a relatively new medium and influenced work by others that achieved wider commercial distribution. Fernand Léger and Dudley Murphy's *Ballet Mécanique* had a first public screening in 1924 (Freeman 1996, 28). Daniel Albright says of this film that it 'has no characters, only femmes-décor; it tells no story; it has no structure except the structure of music' (2000, 240).

Alberto Cavalcanti's *Rien que les heures*, showing one day in the life of Paris, was released in 1926. This film simply documents the life of a city but in a style determined by Cavalcanti the auteur, with deference to the ordinary and the mundane, with political commitment to issues of class and poverty, and with effective moments of humor.[24]

Beyond the detailed observation of a city's daily life, what we notice about Walther Ruttmann's *Berlin: Die Sinfonie der Großstadt/Berlin: Symphony of a Metropolis* (1927), written with Karl Freund and Carl Mayer, is that it is intensely concerned with exploring the 'arts' of cinematography and editing. This is a film about movement, light and shapes, and the interplay of these elements within the composition of shots and sequences. Ruttmann said his aim was to create 'a symphonic film out of the millions of energies that comprise the life of a big city' (Sadoul 1972, 31).[25]

One of the most famous avant-garde films from this period, René Clair's *Entr'acte* (1924), 'deliberately uses the codes of cinematic viewing in order to deconstruct those codes of seeing' (Perry 2006, 67). For audiences this was the effect of all of the films examined here, whether or not this attempt to undermine a mainstream, culturally agreed audience perception was a key motivating force or not. In *Entr'acte* the spectator is confronted by blurred images, superimposed images, upside down images, patterned shot compositions employing movement and unusual angles, and jerky disorientating camera movements. In a film about guns and death and the ludicrous pomposity of human beings, that is released just a few years after the end of the First World War, a funeral cortège features mourners running in slow motion behind a hearse pulled by a camel, and a madcap chase of what becomes a runaway hearse. Clair said the film was met, just as the filmmakers hoped, by 'applause as loud as the catcalls and whistles' (Dale 1972, 12).

One theme that runs throughout the experimentation of the 1920s in European art is the variety of ways in which filmmakers and other artists and musicians worked together and influenced each other. *Entr'acte* was presented between the two acts of a Dada ballet, *Relâche*, devised by Francis Picabia with the dancer and choreographer, Jean Börlin. Both Börlin and Picabia appear in the film, and Picabia is credited with having written the scenario for the film with Clair. Music for both the film and the ballet was composed by Erik Satie, who also appears in the film. R. Bruce Elder suggests that in the early twentieth century, 'the cinema was a pivotal artistic force that gave shape to radical artistic forms across all the arts' (2013, 186).

Other films that exist within that same experimental framework were released towards the end of the decade and into the next, including most famously *Un Chien Andalou/An Andalusian Dog* (Luis Buñuel and Salvador Dali, 1929), *Le Sang d'un Poète/The Blood of a Poet* (Jean Cocteau, 1930) and *À propos de Nice* (Jean Vigo, 1930).[26]

La Passion de Jeanne d'Arc/The Passion of Joan of Arc (Carl Theodor Dreyer, 1928) is not a challengingly avant-garde work but offers an intense experience and was controversial from the outset. There was much debate over how the iconic French saint should be portrayed and a series of versions of the film were released, each cut and censored in various ways, before an original print was re-discovered in the early 1980s and re-released. While showing the sly manipulation and unforgiving brutality of Joan's male inquisitors, Dreyer extracted an intense performance from Renée Jeanne Falconetti that was almost entirely filmed in close-up. This reliance on the close-up is far from conventional but is demanded by the subject matter because, as William F. Woods suggests, '*La Passion de Jeanne d'Arc* is above all an introspective film, a visual accounting of Joan's struggle with herself' (2014, 87). The image of a shaven-headed woman being led towards the inevitability of her death

Fig 3.5 A gun dominates the city skyline (*Entr'Acte*, 1924).

hangs over this film in such a way as to stand for so much that is relevant to the first half of the twentieth century.

FRENCH CINEMA IN THE 1930s

In the early years of sound René Clair created three movies in quick succession, each of which used the new technology. The first, *Sous les toits de Paris/Under the Roofs of Paris* (1930),[27] shows Clair managing to retain much of the visual language developed in the silent era – complicated camera movements range over rooftops and elaborate shot compositions utilize canted lines created by skylight windows – but also employing sound in a creative, often asynchronous, style. The film also captures, within the softening genre constraints of musical comedy, something of the reality of Parisian working-class life. And, all of this is achieved within the increasing commercialization of the industry. The emergence of synchronized sound provided the opportunity for larger companies to invest in the new technology and take tighter control of the film industry. As early sound-on-disc innovations were replaced by sound-on-film processes, smaller film companies that had permitted visual experimentation were squeezed out.

Clair's *Le Million* (1931)[28] is a film-length extended metaphor for the crazy way in which people chase after money which also manages to condemn inequality and the gap between rich and poor, all beneath the sugary coating of a light musical comedy. An all-male chorus line of pickpockets and thieves sings: 'We take back the spoils of social injustice … We redistribute wealth and private property.' *À nous la liberté/Freedom is ours* (1931) ridicules industrialization and commercialism, and in particular those capitalists running the sound technology business, essentially Clair's employers. 'Work is freedom,' a teacher tells children sitting in lines.[29] Employees clock-in in lines and walk in lines to work at an assembly line in a factory that deliberately resembles the opening shots of a production line in a prison. But beyond the social commentary, and somewhere beneath the solace of friendship and laughter that the film displays and advocates, Clair presents life itself as a prison from which we long to escape, and from within which we gain glimpses of beauty which, unfortunately, on closer inspection often turn out to be false. Film being film and this being the early, rather than late 1930s, his heroes, like Jean Renoir's eponymous central character in *Boudu sauvé des eaux/Boudu Saved from Drowning* released a year later, are permitted to escape to the idyll of the freedom of the open road at the end of the film.

The few films Jean Vigo made before his death in 1934, like Clair's films, depend on social commentary, satire, comedy and an underpinning intense seriousness about life. *Zéro de conduit/Zero for Conduct* (1933) puts on screen a full-scale, class-driven revolt under the guise of schoolboys rebelling against the tyranny of the school system, but also includes cinematic innovation as in a dormitory scene of slow-motion, surreal, dream-like anarchy. Vigo's final film, *L'Atalante* (1934), is described by Katherine Groo as being 'at once an exploration of the labour and lives of the French working class and a study of cinematic

Fig 3.6 Surreal, dream-like anarchy (*Zéro de conduit/Zero for Conduct*, 1933).

work and ways of seeing' (2014, 50). With his cinematographer, Boris Kaufman, Vigo explores ways of working within tight spaces and large open expanses, ways of using noir lighting with depth of shot, ways of dividing up inside and outside screen spaces, and ways of expressively utilizing every possible distance and angle of shot. Vigo and Clair took French cinema towards what became known as Poetic Realism; described by Ginette Vincendeau as, 'the lyrical ('poetic') depiction of everyday situations, set in working-class or lower middle-class milieux, acting out tragic or melodramatic stories on the margins of the law' (2002, 348).

Jacques Feyder's *Le Grand Jeu* (1934), the story of a man who joins the Foreign Legion to forget his lover but meets a woman who reminds him of her, is a romantic melodrama but manages to retain something of the reality of day-to-day life. *Pension Mimosas* (1935) makes clear the difference in tone between Feyder and Clair: banknotes blowing in the wind in *À nous la liberté* give rise to comedy as everybody begins to chase after the money, but in *Pension Mimosas* banknotes swirl around a mother weeping over the dead body of her son. Reviews abroad began to identify a dark seriousness as the keynote of films coming out of France in the late 1930s. Describing the reception of these films in America, Dudley Andrew argues:

> As different as they may be, they were taken as sharing a particular sensibility ... Especially after 1935 the Times[30] repeatedly gives the impression that something about French mores, tradition, education, or language destines its better films to be serious, candid, atmospheric, and strangely dark.
>
> (1995, 13)

The films are also politically of the moment: Feyder's *La Kermesse héroïque/Carnival in Flanders* (1935) is a historical drama about a country hospitably welcoming a foreign invader (!).[31]

Julien Duvivier's most well-known film from this era, *Pépé le Moko* (1937), is ultimately as accepting of fate as Feyder's *La Kermesse héroïque*. In the final scene, the central character (played by *the* iconic actor of this time, Jean Gabin) kills himself when he is unable to have the woman he loves. However, confined in Algiers, Pépé's longing is as much for an idealized image of a Paris he remembers as it is for an unattainable woman. The colonial setting raises issues of imperialism and ethnicity but, in terms of the period, it might be as interesting to consider ways in which Pépé's fate might be linked to that of 1930s France. The gritty realism and noir tendencies in the cinematography only further reinforce the pessimism.

In *La Bandera*, released two years before *Pépé le Moko*, Gabin plays a Frenchman who joins the Spanish Foreign Legion in order to escape his past.[32] Again, ideas of place and time seem critically important. Discussing *La Bandera*, Colleen Kennedy-Karpat says, 'the location identified as central to one's identity – in a word, "home" – becomes physically inaccessible while remaining mentally omnipresent (and perhaps omnipotent) during time spent in a new, starkly different location' (2013, 20). As with Pépé, so too this character, Gilieth, is unable to escape his fate in the form of the death that awaits him. In keeping with the scenario typical of Poetic Realism, both these characters are working-class Frenchmen attempting (unsuccessfully) to escape their fate and their past. Edward Baron Turk says Gabin frequently played the role of 'the common working man whose innate dignity is destroyed by social forces beyond his control' (1989, 159). Considering the same political arena but, perhaps, from a different angle, in *La belle équipe/They Were Five* (1936) Duvivier shows five unemployed workers in Paris who through chance – a lottery win – apparently have the opportunity to evade their roots but are unable to co-operate, pool their winnings and work together. Examining the politics of Duvivier's films, Susan Hayward concludes, 'Duvivier, if not an anti-republican, was certainly of the Right' (2006, 125).

Marcel Carné's Left-leaning credentials are much clearer from the outset. In a script by Jacques Prévert, Gabin's character in *Le Quai des brumes/Port of Shadows* (1938), an army deserter, is immediately given the lines:

> Shooting seems easy, like going to a fair and aiming at those little pipes. You shoot and then ... some guy cries out, clutches his stomach and pulls a funny face like a kid who's had too much to eat.

The pessimism identified in much French film from the period, as we can see, persists. Benjamin Martin sees this film as 'the darkest of film noirs':

> In a movie where every character is a *rate* (failure), the dream of Jean and Nelly to flee France and make a new life grants them a single moment of joy before they are enveloped again by an inescapable past.
> (2006, 109–110)

Partnerships with particular writers are often crucial for directors and certainly played a key role in the development of Poetic Realism.[33] Carné, for example, also worked with Prévert on *Le jour se lève/Daybreak* (1939), a film that again places Gabin in a dead-man-walking, working-class hero role. Ben McCann sees Gabin by this point in his career as 'standing for a whole class of people – the decent, hard-working proletarian labourer struggling against forces that seem intent on crushing him' (2014, 18). In this film, Gabin, as François, works in a sandblasting workshop, doing a job that is specifically suggested to be likely to take years off of a man's life. There are interesting potential psychoanalytical approaches that can be taken to *Le jour se lève* – McCann quotes André Bazin describing Gabin's character as 'Oedipus in a cloth cap' (18) – but the strata of society analyzed by the camera's gaze is solid working class.

Jean Renoir's political alignment with the Left is even clearer. His challenge to middle-class values was embodied in films from the early 1930s. *Boudu sauvé des eaux* (1932) has a central character of a tramp who not only pays no heed to social norms, but does not even recognize their existence. Later films, like *Toni* (1935) with its use of location shooting and the casting of non-professional actors, *Le Crime de Monsieur Lange/The Crime of Monsieur Lange* (1936) with its focus on a successful workers' cooperative, and *La Marseillaise* (1938)[34] with its focus on the French Revolution, wear their politics even more openly.[35] Dudley Andrew says of this last film that, rather than the supposedly known grand narrative of the French Revolution, Renoir attempted to record 'representative activities from a period of exceptional social awareness' (2004, 199).

The opening five minutes or more of *La Bête Humaine/The Human Beast* (Renoir, 1938) simply documents through location shooting the speed of a train and the work of the driver and his mate, without any attempt to begin storytelling; and, when the train stops in a station, it is the class system that is immediately emphasized as the station-master is threatened by a factory owner. Moments like this make it clear Raymond Durgnat is correct to assert it is a mistake to see either this film, or Émile Zola's original novel from which the film is scripted, as being intended as 'a Greek tragedy of fatalistic overtones' (1974, 174). The accusation from Zola and Renoir, as Durgnat says, is aimed at 'a social network' (174). How successful either the film, or the novel, might be in connecting with these targets is another question. The faux psychoanalysis of characters[36] offered in both creates two works that are ultimately confused, although the suggestion by, for example, Kate Griffiths that the brutal hereditary ascribed to the central character of Lantier (Jean Gabin) 'parallels the return of the specter of World War I as Europe teeters, in 1938, on the outbreak of World War II' (2009, 113) does make some sense of his much-referenced ancestral past. What we see in *La Bête Humaine* is a maturation of Renoir's auteur signature, not just in his cameo acting role as the scapegoated Cabuche, but more importantly in aspects of filmmaking, such as the use of particular types of shot, like those taken through doorways, and the reprising of elaborate camera movements such as the giddying waltz taken from the earlier *La Chienne* (Renoir, 1931).

It is impossible to fully appreciate the impact *La Grande Illusion/The Grand Illusion* (1937) had on its original audiences who were living amidst growing political tensions in Europe, but its basic aim as an expression of the futility of war is clear. The German woman, Elsa, who hides two escaped French POWs, Maréchal and Rosenthal, has lost a husband and three brothers in the fighting, with the brothers dying ironically at battles viewed as great German victories. But beyond the waste of war the film is, perhaps more importantly, about the failure of people to recognize their common humanity as a result of class, nationalism and prejudice. The episode at Elsa's farm is described by Martin O'Shaughnessy as an 'internationalist idyll' that puts forward the 'possibility of transnational fraternity' (2009, 51). In contrast to *La Grande Illusion* and *La Bête Humaine*, the film Renoir released immediately before the war, *La Règle du jeu/The Rules of the Game* (1939), was a box-office failure. Margaret Butler says the French government wanted films they rated 'healthy and optimistic' but saw *La Règle du jeu* as 'depressing, morbid, immoral and distressing to children' (2004, 26). Renoir felt his satire on society meant the audience was confronted by an image of themselves they did not want to see. 'No one goes to the movies to see themselves ruthlessly exposed for what they are,' argues T. Jefferson

Fig 3.7 The maturation of Renoir's auteur signature (*La Bête Humaine/The Human Beast*, 1938).

Kline, in support of this position (2010, 52).[37] Just as likely, *La Règle du jeu*, a film about aristocratic rural life, simply did not connect with a working-class, urban audience. Furthermore, Renoir himself does not seem to have been at all sure what type of film he was making here as he improvised his way towards its completion:[38]

> During the shooting of the film I was torn between my desire to make a comedy of it and the wish to tell a tragic story. The result of this ambivalence was the film as it is.
>
> (1974, 170)

ITALIAN NEOREALISM AFTER THE SECOND WORLD WAR

For a relatively small body of work, Italian Neorealism has had a strong impact on cinema, influencing not only movements like the

French New Wave and individual filmmakers like Satyajit Ray, but also Hollywood. In a collection of essays on the impact of Italian Neorealism, *Italian Neorealism and Global Cinema*, Laura Ruberto and Kristi Wilson say they are dealing with 'a short period in Italian cultural history that has had and continues to have wide-ranging international influence' (2007, 21). As with all film 'movements' the problem is in the detail: is this or that filmmaker in the movement or on the edge, should this film be included or not, do the key players in the movement believe this or that? Ruberto and Wilson find they are dealing with only a 'loosely' defined set of films, but agree what we see being made in Italy in the period 1945–1952 is a group of 'didactic political films that address social issues' and that these films are made in a style that 'tends to provide ideological and aesthetic alternatives to mainstream Hollywood film narratives' (3). By the early 1950s, according to Bert Cardullo, the moment of Italian Neorealism had passed: 'In a society becoming ever more economically as well as politically conservative, nobody wanted to throw away his capital on yet another tale of hardship and heartbreak on the side streets of Rome' (2011, 27).

In attempting to define Italian Neorealist films, Marilyn Fabe suggests:

> Neorealist films tell stories that take place in the present day, not in the distant past. They also focus on the lives of the lower rather than the upper classes: on workers, not professionals; on the poor, not the rich; on the ordinary man, not the superhero.
>
> (2004, 100)

In a manifesto for neorealism, Cesare Zavattini[39] said: 'We are interested in the reality around us and want to know it directly, reality in American films is unnaturally filtered' (2008 [1952], 152). In summary, these films are generally seen as using simple plots, location shooting, non-professional actors, and a semi-documentary style in an attempt to capture the reality of everyday experience for ordinary people.

Saverio Giovacchini and Robert Sklar suggest what we see as Italian Neorealism may need to be viewed as the 'nationalization' of an 'international conversation about realism and political cinema that had been at the centre of the 1930s' (2013, 9). Others point towards the obvious roots of such left-wing political commitment in 1920s Soviet cinema and see the exploration of realism as drawing on French Poetic Realism.[40] What is clear is that any commonalities of approach or outlook we might find within a body of films made in Italy during this period results from interaction between critics and theorists, as well as practitioners, in particular screenwriters and directors, who 'shared anti-fascist convictions and a leftist politics' (Shiel 2006, 2). Three directors are generally seen as contributing the key works of neorealism: Roberto Rossellini (*Roma città aperta/Rome, Open City* (1945), *Paisà/Paisan* (1946), *Germania anno zero/Germany, Year Zero* (1948)), Vittorio De Sica (*Sciuscià/Shoeshine* (1946), *Ladri di biciclette/Bicycle Thieves* (1948), *Umberto D.* (1952)) and Luchino Visconti (*La Terra Trema* (1948)). But other directors, such as Giuseppe De Santis, make clear contributions to the theoretical and political debates around these films, as do screenwriters and theorists such as Zavattini and Gianni Puccini.[41]

Marcia Landy sums up the difficulties surrounding Italian Neorealism by saying: 'There is no standard definition of neorealism any more than there is a fixed definition of realism' (2000, 13). If we adhere too rigidly to formulaic definitions involving location shooting, non-professional actors, a focus on contemporary events, and 'the privileging of marginalized and subaltern groups', we can miss differences between filmmakers within the movement and also fail to acknowledge that some of these approaches were employed in films from the Fascist era in Italy (14). What is indisputable though, argues Landy, is that 'neorealism introduced new dimensions into the cinema that signaled a move away from classical modes of filmmaking and hence of ways of thinking about the world' (14).[42] If we define achievement in terms of box-office takings and popular appeal, Italian Neorealism (however we finally define it as a body of work) was not a success:

> most historians agree that only a very small proportion of neorealist films achieved that degree of box-office success which alone gives access to the truly mass audience ... The small, international 'art house' audience that they reached brought the producers of Italian neorealist films all-important additional revenues; without this, even this very modest level of production would not have been achieved.
>
> (Reeves 2003, 225)

In Rossellini's *Roma città aperta* (1945) we find ourselves dropped into the midst of a dark and confusing world. We have to attempt to make sense of this place of danger, deciding what the relationships are between various people from snippets of information and, above all, trying to work out who is to be trusted and who is not. We are given no clear central character. Instead, we are presented with insights into the interwoven stories of several men and women, and a boy, as each episodically takes centre stage. The female character with whom we most strongly identified, Pina, is torn from us halfway through the film, shot in the back before our eyes; and, the male character given the strongest characterization, Don Pietro, is executed as the final act of the film. After being a rather aloof, distant figure for much of the piece our nominal central character, Manfredi, a hunted Resistance leader, under torture takes on a role that could be seen as Christ-like.[43] For himself and for the immediate Italian audience, Rossellini reconciles socialist politics with religious belief.

Set in early 1944, the film looks at a period during the Second World War just before the liberation of Rome by the Allies in June of that year. Scenes shot in the streets of Rome are given the look and feel of documentary footage and although events are fictionalized they are heavily based on fact. In particular, events connected with the Ardeatine Massacre of March 1944 are referenced. A group of less than 20 fighters with the Italian Resistance attacked a column of 150 German soldiers, killing 42 and wounding many others. In a reprisal, 335 Italian prisoners were executed in caves on the Fosse Ardeatine in southern Rome (Mikaberidze 2013, 25). Among those killed were Don Pietro

Pappagallo, a priest who had sheltered those wanted by the German authorities,[44] and Colonel Giuseppe Montezemolo, an underground Resistance leader who had refused to break under extreme torture.[45] However, this focus on contemporary events may need to be viewed in relation to the way in which Rossellini 'doctors' this apparently authentic historical perspective. What is revealed by Rossellini, according to Torunn Haaland, is 'an intent to ignore the nation's sins in favor of a conciliatory discourse aimed at unifying the people around ideals of collective rebuilding' (2012, 98).[46]

With *Germania anno zero* (1948) Rossellini takes neorealism and uses it even more fully to his own ends than with *Roma città aperta*. This film is too rich, too full of levels of interpretation, ultimately too poetic, to be seen solely in terms of any film movement. It sets out to be an examination of a defeated country in the immediate aftermath of war,[47] aiming as the opening says 'to be an objective and true portrait of this large, almost totally destroyed city where 3.5 million people live a terrible, desperate life', and much of it is filmed against a backdrop of bombed buildings and rubble. However, for Rossellini, it ends up being an intensely personal attempt to come to terms with the grief caused by the death of his son, Romano, who died from an inflamed appendix, aged nine, the year before he began work on the film.[48] On the one hand, the film presents a slice-of-life look at daily existence for Berliners after the war, a family's day-after-day struggle simply to find enough food to eat. On the other hand, Rossellini gives this a heightened dramatic twist with a son poisoning his father before killing himself. In the final shot, Rossellini reminds us that events like the death of a child, events that we can in any film analysis all too easily dismiss as melodrama, occur against a background of the continuation of 'normal' daily life; and so, combining something of a documentary approach with drama, or objectivity with subjectivity, genuinely does capture something of reality. Rossellini simply tilts the camera up from the boy's dead body to a tram passing, that is to life going on; not only that but he places the boy's body behind a wall so that anybody on the tram would not even see it.[49]

Mira Liehm observes that, although Rossellini develops scenes for his films out of the experience of being in a place, and traveled to Berlin to begin work on this film without any strong storyline in place, he was 'from the outset more concerned with subjective issues than with a faithful rendering of physical reality' (1986, 71). We do get a strong sense of place (although the interiors are filmed in the studio), there is little in the way of plot, the characters are ordinary people leading ordinary lives, and the overcrowding and claustrophobia of tenement rooms is expressed through tight camera shots, and so, to this extent, we do get neorealism; but the intensity of the camera's gaze as it holds the boy, Edmund (Edmund Moeschke), centre frame creates something much more like Poetic Realism.

The most famous neorealist film, *Ladri di biciclette/Bicycle Thieves* (1948), directed by Vittorio De Sica, explores a child's experience of the adult world in its own intense way. Speaking about a moment at the end where the child puts his hand into his father's, Freddie Gaffney says:

> In one simple gesture De Sica captured not a sentimental moment but rather a moment of change in a familial relationship. The moment where the roles reverse, the son realizes his father is not superhuman, and the father realizes he can no longer command the respect of his son, but rather has to earn it.
>
> (2015, 301)

Like Edmund in *Germania anno zero*, experiencing the working-class hardship of the postwar world, the child here, Bruno (Enzo Staiola), also feels a responsibility for attempting to help make money for the family, but De Sica keeps the drama in a distinctly lower key than that employed by Rossellini. The film, scripted by Zavattini, sticks more closely to the classic precepts of neorealist style. It is shot entirely on location, uses non-professional actors throughout (Lamberto Maggiorani, who plays the father, was a factory worker before being offered the role), focuses on the lives of ordinary people, and has a very slight plot amounting to a father and son's search for a stolen bicycle.

Fig 3.8 The camera tilts up from Edmund's body (*Germania anno zero/Germany Year Zero*, 1948).

With *Umberto D.* De Sica and Zavattini shift the focus to consider the postwar experience of the older generation. The central character, Umberto D. Ferrari (Carlo Battisti), is a retired civil servant finding it impossible to live on his meagre pension. The plot is again almost non-existent, simply involving Umberto D.'s dawning realization through a series of mundane events that the only way out of his financial troubles is suicide. André Bazin suggested:

> the story of *Umberto D.* – if one can still speak in this instance of a story or plot – is as much about the times when 'nothing happens' as it is about dramatic events, such as the protagonist's failed suicide.
>
> (2004 [1954], 130)

Discussing a scene which simply follows the routine of the maid in the house where Umberto D. lodges as she gets up in the morning, Bazin points out the way in which 'the camera limits itself to filming the young woman during her habitual morning activities' (130). This film really would seem in scenes such as this to be an attempt at capturing slices of life. On a re-telling, the storyline of an old man moving towards suicide immediately sounds melodramatic, but the inflated possibilities are never pursued by De Sica; each episode of Umberto D.'s life is presented and performed as a simple statement of fact. Particularly by the end, there is something about Umberto D. that reminds one of Charlie Chaplin's famous character, The Little Tramp, but there is no comedy here, only the lonely reality of old age in a failing economy. At the end of the film Umberto D. is literally 'on the streets'. A government minister, Giulio Andreotti,[50] criticized the film for its pessimism and negative representation of Italy (Wagstaff 2007, 457). Millicent Marcus summarizes the position enjoyed in Italy by the neorealists by the early 1950s:

> the neorealists' commitment to social change did not endear them to the guardians of the postwar status quo. Despite their reluctance, for the most part, to embrace a Marxist perspective, the filmmakers maintained a resolute antiestablishment stance and presented an image of Italy that was anything but conforming to Italian officialdom.
>
> (1986, 16)

THE FRENCH NEW WAVE OF THE LATE 1950s AND EARLY 1960s

Without ever being as clearly political as some of the filmmakers involved in neorealism, the group that came to be seen as the French New Wave, or Nouvelle Vague, responded to a mood of youthful rebellion across Western Europe. The revolution instigated by these filmmakers took place within the field of filmmaking itself and had a lasting effect on the future of cinema; although we might ponder whether this impact was permitted only because it worked to reinvigorate the film industry.

> The New Wave dramatically changed filmmaking inside and outside France by encouraging new styles, themes, and modes of production

> throughout the world ... The New Wave taught an entire generation to experiment with the rules of storytelling, *but also to rethink conventional film budgets and production norms.*
>
> (Neupert 2007, xv)

The filmmakers seen as key figures in the movement, François Truffaut, Jean-Luc Godard, Claude Chabrol, Éric Rohmer and Jacques Rivette, who all began as film critics working for *Cahiers du Cinéma*,[51] were passionate about wanting to challenge established norms and conventions in filmmaking without having any political agenda for so doing. Their iconoclastic approach to filmmaking amounted to a conservative elevation of the director as auteur. Their use of male-orientated character perspectives and a male-gendered usage of the camera amounted to conservative gender politics.[52] What was more interesting was the way in which, in attempting to place their own authorial signatures on their work, they responded to the pace and fluidity of modern life and the contemporary audience's increasingly sophisticated awareness of the nature of filmic representation. According to Richard Neupert, the film-going public in France in the period was 'an aesthetically engaged young audience ... with a better education and more disposable income, seeking its own literature, music and cinema' (2006, 44).

What developed was a film style that used location shooting rather than studio sets, available light rather than studio lighting, direct sound rather than dubbed sound, and allowed self-reflexive practices forbidden in mainstream cinema, such as speech direct to camera. Dialogue could be digressive and inconsequential in terms of plot development; camerawork tended towards being fluid, mobile and handheld; and the editing was allowed to draw attention to itself and could result in noticeable, abrupt dislocations of time or place. Referring to early works by Chabrol, Truffaut and Godard, Naomi Greene suggests:

> Like *Les cousins* and *Les Quatre cents coups, À bout de soufflé* captures Paris in a way not seen since the films of Renoir in the 1930s.

> Shot on location in the city's streets, the film conveys the noise and confusion, the crowds and rhythms, of the French capital.
>
> (2007, 84)

Through these stylistic innovations, James Monaco argues New Wave filmmakers 'invented the self-referential postmodernist pose that became the norm for the remainder of the century' (2004 [1976], 340).

The auteur approach to filmmaking and film criticism is usually seen as having been fostered via an article by Alexandre Astruc in *L'Écran français* in 1948, which advocated the concept of 'le caméra-stylo' (or 'camera-pen'), suggesting the director should use the camera to achieve as much personal expression as the writer of a novel[53] and an article by Truffaut in *Cahiers du Cinéma* in 1954, 'Une certaine tendance du cinéma français' ('A certain tendency in French cinema'), that attacked the 'Tradition of Quality' in French cinema and coined the phrase 'la politique des Auteurs'; that is, an active policy to elevate the work of those directors seen as film authors. In French cinema, the work of people such as Abel Gance, Jean Vigo and Jean Renoir was singled out for particular praise, and in Hollywood, directors such as John Ford, Alfred Hitchcock and Orson Welles were seen as having succeeded in placing their distinctive mark on a body of work. This approach to film criticism formed the basis of what became known as auteur theory.[54]

During the late 1950s the Cahiers group began to make short films such as *Le Coup du Berger* (Rivette, 1956) and *Les Mistons* (Truffaut, 1957). The first of these deals with amorous intrigues between bourgeois lovers that in subject matter recalls Renoir's *La Règle du jeu* (1939). The second reveals Truffaut's interest in his childhood that leads into his first full-length feature, *Les Quatre Cents Coups/The 400 Blows* (1959). *Les Quatre Cents Coups* opened the 12th Cannes Film Festival, won Truffaut the award for best director at that festival, and became the commercial breakthrough film for the New Wave directors. The film, which is only semi-autobiographical,[55] reflects a view of childhood as being oppressive and restrictive. The central character, Antoine Doinel (Jean-Pierre Léaud) is constantly attempting to break out of the confined spaces offered to him by the adult world, only to find society consistently working to curb his instinctive efforts to attain freedom. This culminates in the famous final freeze-frame shot of Antoine staring into the camera with the sea lapping behind him, an image that in itself works on several levels of potential meaning but which also references, and thus operates as a *homage* to, Jean Vigo's *L'Atalante*. The film as a whole pays tribute to Vigo's *Zéro de conduit*, developing the central idea beyond merely the restrictions imposed on young people by a schooling system as in Vigo's film but, at the same time, producing a much less politically charged work.

Truffaut's next film, *Tirez sur le pianist/Shoot the Pianist* (1960), a take on the American gangster genre that mixes tragedy and comedy, was in many ways his most adventurous in terms of challenging mainstream filmmaking conventions. The abrupt changes of mood disrupt the conventional expectation of genre continuity, offering a postmodern experience audiences in the early 1960s found difficult to understand. This is a film that continually draws attention to itself as a film. When the central character, Charlie (Charles Aznavour), is in bed with a woman he uses a sheet to cover her breasts and says this is what they do in films; when one of the gangsters swears on the life of his mother we cut to a shot of an elderly lady dying; when the treachery of a bar owner is being discussed we are given a triptych-style single frame with three iris shots of the man in question; and when a gangster is about to shoot and kill Charlie's lover, Léna (Marie Dubois), he twirls his gun as if he is a cowboy in a Hollywood 'B' western. Truffaut's *Jules et Jim* (1962) was more successful in marrying a Nouvelle Vague cinematic style with commercial success. Two friends, Jules (Oskar Werner) and Jim (Henri Serre), one Austrian and the other French, live a bohemian lifestyle in Europe before the First World War and fall in love with the same woman, Catherine (Jeanne Moreau). Catherine's character and Moreau's performance are central to this film, defining the trajectory of events and creating a powerful image of an unrestrained woman. The performances of certain actors was crucial in defining the look of the New Wave, but the creation of a coherent body of work was also down

Fig 3.9 The final freeze-frame of Antoine staring into the camera (*Les Quatre Cents Coups/The 400 Blows*, 1959).

to contributions made by others. The soundtracks for both *Jules et Jim* and *Tirez sur le pianist*, for example, were composed by Georges Delerue and the cinematography for both films was the work of Raoul Coutard.

Coutard also worked with Jean-Luc Godard throughout the early 1960s, filming the most famous film from the New Wave, *À bout de soufflé/Breathless* (1960), as well as *Le Petit Soldat/The Little Soldier* (1960), *Une femme est une femme/A Woman Is a Woman* (1961), *Vivre sa vie/My Life to Live* (1962), *Les Carabiniers/The Carabineers* (1963), *Pierrot le Fou* (1965) and *Alphaville* (1965). Jean-Paul Belmondo, another key definer of the New Wave, acted in several of these films and Anna Karina took key parts in all of them apart from *À bout de soufflé*. Godard's New Wave films range across genres. As with his fellow directors originating from *Cahiers du Cinéma* he shows an interest in exploring existential philosophy and in challenging filmmaking conventions; but, beyond that, he also begins to reveal a personal interest in the politics of the period. *Le Petit Soldat* deals with the 'dirty war' of infiltration and torture that went on around the struggle for Algerian independence. This film was made in 1960 but banned in France and not released there until 1963 (Betz 2009, 104). The politics, however, is not a committed form of politics; Godard is not 'for' one side or the other. Mark Betz points out that for the central character, Bruno (Michel Subor), 'politics have become meaningless' and in the film 'the right and the left are indistinguishable in their politics' (104). He goes on to quote Godard: 'I spoke of what concerned me, a Parisian in 1960, belonging to no party. And what concerned me was the problem of war and its moral repercussions' (104). *Les Carabiniers* indicates clearly Godard's trajectory towards his radical left-wing films of the late 1960s and early 1970s. Two nondescript everyman characters are recruited to fight for the king, enabling Godard to explore in Brechtian style the brutality of war, but more importantly the illusions society sells to ordinary people. In *Le Petit Soldat* torture was filmed in such a way as to make it seem 'normal'; here, death is presented as being 'as everyday an activity as making one's bed or drinking a cup of coffee' (Dixon 1997, 36).

Ultimately, although they hail from the same background at *Cahiers du Cinéma*, and share a moment of quite sudden eruption in film creativity and challenge to the old film order – Claude Chabrol's *Le Beau Serge* was released in 1958, Éric Rohmer's *Le Signe du lion/The Sign of Leo* was filmed in 1959 although not released until 1962, and Jacques Rivette's *Paris nous appartient/Paris Belongs to Us* was released in 1961 – those directors associated with La Nouvelle Vague were very individual filmmakers who would quite quickly begin to move in their own filmmaking directions.[56]

These critics-turned-filmmakers emerged in Paris at around the same time as another group, sometimes associated with them, known as 'The Left Bank School', or 'Rive Gauche'. Directors generally seen as part of this 'movement' include Chris Maker, Alain Resnais and Agnès Varda. These people had been making films prior to this late-1950s watershed. Maker and Resnais had worked together, for example, on film essays on colonialism and race (*Les statues meurent aussi/Statues Also Die* (1953)), and on Nazi concentration camps (*Nuit et brouillard/Night and Fog*

(1955)). Maker's *La Jetée* (1962) was a short post-apocalyptic science fiction film constructed almost entirely from stills. Resnais worked collaboratively with the writer, Marguerite Duras, on *Hiroshima mon amour* (1959), and with the novelist, Alain Robbe-Grillet, on *L'Année dernière à Marienbad/Last Year in Marienbad* (1961). Agnès Varda's debut film, *La Pointe Courte* (1955), was made on a low budget, used location shooting, and featured characters wrestling with the existential question of defining meaning in their own lives. For these reasons, *La Pointe Courte* is often seen as contributing to the emergence of the French New Wave, but the film's strong sense of intense documentary interest in the social life of the local community also highlights an important way in which Left Bank filmmakers can be seen as distinctive from their New Wave counterparts.

> Varda conveys basic facts about the conditions of life in the region: its human and natural environment, its material poverty, and its relationship to the trends and powers emanating from the major cities that seem like distant lands.
>
> (Tweedie 2013, 125)

Existentialism, the need to address the issue of individual mortality and our sense of confusion when faced with the seeming meaninglessness of life, is at the heart of Varda's *Cléo de 5 à 7/Cléo from 5 to 7* (1962). What we see, as Valerie Orpen describes it, is 'Cléo's existential angst at the beginning and her journey towards serenity at the end' (2007, 29). In deciding our reading of the film, one important question is the extent to which we are able to see *Cléo de 5 à 7* as a feminist film. Related to this is the question of how Varda's representation of a central female character might be seen to differ from that of Godard, or other New Wave directors. Phil Powrie quotes Varda herself as suggesting that, during the course of the film, the central character moves from being 'the object of the look' to become 'the subject who looks' (2006, 115).

THE BRITISH NEW WAVE OF THE LATE 1950s AND EARLY 1960s

As with La Nouvelle Vague, the British New Wave owed something to developments in documentary filmmaking. In France, cinéma vérité, pioneered by Jean Rouch,[57] 'took lighter, 16mm equipment into places that had not been seen before – the interiors of ordinary people's homes, on the dance floor with teenagers' (Aufderheide 2007, 45). The chance to shoot on location and record sound directly during filming was taken up by filmmakers across Europe. In Britain, Free Cinema emerged in the mid-1950s. Those who instigated this approach to documentary filmmaking, Lindsay Anderson, Karel Reisz and Tony Richardson, became key figures in the later British New Wave. As with French New Wave directors, Anderson and Reisz first emerged as film critics. In writing for the magazine, *Sequence*, they criticized British film for its conformity, conventionality and lack of experimentation (Hayward 2013, 164). Susan Hayward characterizes these filmmakers as being 'committed to representing working-class life as it was lived, not as it was imagined' (165). The attitudes towards cinema shown by both the French and British new waves also resulted in part from increased interest in the work of Jean Vigo and to postwar Italian Neorealism. In Britain, the documentary films of Humphrey Jennings[58] were another crucial influence. Impetus was also given to the British New Wave by a raft of challenging plays and novels written in Britain in the 1950s. Jim Fowler says the staging of John Osborne's play, *Look Back in Anger*, at the Royal Court Theatre in London in 1956, 'ushered in an era of new drama that challenged the escapism of post-war entertainment and tackled the reality of post-war, post-colonial Britain'. The play, he argues, 'articulated the impatience and anger of a generation' (2005, 9).

Novels and plays from the period addressed working-class life and experiences directly, and this was reflected in the films. *Room at the Top* (Jack Clayton, 1959), focusing on Joe Lampton's (Laurence Harvey) efforts to 'better himself' and climb out of the working class, adapted

John Braine's novel published two years earlier. Neil Sinyard suggests this film was 'part of a tide of change in art and society that was pushing so hard against the British Establishment that something eventually had to give' (2000, 38). *Look Back in Anger* (1959) adapted John Osborne's stage drama for the screen. It was directed by Tony Richardson who had also directed the play. Both *Room at the Top* and *Look Back in Anger* give a strong sense of a working-class environment in an industrial town, a feature of British New Wave films.[59] Films could deal with 'locations that are only referred to in the plays' (Lacey 2002, 168).[60] Importantly, increasing competition from television meant the film industry was prepared to back innovation. Laurie Ede suggests: 'The New Wave represented a rare moment when filmmakers' ideological concerns made a felicitous match with the desire of British producers for cheap but fashionable product' (2010, 95).

Saturday Night and Sunday Morning (Karel Reisz, 1960) adapts Alan Sillitoe's novel from 1958 that looks at the life of a young factory worker in Nottingham. Again, much of the filming is done on location and there is an effort to achieve what was described as 'social realism'. Richard Bradford claims Sillitoe's book was 'like nothing written before and it changed the history of the English novel' (2008, 1). It 'disclosed without apology or pity the worlds of ordinary people in 1950s England' (3). What is being reflected may be a real shift in social attitudes, with young working-class men increasingly feeling, like the central character here, Arthur Seaton (Albert Finney): 'There's a lot more in life than me mam and dad have got.' Two years later, a short story by Sillitoe was made into the film, *The Loneliness of the Long Distance Runner* (Tony Richardson, 1962). The oppressive nature of the class system is challenged in both of these films. This is very clear in the central scene in *The Loneliness of the Long Distance Runner*, which cuts between a young working-class prisoner being pushed into a cell to be beaten by a prison warder and the rest of the inmates in an assembly hall singing a perverted, Establishment-version of William Blake's poem, *Jerusalem* (*'And did those feet in ancient time'*). Some critics have suggested that by focusing on the individual lives of single central characters, these films detracted from any analysis of the collective economic experience of the working class. For Kenneth Nolley, the result was:

> to turn attention toward the personal and away from the collective and structural and to construct the behavior of the poor as driven by their own self-destructive impulses at least as much as by the lightly examined nature of their situation.
>
> (1999, 232)

But this is to neglect the strength of the 'rebellion' of young people at the time, who would have been with Sillitoe's characters in their defiant chanting of the mantra, 'Don't let the bastards grind you down'; an individual attitude that made possible the collective industrial action and political protest that was soon to materialize in Britain.

Having said that, there is probably some truth in the argument that *This Sporting Life* (Lindsay Anderson, 1963), based on a novel by David Storey and adapted by him for the screen, 'pushed social realism toward psychological realism' (Phillips 1999, 212), and that this was a film that was 'more concerned with examining … the inner conflicts that motivate a character's actions than with exploring the external social pressures that influence their behavior' (212). Ken Dancyger argues, 'Anderson seems most interested in existential, rather than social or political elements' (2013, 140). We are taken away from social realism, particularly through the editing, which 'aimed not simply at telling a story but at evoking, by associations and juxtapositions, ideas and emotions integral to mood and theme' (Sussex 1969, 54). Despite working within the working class/industrial town context inhabited by other films, Anderson is seen as having created a distinctively individual film. But, in fact, each of these 'new wave' films exists first and foremost in and of itself, and amid any talk of film movements it is always useful to remember this. As B.F. Taylor reminds us: 'There are

Fig 3.10 The singing of *Jerusalem*/'*And did those feet in ancient time*' (*The Loneliness of the Long Distance Runner*, 1962).

significant differences among these films, and it is through an examination of style and meaning in each film that these differences will be most clearly demonstrated' (2006, 7).

NEW GERMAN CINEMA

People born in Germany just before, during, and immediately after the Second World War had a very particular, intense awareness of that conflict. For these generations there was a pressing collective, and often familial, need to come to terms with not only the emergence of Hitler in the 1930s and the resulting consequences, but also the bleak Cold War aftermath. The director Wim Wenders has talked of how 'desperate' he was as a child 'to go to a different country than my own for instruction on such vital things as 'fun', 'laughter' and 'adventure'. The words might exist in German, but not the things they stood for' (1997, 157).

By 1949 pre-war Germany had been divided into West Germany (the Federal Republic of Germany) and East Germany (the German Democratic Republic), and the Iron Curtain was in place. Simultaneously, in West Germany, the so-called 'economic miracle' was starting, funded by aid from the Marshall Plan. The postwar generation found itself living through a complex present, fueled by being on the front line of the political divide between East and West, while also needing to come to terms with the trauma of the recent past, the evidence for which was inescapably all around them. At the same time, this politically radicalized generation became part of a wider challenge to the past that was being offered by young people throughout the Western world. By the 1970s, the whole democratic process seemed under threat in West Germany as some on the political left began to pursue increasingly violent means and the government began to follow an increasingly authoritarian course. Wallace Steadman Watson claims one of the key filmmakers from the period, Rainer Werner Fassbinder, 'was acquainted with two of the early terrorists, and he sympathized with their ideological position even though he had serious doubts about their tactics' (1996, 25).

Against this dynamic political backdrop a new generation of filmmakers began to emerge. In 1962, a group of young directors at the International Short Film Festival Oberhausen signed a manifesto that declared: 'The old cinema is dead. We believe in the new cinema' (Reimer and Reimer 2008, 217). Two of those who signed, Alexander Kluge and Peter Schamoni, had recently completed a short, 12-minute film, *Brutalität in Stein/Brutality in Stone* (1961) that presented images of stark, monolithic Third Reich architecture overlaid with a soundtrack of Nazi propaganda. Kluge went on to script and direct *Abschied von gestern/Yesterday Girl* (1966) featuring an East German migrant adjusting to life in the West. Something of the interests that would be pursued by the emerging generation of filmmakers is suggested by these works – the traumas of the recent past and their continuing repercussions. During the 1970s and into the 1980s, directors such as Hans-Jürgen Syberberg (born 1935), Volker Schlöndorff (born 1939), Helma Sanders-Brahms (born 1940), Werner Herzog (born 1942),

Margarethe von Trotta (born 1942), Rainer Werner Fassbinder (born 1945) and Wim Wenders (born 1945), almost all a little younger than those who signed the original manifesto, began to work with this type of subject matter and to develop a stronger sense of the auteur within German cinema. Helma Sanders-Brahms identifies the starting point for these filmmakers:

> The Germany in which I grew up was no longer recognizable, after two World Wars for which it had been responsible. The air raids had turned its cities, large and small, into piles of rubble. The lies of the Nazis about the superiority of the German race had been exposed. Millions of disillusioned, shamed people had lost their face.
>
> (2005, 160)

Syberberg's most controversial film, *Hitler, ein Film aus Deutschland/Hitler: A Film from Germany* (1977), is an experimental work that runs to just over seven hours. This is a highly theatrical film employing a series of staged scenes and set-pieces, which rely heavily on character monologues and/or overlaid soundtrack narration allied to a suggestive use of costume, props, lighting and set design. Susan Sontag categorized it as a film that 'tries to say everything' (1983, 421); for Sontag, it was a work that was 'on another scale than anything one has seen on film' (421). But, for others, the film worryingly 'reproduces and reenacts Hitler's appeal to his public and his followers' and contains 'a kind of mourning, a kind of mythologizing and an empathy which make no distinction between victim and sacrifice, between victim and murderer' (Stern 1980, 47). Ian Aitken attempted to clear up the controversy:

> Syberberg has been criticized for turning to such politically controversial subject matter, and has even been accused of harbouring Nazi sympathies. However, Syberberg is not a proto-fascist, but a critic of the way that attempts to understand romanticism have been marginalized within West German establishment and intellectual culture.
>
> (2001, 147)

Aitken suggests the real point Syberberg is making is that the utopian ideals at the heart of romanticism remain important for contemporary society and need to be reclaimed.

Volker Schlöndorff became most well-known for the surreal, darkly comic *Die Blechtrommel/The Tin Drum* (1979) which brought Günter Grass's novel of the same name to the screen. The film examines the pre-war rise of the Nazi party and the war itself, with a strong emphasis on exploring the historic relationship between Germany and Poland. Such a re-examination of the past, indeed, a refusal to look away from the past, is at the heart of New German Cinema. Referring to the novel and the film, Hans-Bernhard Moeller and George Lellis say: 'As political discourse, these works of art deal with German-Polish relations in a fresh, frank and enlightened manner' (2012, 168). Schlöndorff's first film, *Der junge Törless/Young Törless* (1966), was based on a novel by Robert Musil, *Die Verwirrungen des Zöglings Törleß/The Confusions of Young Törless* (1906). Set in a boarding school, the central character observes in a detached manner the brutality of the world around him, remaining aloof even when a victim of bullying asks for his help. Törless's struggle throughout is, as he expresses it towards the end of the film, with the fact that given certain circumstances 'perfectly normal people can do terrible things'. Stephen Brockmann argues Schlöndorff was clear that at some level Törless should be seen 'as a representative of the passive complicity of the German people during the Nazi period' (2010, 320).

Helma Sanders-Brahms's debut feature, *Unter dem Pflaster ist der Strand/Under the Pavement Lies the Strand* (1975), looks at issues affecting working mothers against the backdrop of the failure of the 1968 student rebellions to achieve real social change, and became a feminist cult classic. *Deutschland bleiche Mutter/Germany, Pale Mother* (1980) shows how the lives of an ordinary couple, Hans (Ernst Jacobi) and Lene (Eva Mattes), are torn apart through the war. This film, directed and written by Sanders-Brahms around autobiographical material, examines the difficult ground of the relationship of everyday citizens to major political events. For Barbara Kosta, the opening to the film 'affirms the couple's innocence' (1994, 124). She argues, 'the reflection of Hans and Lene together in the three-panelled mirror visually consummates their unity in an idealized existence as unsuspecting, even blameless, participants in the fictions that inform their lives' (124). The focus of this film is clearly on the central female character, Lene, and Sanders-Brahms faced criticism from some for, as they saw it, allowing this character to be seen simply as a victim of German history.[61]

Werner Herzog's films do not deal with recent German history in the direct way adopted by many filmmakers under discussion here. His films tend to focus on intriguing individuals in extreme situations. *Aguirre, der Zorn Gottes/Aguirre, Wrath of God* (1972) follows a megalomaniacal Spanish conquistador with plans to found his own Amazonian empire.[62] *Jeder für sich und Gott gegen alle/The Enigma of Kaspar Hauser* (1974) is based on the story of someone who appeared in Nuremberg in 1828 claiming to have lived the first 17 years of his life confined in a cell. *Fitzcarraldo* (1982) focuses on a driven man who sets out to pull a steamship over a hill between two rivers to reach a rubber-rich area of Amazonian jungle. Herzog's characters are outsiders who, through their existence outside of the mainstream within some dream-like dimension, throw the ordinary and the normal into relief (Franklin 1986, 110–114).[63]

Margarethe von Trotta began her career by working in collaboration with Volker Schlöndorff. *Die verlorene Ehre der Katharina Blum/The Lost Honour of Katharina Blum* (1975), for example, examining the way organs of the state, such as the police and the media, can hound an innocent woman, was co-directed and co-written from a novel by Heinrich Böll. As von Trotta began to develop her own projects her determination to explore the female experience from a feminist perspective began to emerge more clearly. *Das zweite Erwachen der Christa Klages/The Second Awakening of Christa Klages* (1978) looks at a young woman who robs a bank in order to fund a children's daycare centre. Von Trotta places relationships between women, and particularly between sisters, at the heart of her films. *Schwestern oder Die Balance des Glücks/Sisters, or the Balance of Happiness* (1979) and *Die bleierne Zeit/Marianne and Juliane* (1981) emphasize 'the emotional flow between two women, their mutual dependency and intersection of internal worlds' (Rueschmann 2000, 147). Eva Rueschmann identifies von Trotta's debt to Ingmar Bergman, seeing her as using her female characters to explore 'modern consciousness and memory' in a manner reminiscent of Bergman (2000, 118).

Rainer Werner Fassbinder directed more than 40 films before his death in 1982. *Die bitteren Tränen der Petra von Kant/The Bitter Tears of Petra von Kant* (1972) is developed from his own play and retains an essential theatricality, taking place entirely in one room in Petra von Kant's (Margit Carstensen) apartment. The film considers the loneliness of the individual and the power struggle Fassbinder sees as existing within our relationships with others. *Angst essen Seele auf/Ali: Fear Eats the Soul* (1974) demonstrates how each of Fassbinder's films demands an awareness of the contemporary political landscape in West Germany.[64] Ali, from Morocco, is a gastarbeiter, a guest worker or migrant worker. These workers moved to Germany for the chance of a job and a better life but, following a classic pattern experienced by migrants, they were frequently the victims of extreme prejudice. *Die Ehe der Maria Braun/The Marriage of Maria Braun* (1979) is the story of someone who becomes a successful businesswoman in the postwar years. Her success parallels the wirtschaftswunder, or 'economic miracle', of West Germany's recovery from the devastation of the war (Elsaesser 1996, 292). The central question posed by both Maria Braun's and West Germany's postwar 'success' might be: at what cost has this been achieved?

Wim Wenders formed a particularly strong collaboration with cinematographer Robby Müller. They made *Die Angst des Tormanns beim Elfmeter/The Goalkeeper's Fear of the Penalty* (1972), *Alice in den Städten/Alice in the Cities* (1974), *Im Lauf der Zeit/Kings of the Road* (1976), *Der amerikanische Freund/The American Friend* (1977) and *Paris, Texas* (1984) together. *Die Angst des Tormanns beim Elfmeter* documents the isolation of a goalkeeper, Josef Bloch (Arthur Brauss), who exists detached from those around him. In our observation of his in many ways mundane life we are as coolly distant from him as he is from the world. In the slow unfolding of a sequence of episodes from an enigmatic life we are faced with the existential meaninglessness of it all.

Fig 3.11 Isolation (*Die Angst des Tormanns beim Elfmeter/The Goalkeeper's Fear of the Penalty*, 1972).

Wenders claimed that, 'With *Alice in the Cities* I found my individual voice in the cinema' (Brady and Leal 2011, 196). This film, because he was working with his own script, allowed him 'to explore the individual's relationship to reality from a more personal and autobiographical perspective' (196). In literature in West Germany in the 1970s it has been suggested there was a movement towards Neue Subjektivität (New Subjectivity). In this understanding of the period, disillusioned by the failure of political action to bring about social change, there is renewed focus on the individual experience. These films might be seen to follow a similar trajectory. *Im Lauf der Zeit*, like *Alice in den Städten*, is a road movie built around the concept of the journey. The route takes us directly into German history as it follows the border between East and West Germany. With this film, Wenders's working pattern was to write the script overnight for filming the next day. As Alexander Graf describes it, 'The story was "found" on location' (2002, 14). The characters Wenders creates often seem to be searching for something ill-defined and uncertain but which they feel is important, and their quest in some way mirrors that of Wenders himself. Referring to this film, he said, 'I felt that I needed to come up with a story in which I could investigate myself and my country' (Cook and Gemünden 1997, 38).

New German Cinema of the 1960s and 1970s produces a series of intensely serious works. As James Franklin says: 'The world of the New German Cinema is no laughing matter. These films, however, compensate for their lack of humor with an intense sense of social justice' (1986, 39). The films consider philosophical issues and operate in political dialogue with recent German history: the pre-war rise of fascism, the hardships and horrors of war, the postwar economic recovery, increasing social dissent in the 1960s, and violent attacks on the social establishment in the 1970s as epitomized by the actions of the Red Army Faction.[65]

DEVELOPMENTS IN EUROPEAN ART CINEMA POST-1989

In 1995, two Danish filmmakers, Lars von Trier and Thomas Vinterberg, instigated the Dogme 95 film movement. They said the French New Wave was correct to attempt the resurrection of movies, but the problem was their approach was based on 'the bourgeois perception of art'. The individualism attaching to the idea of the auteur was 'bourgeois romanticism'. 'Today a technological storm is raging,' they declared, 'the result of which will be the ultimate democratization of the cinema. For the first time, anyone can make movies. But, the more accessible the medium becomes, the more important the avant-garde' (Trier and Vinterberg 2000, n.p.). As a filmmaker, they suggested, the way to counter the cult of the individual auteur was to submit yourself to a set of collectively agreed rules. This was the basis of the manifesto they put forward, which said shooting had to take place within authentic locations that had not been altered for the filming, sound and images had to be recorded together and without music unless it occurred from within the scene, and only filming that could be achieved with a handheld camera should be allowed (Hjort and MacKenzie 2003, 199). The extent to which we should take this manifesto seriously can be debated, but it does recognize a changed socio-technological space within which filmmaking begins to take place from the 1990s. Susan Hayward sees a parallel with the French New Wave: 'As with the earlier Cahiers manifesto, Dogme 95 produced a new radical film practice … we have Dogme films in the digital age and New Wave cinemas with Cameflex cameras in the 1950s and 1960s' (2013, 116).

For André Bazin, film attempted 'to give the spectator as perfect an illusion of reality as possible' (2005 [1971], 26) within the demands of the storytelling necessity of moving between characters and places. Bazin praised Orson Welles for his use of deep focus and the long take, which he suggested 'restored to reality its visible continuity' (28), allowing the spectator to take in for themselves the whole 'dramatic field'. However, proponents of Dogme 95 were interested in presenting the viewer with a very different experience of this awkward concept of 'reality'. Their films are in some ways much more like watching amateur home-movies. And yet, there is something more. At the point at which detached observation of the filmmaking process is left behind, we are absorbed into the action and into the narrative world with increased intensity. In some sort of contradictory state, we are unaware of the in-your-face presence of the filmmaking, so sutured into the fabric of a 'real' imagined world have we become.

Holly Willis sees a connection between ideas in the Dogme 95 manifesto and the concept of Third Cinema, outlined as long ago as 1969 by Argentinian filmmakers, Fernando Solanas and Octavio Getino, in their essay *Hacia un tercer cine/Towards a Third Cinema*,[66] where the need to go beyond not only Hollywood but also auteur film practices is advocated (2005, 25). Willis highlights the call from Solanas and Getino for films that 'the System cannot assimilate and which are foreign to its needs', a cinema described as 'outside and against the System' (1997, 42–43). Willis immediately, quite rightly, points out that Dogme 95 productions still tend to be linked to the idea of the auteur; but she is also right to identify more radical possible interpretations of the manifesto, because this is something that has excited the interest of filmmakers well beyond the original few Danish moviemakers who joined Trier and Vinterberg. Can simplifying the filmmaking process, breaking down the formalities of camera setups and other on-set arrangements, create a stronger sense of collaborative, collectivized filmmaking? Ultimately, it is disingenuous of Trier and Vinterberg to suggest they are moving away from an auteur perspective; nevertheless, they have wanted to question and challenge both the filmmaking 'System' and the social 'System'.

Judith Weston suggests the first film to be made as a Dogme 95 production, *Festen/The Celebration* (Vinterberg, 1998), is based on 'a premise that could be equally at home in soap opera as it is in a European art-house movie' (2003, 28), the idea that 'victims of incest pay the emotional costs for the rest of their lives'. This is, indeed, something of the premise of the film, but it is not what the film is primarily 'about', any more than the second Dogme 95 production, *Idioterne/The Idiots* (Trier, 1998), is 'about' disability or pornography. The story of *Festen* revolves around a father's sexual abuse of his children coming to light during a party for his sixtieth birthday. *Idioterne* follows a group who spend their time acting as if they have various developmental disabilities, what they call 'spassing', and who at one point take part in group sex. Both films, however, exist within a wider context in that they are essentially 'about' capitalism and the type of society that exists under capitalism, in particular the repressive and abusive nature of the institution of the family under capitalism.[67] Referring to *Idioterne*, Caroline Bainbridge points out how 'we are forced into a number of encounters with bourgeois ideals and attitudes that are discomforting for the spectator and which seem to demand self-reflexive scrutiny on the part of the audience' (2007, 124).

Tanya Horeck and Tina Kendall focus on 'a trend towards "new extremism" in contemporary European filmmaking' (2011, 1) within which some of Trier's work might be seen to fit.[68] They refer to 'art-house films, whose brutal and visceral images appear designed deliberately to shock or provoke the spectator' (1). And, they suggest, the effect these films has on audiences creates a need for us to rethink the nature of spectatorship in relation to the contemporary cinema experience.[69] One way of looking at art cinema is to see it as setting out to challenge accepted norms, to push at the perceived boundaries of cinema and filmmaking, to deliberately transgress social boundaries of 'taste' and correctness, to offer new possibilities for what might be seen as 'art', and in the process to renew discussion and debate around aspects of the human condition. Within this context, any 'tendency' towards the presentation of extremes of graphic sex and violence would be something to be expected within art cinema.

As with all 'trends', 'tendencies', 'movements' and 'genres', which films should be included and which move beyond the bounds of the type of film we are attempting to delineate is, as we have suggested, problematic. It does seem to be the case, however, that a range of European films from recent times, while not being classifiable as 'porn', do make use of graphic sex and, while not easily classified as 'horror', do make use of easily recognizable aspects of the violence on which horror films trade. Arguably, the consistent purpose of all of this within these ultimately art-house movies is to explore gender issues of critical importance to feminist perspectives on society. Some of the films (Gaspar Noé's *Irréversible* (2002) and Bruno Dumont's *Twentynine Palms* (2003), for example) brought together within this 'trend' are the work of male directors, but other films show female directors and other creative personnel appropriating 'male' genres for their own uses. These women have turned the porn and horror genres back on a male-dominated film industry and upset male-dominated circles of film critics, while challenging the norms and expectations of a patriarchal society in a strongly visceral and affective style.

Romance/Romance X (1999), written and directed by Catherine Breillat, is one film amongst a series of works by this director that looks at female sexuality in a frank and challenging way. Emma Wilson asks whether such 'a liberal exploration of female sexuality' by not only Breillat but other French women might not be 'crucial to an understanding of women's identity and their independence' (2001, 146). Certainly, the viewer, of whatever gender or sexuality, is invited through their spectatorship to reflect both on the ways in which society might represent female sexuality and their own understanding of female sexuality, as they follow the central character, Marie (Caroline Ducey), through a series of sexual relationships. The film does what art cinema always does: it offers an entirely different 'take' to that found in mainstream movies dealing with 'romance'. Breillat's *À ma sœur!/Fat Girl* (2001) again deals with female sexuality and 'provides an implicit analysis of traditional gender roles among the bourgeoisie' (McDonald 2010, 249). Within this context, 'a woman's desirability determines how much she is loved, and she is desirable to the extent that she conforms to beauty standards and can tease and please men' (249). The sudden genre twist in this film propels the spectator into a dark world of horror, and jolts the viewer into further consideration of the representations of female sexuality on offer within contemporary Westernized society.

In *Baise-moi* (2000), directed by Virginie Despentes and Coralie Trinh Thi, it is payback time for the abuse women have suffered at the hands of men both in films and in real life. Two women, Nadine (Karen Bach)[70] and Manu (Raffaëla Anderson), take to the road for a violent crime spree that allows a certain sort of feminist revenge to be taken against men and a succession of warped male attitudes towards women.[71] The inclusion of real rather than simulated sex aroused entirely predictable media interest,[72] but the film 'both cites and subverts the genre of porn' (Fox et al. 2015, 471). *Baise-moi* confronts the spectator with an entirely different imaginative perspective than that offered by the constructed sexual fantasies of porn, presenting us with some small insight into the grim, poverty-lined abuse offered to women within the twin sex industries of prostitution and pornography.[73] Alexandra Heller-Nicholas perhaps sums up the most interesting way to approach this film: '*Baise-moi* seeks to actively defy the normative "male gaze" of Hollywood narrative cinema as identified by Laura Mulvey in 1972' (2011, 165). In *King Kong Theory*, Despentes says: 'Men alone conceive of porn, direct it, watch it and profit from it. And female desire is subject to the same distortion: it must only occur via the male gaze' (2009, 90).

Some spectators booed and left the theatre when *Trouble Every Day* (2001), directed by Claire Denis and filmed by Agnès Godard, was screened at the Cannes Festival (Beugnet 2004, 1). This film confronts the viewer with a disturbing story and disturbing images. The images challenge, not only because they can be graphic but also because the human figure 'is broken up or driven to the periphery of the images while empty spaces and inanimate objects (or objects that are mechanically animated like the rotating flasks in the neurological labs) take over the screen' (31). The story is disturbing not only because of the monstrous and tragic nature of the characters at its heart, but also because the plot 'is based on the simultaneous unfolding of several story lines which the parallel editing, and the loose mingling of a multitude of individual trajectories, allow to unfold in an elliptical fashion' (166). In other words, the viewer is continually on shifting ground, faced with a kaleidoscope of images and storylines. As Horeck and Kendall's *The New Extremism in Cinema: From France to Europe* suggests, at the heart of any critical evaluation of this trend in art cinema is the need to examine the nature of the form of spectatorship being offered to the viewer (2011, 7–10).

As a complete contrast, it is worth mentioning the concept of 'slow cinema', or 'contemplative cinema', described by Thomas Elsaesser as filmmaking that

> counters the blockbuster's over-investment in physical action, spectacle and violence with long-takes, quiet observation, an attention to detail, to inner stirrings rather than to outward restlessness, highlighting the deliberate or hesitant gesture, rather than the protagonist's drive or determination.
>
> (2011, 117)

This too is a recent 'trend' in European art cinema, not as noticeable as 'new extremism' perhaps, but precisely the sort of counterpointing of

Fig 3.12 Different, unsettling uses of screen space (*Trouble Every Day*, 2001).

approaches one might expect to find within art cinema. In his address to the 46th San Francisco International Film Festival in 2003, Michel Ciment explained this particular 'trend':

> made impatient by the bombardment of sound and image to which they are submitted as TV or cinema spectators, a number of directors have reacted by a cinema of slowness, of contemplation, as if they wanted to live again the sensuous experience of a moment revealed in its authenticity.
>
> (Ciment 2003, n.p.)

The films of Andrei Tarkovsky, who made five feature films in the Soviet Union between 1962 and 1979 and then a further two in Western Europe, have been described as 'slow, dreamlike searches for faith and redemption' (Martin 2011, 13), and it is in his work that the origins of 'slow cinema' have commonly been seen.

The Hungarian director, Béla Tarr, another filmmaker well known for using long takes, is also seen as critically important for this approach. Discussing *Damnation* (Tarr, 1988), András Bálint Kovács says this film's 'visual qualities together with its handling of time ran radically and spectacularly counter to the fashion of short-take, fast-paced non-linear editing' (2013, 4). Tarr's film *Sátántangó* (1994) is shot in black and white and has a running time of over seven hours, and *Werckmeister harmóniák/Werckmeister Harmonies* (2000), in length a more normal 145 minutes, is composed of just 39 long takes.

Among more recent films of this ilk, Philip French describes *Le Quattro Volte* (Michelangelo Frammartino, 2010) as 'an essay, a cinematic poem, a spiritual exploration of time and space,' which is 'designed to make us think and feel about the world around us and our place in it' (2011, n.p.). The camerawork and editing in this film take up the pace of life of the central character, an old goat-herder living in a rural Calabrian village in Italy. In *Two Years at Sea* (2011) the director, Ben Rivers, follows the rambling, unhurried life of Jake Williams, who lives alone in a clearing in a pine forest in Scotland. *Silence* (Pat Collins, 2012) has a little more of a plot – after living in Berlin for some years, a sound recordist returns home to Ireland with a commission to record soundscapes without human noise – but is, essentially, another slow, highly contemplative film offering plenty of time and space for the viewer to engage with the work.

4

KEY CRITICAL APPROACHES TO EUROPEAN ART CINEMA

ART CINEMA AND SEMIOTIC ANALYSIS

Focus films: *El espíritu de la colmena/The Spirit of the Beehive* (Erice, 1973, Spain) and *Im Lauf der Zeit/Kings of the Road* (Wenders, 1976, West Germany).

As we watch a film, a series of visual images and an array of sounds – a film language – convey a complex range of meanings to us. Whatever theoretical approach we adopt towards film analysis, whether it be feminist, psychoanalytical, postmodernist, or some other attempted method of accessing meaning, an awareness of this fundamental communication process is critically important. Every film should be seen to be employing film language as a sign system creating layers of potential meanings. The better we understand the language, the greater will be our understanding of meaning.

Semiotics, or the study of sign systems,[1] provides the basis for other forms of analysis. Our apparently 'instinctive' understanding of much of what we see on the screen, in fact, derives from our knowledge of the nuances of the language used. Every element of mise-en-scène, cinematography, editing and sound employs sign systems in order to communicate with the viewer. Body movements (whether of an actor, or of somebody 'performing' in everyday life), for example, only make sense within a culturally agreed sign system. Individual shots, scenes and sequences in films are constructed out of 'signs' that are being used to communicate with the audience. Close reading enables us to 'unpack' the film text, exploring potential meanings and associations.

The philosopher, Charles Sanders Peirce (d.1914), suggested three types of sign:

- an 'icon' directly resembles the object – a photograph, for example, indicates something beyond itself by direct resemblance to that object;
- an 'index' is directly linked to the object – smoke, for example, indicates something beyond itself by direct linkage, i.e. fire;
- a 'symbol' has only a culturally agreed connection to the object – in some cultures a red rose, for example, is culturally linked to the idea of love.[2]

Film clearly depends on 'icons' at a fundamental level, but indexical signs and symbolic signs are also at work in screen images. Vehicles in a road movie such as *Kings of the Road* have a direct indexical link to the idea of travel and movement, but also a symbolic link to the cultural concept of the journey as a means of individual exploration and discovery. The use of cinemas, projectors and screens (as in *Kings of the Road* and *The Spirit of the Beehive*) indicates the idea of films being shown, but also suggests the whole concept of human communications as a method of control or as a means of allowing freedom of expression.

Developing these ideas in the 1970s, Roland Barthes suggested a sign had a simple, surface, or literal meaning at the level of 'denotation', and a further potential set of meanings at the level of 'connotation' consisting of the social and cultural associations linked to the sign.[3] The mechanical process of photography (or cinematography) produced denotative meanings, displaying simply the surface fact of, for example, 'this is a table', or 'this is a chair'. But the image maker's intervention – the use of camera angle or distance, shot composition, editing, props, costume, lighting, etc. – produced connotative meanings. Within the second level of meanings, 'myth' was also at work, where 'myth' was an interlocking set of concepts widely accepted within a culture as expressing their understanding of some aspect of social experience. In *The Spirit of the Beehive*, when we see Ana's father, Fernando, alone in the library he is 'denoted' as a man on his own in a room lined with books, but the connotations are those of learning and intellectual activity. The scene might be said to reinforce socially shared, dominant Western beliefs in the concepts of the quiet, studious intellectual and the distant, aloof, father figure. The director, Victor Erice, is here going beyond these 'myths' to suggest the isolation of the father, cut off from, or cutting himself off from, the family in the sanctuary of the library, and then further cutting himself off through the use of headphones to listen to the radio. This situation is reinforced when in the next scene we see Fernando's wife, Teresa, in bed. She is denoted simply as a woman in bed, but the empty space beside her carries connotations, as do the bars on the headboard of the bed behind her. What we have is the classic unhappy couple, but Erice places them within a firm historical context, so that the third point of the classic 'love triangle', Teresa's lover, has been torn from her by the Spanish Civil War, and we are left uncertain whether Fernando is listening to the banned BBC[4] or the propagandistic RNE (Radio Nacional de España).[5]

Other theorists approaching semiotics (Fiske and Hartley 1978) suggested connotations and myths attaching to visual images expressed a further level of signification or meaning: that of ideology. Also, Stuart Hall (1973) suggested that in the process of decoding images, there were three options. The reader might adopt the socially dominant, preferred meaning; or, construct a negotiated reading, accepting some parts of the preferred meaning but rejecting others; or, adopt an oppositional reading, totally rejecting the preferred reading.[6] What is emphasized by semiotics is the importance of basing any critical analysis on close attention to individual signs and the relationship of these signs to social, cultural and historical contexts. Finally, the meaning of any sign will also depend on the context within which the audience experiences it. If, for example, the viewer is watching a film at a time when the country they are living in is one half of a previously united single country, as with watching *Kings of the Road* in West Germany in 1976, then the visual display of border fences and watch-towers on the screen takes on a particular resonance. If the same person watches the same film after 1989, when the divided country has been successfully reunited and the paraphernalia of the internal border dismantled, then those same images assume a re-constituted significance. Similarly, watching *The Spirit of the Beehive* in 1973 is a different experience to watching it after Franco's death in 1975.

The Spirit of the Beehive begins with a lorry coming along a road and then entering a small village. We are presented with simple iconic signs, in Peirce's terms, images that directly resemble implied objects – the flat, Castilian plateau landscape with a road and a lorry, followed by the buildings of a settlement. The photographic images stand for implied objects in the real world. Using Barthes's terms, what we have are objects that are simply denoted, e.g. road, lorry, buildings. But, maybe, the buildings are also indexical, in Peirce's terms, in that they suggest the presence of a village/settlement without showing it, giving us a mental concept of 'settlement' without as yet showing us the whole thing. The words we see on the screen, though, form a symbolic phrase: 'Once upon a time...' Culturally agreed connections with children's stories, folk tales, fantastical events and imagination come to the fore in the meanings we are being expected to create. The sign on the wall as the lorry passes into the village is clearly symbolic. Perhaps we recognize within the symbol the image of a 'yoke', relating to a specific object in the real world, and overlain by the yoke, an image of a 'set of arrows'; but, through symbolism, this sign stands for much more than a yoke and some arrows. The connotations, to use Barthes's term, suggest much more. This is the symbol of the right-wing, Falangist organization; a symbol that became the insignia of the only official political organization in Spain under Franco. The myths Barthes's theory might see as underpinning this particular sign might include a myth of Franco as the 'father' of the Spanish people and the accompanying myth of a

Fig 4.1 The symbol of the only official political organization in Spain under Franco (*El espíritu de la colmena/The Spirit of the Beehive*, 1973).

happily united Spanish national 'family'. Finally, if we return once more to the central image of the opening, a covered lorry entering a village, and we place this image in the context of Franco having gained full control of the country by April 1939, we realize the power of this image in a way that may not have at first occurred to us. In the context of the Civil War, out of the back of a lorry entering a village would come troops who would in all likelihood gather together supporters of one side, or the other, to be shot and buried in a mass grave. What is important about a semiotic approach is not so much that we should recognize the various theoretical understandings of sign systems that have been put forward, but that we should 'read' films with an awareness that something like 'lorry entering village' might signify more to the audience than simply 'lorry entering village'.

The opening to *Kings of the Road* shows a man (Bruno) repairing a projector while chatting to the elderly cinema owner. The scene is shot as if it were a documentary, with Bruno interviewing the cinema owner about the history of film in Germany. What we have denoted is simply an older man and a younger man with a projector between them. The projector functions as an indexical sign to suggest the twin concepts of 'cinema' and 'films being screened for an audience'. The connotations attaching to it might be to do with the ways in which the media in general, and film in particular, represent the world, and understandings of the world, for audiences. The connotations attaching to the presence here of 'older man' and 'younger man' may be to do with the idea of knowledge and the passing on of knowledge, and may be underpinned in some way by a myth of socially agreed roles of 'father' and 'son'. The connotations may also relate to the concept of history, or knowledge of the past, and the passing on of this to a younger generation. Certainly, the film *Kings of the Road* may be said to be 'about' the recent history of Germany and the resultant relationship between the older and the younger generation. Before any images have appeared on screen the viewer has been told this film was shot 'along the frontier with East Germany, between Lüneburg and Hof'. Documents formalizing the German Army's surrender and ending World War Two in Europe were signed near Lüneburg in May 1945; Heinrich Himmler's body was buried on a military training area near the town after he had taken his own life; the local mental health hospital is thought to have taken part in the Nazi euthanasia programme; and the first war crimes trial after the war, the Belsen Trial, began here in September 1945. And so, the sign 'Lüneburg' takes on additional connotations, marking it out as something more than simply the denoted place of Lüneburg. The films the cinema owner talks about with affection from the 1920s were directed by Fritz Lang, who fled Hitler's Germany in 1934 to work in the United States; but the works discussed, *Die Nibelungen* (1924), two silent films written by Lang and his then wife, Thea von Harbou, are expressions of pride in a Germanic heritage. A moment or so later, the cinema owner offers the information to Bruno that he was himself a member of the Nazi Party.

There has been tremendous critical debate about *Die Nibelungen* and how they should be viewed. Certainly they focus on an intense warrior culture: *Die Nibelungen: Siegfried* is a film in which the hero becomes invincible through bathing in the blood of his enemy. The cinema owner in *Kings of the Road* seems clear that *Die Nibelungen* should be seen as a nationalist epic. Nevertheless, there are no culturally agreed associations attaching to the sign *Die Nibelungen*, only controversy and disagreement, and a search to try to understand the 'true' position of people from the period involved in the production, critically Lang and von Harbou. Lang has been seen as an enigma surrounded by questions, uncertainties and ambiguities – much like the character of the cinema owner. Mention of *Ben-Hur: A Tale of Christ* (1925) clearly denotes a particular film but also carries even deeper connotations of ambiguity, uncertainty and confusion than those raised by *Die Nibelungen*. Based on a novel by Lew Wallace, published in 1880, *Ben-Hur: A Tale of Christ* follows the heroic story of a Jew enslaved by the Romans whose tale is interwoven with that of Christ. Culturally agreed myths attaching to Christianity, Judaism and Jews within different societies at different historical moments through the late nineteenth century and the first half of the twentieth century, but centring on the Jewish experience in Europe in the 1930s and 1940s, are all potentially playing out within a rich layering of ideologies. Again, what is critically important is that we should recognize the fact that a sign such as '*Ben-Hur: A Tale of Christ*' does so much more than simply denote a particular silent movie since it carries with it a rich hinterland of complex associations.

Proper nouns, as in film titles or the names of people, operate as significant signs in both *Kings of the Road* and *The Spirit of the Beehive*. In the second of these films, the poster announcing the film *Frankenstein: the Man Who Made a Monster* (James Whale, 1931) carries the name of the producer Carl Laemmle, but (particularly since it does not announce that this is actually Carl Laemmle Jr.) it also evokes the Jewish German father of the producer, Carl Laemmle Sr., one of the founders of Universal Studios, who helped hundreds of Jews to emigrate from Germany in the 1930s. In Saussurean (Ferdinand de Saussure was a Swiss linguist and semiotician) semiotic terms, the signifier composed of the letters making up 'Carl Laemmle' simply links to the signified mental concept of the person(s) of Carl Laemmle; but in the semiotic terms of Barthes the connotations here of Jewishness and German Jewishness, related to the socially agreed myths attaching to the concept of Jews and Jewishness in the 1930s, create an altogether richer interplay of ideologies, particularly in relation to Fascism in Europe in the period. Similarly, when we see 'Segovia' written on the wall of the village hall that is being used as a cinema and we know the Civil War background to the film, we might immediately think of an attempted Republican campaign during the early summer of 1937, the Segovia Offensive. This simple sign with a signifier, 'Segovia', evoking a signified place in Spain, might even trigger an association with the early sixteenth century Guerra de las Comunidades de Castilla/Revolt of the Comuneros, essentially an anti-feudal, peasant rebellion.[7] We may not recognize the painting on the wall between the beds of Ana and her sister, Isabel, as *The Guardian Angel* by Bartolomé Esteban Murillo, nor associate it with the related Roman Catholic litany, but we will see, in Peirce's terms, a simple iconic sign of a person with wings leading a child by the hand. Maybe the presence of wings evokes the concept of an angel and immediately sets this image within the sphere of Peirce's symbolic signs. Or, maybe, it is more complex still since we have a film image of a painting and, therefore, a representation of an object (a painting) in the real world; in Peirce's terms, an iconic sign. The point is, all of this carries (to use Barthes's terminology) connotations, relates to a series of myths on which society[8] is based, and links to ideology. How should society look after children: through the Church and teachings relating to guardian angels and the like? In this film, how does the image of the angel sit in relation to the image of the monster? When, a little later, Ana comes across a large footprint near the barn in the countryside where a Republican soldier has been hiding, we have an indexical sign, in that the sign of the footprint has direct linkage to the object of the man. But, of course, for Ana and for us it is more complex than this since the footprint links, both in Ana's imagination and in our conceptualization of the framework of ideas on which the film is built, to the idea of the monster and monstrosity.

Again, the simple sign is a stepping-off point for a rich layering of complex possible meanings and, therefore, potential understandings. In the following scene where the children help their father to search for mushrooms, there is a close-up of the father's boot, like the foot of a giant, an ogre, or a monster, coming down heavily on a mushroom; but this particular mushroom is a poisonous mushroom, a monstrous mushroom that has the potential to kill children. The image is simple, a boot coming down on a mushroom, but the connotations are rich and reverberate through the complex sign system of the film. Again, this same scene is filled with light, particularly when seen against the darkness of so many other scenes in the film. Light carries a certain, very obvious, and often used, array of connotations, but the trunks of the trees, between which Fernando and his children search for mushrooms, cast noticeable shadows and the scene has these darker undertones as indicated above. It is the signs of light and shadow, together with the darker connotations carried by signs such as the black boot, that create contradictory meanings and, therefore, contradictory responses in the audience.[9]

When in *The Spirit of the Beehive* the village children are in a schoolroom with their teacher and one of them is standing at the front reciting a poem, the cinematography simply denotes these things for us: 'children', 'schoolroom', 'teacher', 'one child standing'. But the connotations to what we see and the myths that underpin what we are shown are extensive. The chalk image behind the girl reciting the poem is of the Madonna and the words on the board are the title of a particular prayer, 'Oh, Señora mía'. There are, therefore, powerful religious connotations to the scene, particularly relating to Roman Catholic beliefs surrounding the Virgin Mary. The key line in this Marian devotion is when the devotee says, 'I offer myself entirely to you'; but, we should note that the child then asks to be 'guarded' and 'defended' as Mary's 'possession'.[10] The key myths, or cornerstone social beliefs, here are clearly to do with the Church, the Virgin Mary and Christ. The poem being recited in Castilian is Rosalia de Castro's *Follas Novas. Vaguedás.* Poem XIII.

Now, neither malice nor hatred.
Not even the fear of change.
I only feel thirst, a thirst for I know not what.
Rivers of life, where have you gone?
Air, I need air.
What do you see in the darkness that makes you so tremble?
I have the eyes of a blind man who stares at the sun's face.
I will fall where the fallen never rise.

What are the connotations to this: schoolchildren being taught to celebrate Spain's literary and cultural heritage? There is a photograph of Franco, the nation's leader, behind the teacher. And so, we have a celebration of the related underpinning myths of this society, the nation and the nation's cultural heritage. Or, do the connotations run deeper, and in relation to this do we need to invoke the notion of ideologies and the clash of ideologies? Notice the complex sign Erice gives the viewer as the line, 'What do you see in the darkness that makes you so tremble?' is read. The sound is the girl's voice reading this line but the visual image is the teacher's (thoughtful/pained?) face with the portrait of Franco behind her. The presented ideologies are primarily those of the Roman Catholic Church and the fascist state, but what is the film's implied ideology in relation to these belief systems? If we return to the denoted space in which we find ourselves, the schoolroom, what are the connotations of this setting? Presumably, they are to do with a society's responsibilities to educate, nurture and look after children. There is no narrative reason for Erice to take us into this school other than to raise these sorts of issues. Is the Church 'guarding' and 'defending' these young children as the prayer to Mary asks? Depending on your own ideology you might answer this in very different ways. If you were of a certain ideological persuasion, and recalling the theme of 'monsters' and 'monstrosity', you might ask whether the Roman Catholic Church was not rather monster-like in its relationship to children? Or, you might ponder whether Franco and the fascist state were not now demanding of children and citizens that same 'offering of myself entirely' as the Church had always required? And, these sorts of questions might seem more likely to be the correct ideological tack to be taking for the whole film if you realized that de Castro had originally, very deliberately, written her poem in Galician, the language of the poor and illiterate in the area where she grew up, and furthermore that both written and public use of Galician was banned in Spain under Franco.

The classroom scene before this one opens with children reciting in chorus as they learn mathematics by rote. There is a cross on the wall and two maps of Spain.[11] The children then learn human biology by hanging various parts of the body on a cardboard cut-out character, 'Don José'. There is a photograph of Franco on the wall. All of this is what is denoted for us by the use of images and sounds, but what are the connotations? The ordered conformity of learning by rote would seem to be clear. The connotations of religion, the Church and nationalism would seem obvious from the props placed on the classroom walls. The connotations of the cardboard 'Don José' as a 'monster' would seem at least possible within the context of this particular film. The ideological linking of the 'monster', 'Don José', who the children work out is missing 'his heart', to Franco, who is shown on the wall, might also be possible.[12] Here, the juxtaposition of one simple sign denoting 'teaching aid with missing heart' with the following simple sign of a photograph denoting 'Franco', could be said through their alignment to carry the additional connotation of the teaching aid and Franco being alike in not having a heart. Similarly, the linking, through closely following shots, of the cross on the wall with the two maps of Spain might be said to carry the connotation of some linkage between the Church and nationalism, and even between the Church and fascism.

Clearly, all of this implies sign systems can never be seen as simple and can never be interpreted fully outside of ideological contexts. The filmmakers use signs in this film to show they are aware of the difficulties facing those living in this particular society. A photograph of a young Teresa, a simple iconic image in Peirce's terms of 'Ana's mother as a younger woman', is inscribed 'To my dear misanthrope'. It carries an array of potential connotations relating to the concept of the past, to the passing of time and to the relationship of each successive generation to the next. But there is potentially much more here: a misanthrope's answer to the fact that they do not much like the way human beings conduct themselves is to cut themselves off from other people. Further, if we take Moliere's central character, Alceste, in *The Misanthrope* (1666) we are not sure whether we should admire him for his high moral outlook or see him as stupid in expecting such standards from human society. Again, a simple shot within a film and a simple single word can operate as complex signs carrying a range of potential associations and meanings. Take St Jerome, who we keep seeing in the main painting in Fernando's study. This is a critically important Catholic saint, but is he to be admired as the person who translated Greek and Hebrew scriptures to produce a standardized Latin Bible, or is he to be seen as a Dr Frankenstein character who created the oppressive monster that is the Church?[13]

Proper nouns, and their ramifications beyond operating simply to denote objects in the world, are also important in *Kings of the Road*. Bruno (Rudiger Vogler) first becomes aware of Robert (Hanns Zischler) as the driver of a car hurtling along a road towards a river. We are given a simple arrangement of images displaying signs standing for objects we recognize from the real world: 'driver', 'car', 'road', 'river'. However, the car is a Volkswagen Beetle, the driver is a West German, and the river is the heavily guarded border between West and East Germany; and, at this point, the denoted objects begin to carry heavy connotations, or associations. The VW Beetle was originally designed and made after Hitler ordered that a cheap and simple car for ordinary people should be mass-produced.[14] That the type of car is not insignificant is confirmed by the use of the sign 'Wolfsburg' a little later in the film. In one sense, this is simply the name of a town through which Bruno and Robert pass, but it was specially created in 1938 to house workers producing the VW Beetle.[15]

Camera shots can also, of course, operate in particular ways as signs. When we see Bruno and Robert in bunk-beds in the cab of the lorry in which they are traveling, the image simply shows, or denotes, one man in one bunk-bed with another man in another bunk-bed below. However, the strong horizontal line of Robert's bed across the screen divides the men from each other and connotes something of the tension in their relationship. Throughout the film, with varying degrees of success, we see them attempting to communicate with each other across the divide that keeps them (inevitably as individual beings) separate from each other. When they perform an (in the narrative) improvised slapstick routine as shadows behind a cinema screen, they seem to come together in an intensely bonded moment. But afterwards Bruno recalls how he actually felt: 'I wanted to stop. I was in a rage … Why did I get involved in this? But you went on acting the fool, so all I could do was join you again. That made me even angrier.' Robert's simple response is: 'Same thing with me.' These are simple sentences denoting a particular series of events and emotions, but the connotations are much deeper and are connected to the effort of the filmmakers (particularly, presumably, director Wim Wenders) to explore the nature of human relationships. During this exchange Wenders positions his two characters next to each other, so that in simple denotation terms we have 'a man standing next to another man'; but the shot places the two men before a white van with a split windscreen, so that the two men are boxed either side of the strong central line of the windscreen. The connotations are clear for both the relationship between Bruno and Robert, and human relationships more generally. When they stop speaking, Wenders has Bruno coming round one side of the fast-food van in front of which they have been standing, while Robert walks around the other side. He then shows Bruno walking down one side of his van while Robert walks down the other side. They climb in opposite sides of the driver's cab and then are separated in the shot by the central line of a split windscreen. In other words, a series of shots denote simple movements and placements of actors within the screen space, but each shot is structured so as to connote isolation and division.

Fig 4.2 The divide between Bruno and Robert (*Im Lauf der Zeit/Kings of the Road*, 1976).

One difficulty is always deciding how far to pursue connotations. For example, Bruno and Robert pass through Hassfurt, the hometown of Fritz Sanckel. This was the man responsible for ensuring Nazi Germany had a large enough labour force to continue war production. He directed the mass deportation and enslavement of more than five million people and was hanged for war crimes in 1946. One of the things Bruno and Robert have to deal with, in common with the rest of their postwar generation, is the legacy of the war. Connotations of that war are inescapably present everywhere. Should we also be aware that 'Hassfurt' may carry more positive connotations in that the first cantilever bridge was built here in 1867? This uses the cantilever engineering principle to place two halves in perfect balance, enabling a bridge to span what would seem an impossible divide. And, the complex connotations potentially attaching to references continue when we see another image of Fritz Lang. In the photo from a film magazine he is on the set of *Le Mépris/Contempt* (Jean-Luc Godard, 1963). Here, Lang is playing himself in a film in which a director tries to make an art film relating to the story of Odysseus. In Homer's *Odyssey*, Odysseus and other Greeks involved in the Trojan Wars find that, as a result of their own arrogance, Poseidon has stirred the seas against them when they attempt to return home. Odysseus has to journey for ten years before he is able to return to his home. The potential connotations in relation to the German experience of the aftermath of the Second World War would seem obvious. On the wall of Bruno's van near the image of Lang is one of Robert Mitchum. This Hollywood actor's first film was a Western entitled *Border Patrol* (1943). Perhaps his most famous Western role was in *Pursued* (1947) in which he played an orphan who grew up haunted by the moment in his childhood when his family was killed as he hid in the cellar. The poster from which this particular image was taken was for *Young Billy Young* (1969) in which Mitchum played an older man whose son has been killed. He seeks revenge and in the process forges a bond across the generational divide with a younger man who becomes something like an adopted or replacement son. What we have on the wall of Bruno's van is simply an image of a man's face, which if we recognize it as Mitchum may become a symbol taking on cultural meanings. But if we place this image within the particular context of this film, the picture torn from a film poster takes on specific connotations relating to the particular themes and interests of the film. The only question then becomes how far we should take our investigations into the associations that might be seen to be attaching to particular signs. When Bruno, who never had a father because 'he got lost in the war', takes Robert to a summerhouse on an island on the Rhine where he spent time as a child, the eerie atmosphere may remind the viewer of *Night of the Hunter* (Charles Laughton, 1955). For this viewer these scenes will acquire particular connotations. Will these connotations be a legitimate part of any analysis we might offer of these scenes? And, will that legitimacy be reinforced by recognizing the continued symbolic presence of Robert Mitchum as the sinister central character in *Night of the Hunter*?

ART CINEMA AND AUTEUR THEORY

Focus films: *Wild Strawberries* (Bergman, 1957, Sweden), *Winter Light* (Bergman, 1962, Sweden) and *Persona* (Bergman, 1966, Sweden).

Art cinema has tended to be seen as the creation of a 'work of art' embodying the vision of an individual (male) filmmaker. Studying film as the work of an artist, or artists, while continuing to employ an analysis of sign systems as the basis for our search for meaning, is crucial to our project of exploring European art cinema.

The concept of the 'auteur' emerged in France in the late 1940s/early 1950s when critics began to suggest there were certain directors who took such creative control over films as to leave their distinctive stamp on them. It was argued this effectively made these directors the 'author' of the films. The status of 'auteur' was accorded to directors such as Orson Welles and Jean Renoir because of the 'signature' marks to be found across the range of films they made. Directors such as these were seen as working at a higher level of creativity than those who were more workman-like and simply put scenes together without imbuing the results with anything of their own personal vision. Alexandre Astruc suggested in an essay on la camera-stylo (the camera-pen) in 1948 that the auteur 'writes with his camera as the writer writes with his pen' (1967, 23). The term was used more provocatively in an article by Francois Truffaut, 'Une certaine tendance du cinema francais', in the magazine *Cahiers du Cinema* (Cinema Notebooks) in 1954, in which he put forward the idea of the politique des auteurs. This amounted to an artistic stance on how filmmakers should approach filmmaking and formed the basis of what in the 1960s became 'auteur theory'. Through the use of a unique, identifiable style certain directors working within Hollywood, such as Howard Hawks, John Ford and Sam Fuller, were said to have left their mark on a body of work. Despite the strictures of the Hollywood system of production, directors such as these were said to have given a distinctive signature to their work.[16] The concept was subsequently extended to include the idea that certain stars, studios, or production teams working together over a period of time, could be said to achieve the same sense of there being a distinctive unity of theme and style attaching to their work.

We will consider three films, *Wild Strawberries* (1957), *Winter Light* (1962) and *Persona* (1966), directed by Ingmar Bergman over a ten-year period, to illustrate the possibilities of this approach to art cinema. Any number of films directed by Bergman over a career spanning more than 30 years, including *Summer with Monika* (1953), *Smiles of a Summer Night* (1955), *The Seventh Seal* (1957), *Through a Glass Darkly* (1961), *The Silence* (1963), *Cries and Whispers* (1972) and *Fanny and Alexander* (1982) could be used by anyone wanting to extend the analysis. Essentially, we will be looking for recurring themes, types of character, narrative structures and filmmaking techniques that together might be said to produce a unity of form and outlook that could be attributed to the director exerting a controlling vision.

Each of these films focuses at heart on the nature of the human condition. The central character in *Wild Strawberries* is reassessing his life in the face of old age. In *Winter Light* a Lutheran pastor is wrestling with his loss of faith. And, in *Persona*, faced with the cruelty of the world the central character decides the only possible response is silence. Effectively, the films deal with the human condition in terms of the inescapability of death, the seeming meaninglessness of life, and the malignity of the world with which the individual is faced. All three films confront the idea that each of us exists in relation to other people and each of us attempts to communicate with other people, but in the final analysis each of us is isolated and alone.

Wild Strawberries begins with the central character, 78-year-old Professor Isak Borg (Victor Sjöström), alone in his study with the clock ticking and ends with him alone in bed. Borg's voiceover narration in the first scene assesses the very idea of the relationship of the individual to other people. 'Our contact with others consists mainly of discussion,' he says. 'We evaluate the character and conduct of our neighbour. That is why I have refrained of my own free will from almost all so-called social life.' The implication of the final phrase, 'so-called social life', is that communal life can only fail to achieve communion between people. Yet, Borg has also chosen of his own free will to write an autobiographical assessment of his life, that is, to attempt to communicate with others in some way. We are the recipients of his attempted communication, and we are also the audience for Bergman's efforts to bridge the divides between human beings. In bed at the end of the film, Borg (and Bergman) offers us some small comfort: 'Whenever I feel anxious or worried during the day I usually relax when I recall childhood memories.'[17]

Winter Light, perhaps, offers less comfort for the viewer. There is, though, a suggestion that 'love' may provide some relief from loneliness. At the end of an intensely choreographed scene in which Märta (Ingrid Thulin) has repeatedly pursued, moved towards and looked towards Tomas (Gunnar Björnstrand) while he has repeatedly moved away from, turned his back on and looked away from her,[18] Märta tells Tomas not only that he 'has a lot to learn' but that specifically what he must do is 'learn to love'. This film opens with the central character of Tomas, the local pastor, in church and seemingly at the heart of his congregation as he conducts the Eucharist. Yet, everything about the construction of this scene contributes towards demonstrating how isolated and cut-off Tomas really is. Instead of the clock ticking, as in *Wild Strawberries*, what we have in the opening to *Winter Light* is the steady, relentless tolling of a church bell. Like the church itself, shown in a series of long shots as a backdrop to the pastor's voiceover, Tomas is isolated in a cold, snowy, winter landscape. Within the church, he is divided from the congregation by a heavy altar-rail.[19] The individual members of the congregation sit boxed within pews and the whole space with its low, overbearing arches feels tomb-like. *Winter Light* comes full circle to end with Tomas, a man whose loneliness has been fully explored, in another church in his parish reciting with heavy irony, the Sanctus, 'Holy, holy, holy, is the Lord of hosts: the whole earth is full of his glory.'[20] At the core of *Winter Light* is an intense and bitter relationship between Tomas and Märta, a schoolteacher, as Bergman explores the impossibility of genuine union between people who must necessarily remain individuals and, by definition, divided from others.

This examination of the fervor of relationships, that Bergman always sees as existing in relation to the ultimate isolation of the individual, continues in *Persona*. Here the editing and cinematography, as well as the script and events within the narrative, work together particularly strongly to show the detachment of characters one from another, but also the sense in which individuals may at moments feel as if they are able to merge into each other. As Alma (Bibi Andersson) tells Elisabet (Liv Ullmann) about her sexual adventures with young boys on a beach, the two women are shown in separate shots and we cut between the two, but immediately after this they are shown together in a two-shot culminating in Elisabet holding Alma and comforting her by stroking her face. Next, we see the two of them very close to each other in close-up at a kitchen table. 'I've talked and you have listened to me. How boring for you. Of what interest can my life be to you?' says Alma, highlighting the idea of the difficulty of communication in the face of the self-centredness of human beings. This passage of the film then culminates with Elisabet entering Alma's room and the two of them standing together facing the camera. The camera moves in slowly towards an increasingly tight close-up of their faces and eventually a merging of the two into one as Elisabet's face moves behind Alma's head and we fade to black. All of this, however, contrasts with the opening of the next scene, which fades in straightaway from the black screen. Alma is, first of all, shown in long shot, small within the frame on a rocky seashore, before Elisabet suddenly, unexpectedly and dominantly rises into the foreground of the shot in close-up, with Alma small and in the distance over her right shoulder. Over the series of shots that follow, we see the two of them moving together and then apart again as they traverse the boulder-strewn terrain, and we see Elisabet apparently lying twice to Alma. It is in the coming together of dialogue, actions, location, cinematography and editing that the particularities of this relationship are given to us.

The nature of the human condition for Bergman means we are all inevitably egocentric. *Wild Strawberries* begins with Isak's autobiographical description of himself. *Winter Light* has a central character who is totally focused on himself and his relationship with God. *Persona* revolves around the story of Elisabet who, apparently because of the unavoidability of doing anything other than moving within the realm of half-truths, untruths and downright lies as soon as you speak, has decided to remain silent. The effort, it seems, is to elevate herself above the commonplace, sullied nature of human existence. She is to some extent like Isak's son, Evald (Gunnar Björnstrand), in *Wild Strawberries*, who sees life as 'absurd'. 'This life turns my stomach,' he says. 'I won't be committed to it ... I need to be completely, immovably dead.'

Explaining Elisabet's decision to opt for silence, the doctor talks of 'the chasm between what you are to others and to yourself ... Every tone of voice a lie, every gesture a falsehood, every smile a grimace.' But the doctor warns that life, or the human condition, is not that easy to escape. A close-up of Elisabet has the doctor's words given as a voiceover: 'Your hideout isn't watertight. Life seeps into everything.' And then, the doctor comes into the close-up beside Elisabet in order to give emphasis to the words: 'You're forced to react.' What Elisabet cannot evade is her ego; remaining so steadfastly mute only confirms her self-awareness and sense of self-importance. Her arrogance and cruelty, that is, the inescapable arrogance and cruelty of the human condition, is confirmed in her letter to the doctor in which discussing Alma's devotion to her she says: 'I think, by the way, she's enjoying herself and is quite taken with me, even smitten in an unconscious and delightful way. It's fun studying her.'

Isak, in *Wild Strawberries*, is followed on a journey of self-discovery in which his daughter-in-law, Marianne (Ingrid Thulin), in particular, confronts him with 'the chasm between what you are to others and to yourself' as proposed by the doctor in *Persona*. 'You're a rigid egoist, even if you are applauded as a friend of humanity,' she tells him. She goes on to condemn him as 'categorical' in his 'judgements', while failing to realize, of course, that she is being equally assertive in her judgements. This is the messiness of human relationships in which, as Isak puts it, 'We evaluate the character and conduct of our neighbour', and that, from the beginning of the film, he has (egotistically) seen himself as rising above. But, as with Elisabet's attempted retreat into silence, so too Isak's refraining (of his 'own free will') from 'social life' is actually an impossibility. Each of Bergman's characters seeks some way of dealing with the unsolvable binds into which each of us is locked by

Fig 4.3 The impossibility of shutting out the world (*Persona*, 1966).

the human condition. Tomas in *Winter Light* has constructed his own space of withdrawal from the confusingly unanswerable conundrums of life. He has retreated into Christianity. 'My God and I lived,' he says, 'in a world where everything fitted in.' In this place, he says, he had his own 'private' God, who 'loved people but most of all me.' He has, he says, 'refused to accept reality', instead he has constructed his own God 'who gives benevolent answers and soothing blessings'. Confronted by 'God's silence', and illuminated by winter light streaming through a heavily barred church window, all Tomas can egotistically do is recite Christ's words on the cross, 'My God. Why has thou forsaken me?'

Jonas Persson's (Max von Sydow) retreat from the realities of the world in *Winter Light* is into death itself through suicide. The presence of death hangs over this film, not only in this central event of suicide, but also through the key image of the crucifixion. Tomas is repeatedly positioned within shots in relation to icons of Christ on the cross. In

Fig 4.4 Tomas between Christ and the world (*Winter Light*, 1962).

one shot, for example, three figures are shown in the church vestry in relation to each other. The sexton, Algot Frövik (Allan Edwall), is in the foreground counting money from the church collection and with a flask prominently positioned on the table at which he is sitting, in the background is a figure of Christ slumped on the cross, and between the concrete reality of the foreground and the background imagined 'reality' of religion is Tomas. A little later, Tomas emerges into the church from the vestry and is 'surrounded' by carved religious images on the altar to his right and on the pulpit to his left. He then walks towards a coat of arms on one wall of the church on which a skull and crossebones is conspicuously displayed. As he walks past this his face passes over the image of the skull and, in case we have missed this, he then turns and walks out from the wall with the skull visible to his right. Perhaps some of these things are too obviously handled but they do reveal the extent to which the concept of death is present within the filmmaker's vision.

Death is present in *Wild Strawberries* in every scene in which we see 78-year-old Victor Sjöström playing Isak Borg.[21] When we see him in bed early in the film, emphasis is placed on his aged, wrinkled face and he is positioned in a classic pose in which a dead body would be laid out. The key event in Isak's first dream, or nightmare, is a coffin breaking open after falling from a horse-drawn hearse to reveal, first of all, a hand that attempts to pull him towards the coffin, and then, the staring face of Isak himself.[22] In *Persona*, Elisabet is expressly said to have declined suicide in favor of silence; in effect, as an actor (egotistically) taking on the challenge of the ultimate performance. Dead bodies and bodies that appear to be dead, and concepts and images relating to death and the fear of death, are found throughout this film. As part of a challenging opening sequence, for example, and less than two minutes into the film, we are shown in close-up the lifeblood running from a sheep's throat that has been cut. An old man's hands hold the head of the sheep firmly as it struggles in its death throes before the viewer is given an extreme close-up of the animal's lifeless eye. After a couple of quick shots that appear to be of the butchery of this animal, there is an extreme close-up of a nail being driven through a hand.[23] There are then a series of shots of dead bodies on mortuary tables before a young boy, also apparently on a mortuary table, or an operating table, wakes.

All of this would suggest Bergman's work is completely angst-ridden; but, while there would certainly be some justification for taking this view, this might be to miss the humour. The young boy who wakes in the opening sequence to *Persona* begins to read from *A Hero of Our Time*, a Russian novel written by Mikhail Lermontov in 1841. The 'Author's Preface' to this book says:

> The preface to a book serves the double purpose of prologue and epilogue. It affords the author the opportunity of explaining the object of the work, or of vindicating himself and replying to his critics … The public of this country is so youthful, not to say simple-minded, that it cannot understand the meaning of a fable unless the moral is set forth at the

end. Unable to see a joke, insensitive to irony, it has, in a word, been badly brought up...

(2006 [1841], v)

Before the images of death in the opening to *Persona* there are various images of a projector and of film running through a projector. The audience is being taken back to their own earliest experiences of film and, at the same time, back to the experience of the earliest audiences for film. The image the projectionist appears to be trying to show is, first of all, upside down (i.e. the projectionist has got it all wrong), and secondly, in having a woman in a bathing costume on a rocky seashore, parodies what is to happen in the normatively substantive narrative. Of course, the joke is ultimately on us as well because, as viewers, Bergman knows we will be desperately trying to make sense of the succession of images he is giving us; that is to say, we will be parodying our own human existence predicated as it is on the seemingly inescapable desire to make sense of the world around us. Bergman does not exempt himself from all of this: a clip he made in silent comedy film-style for *Fängelse/Prison* (1949) is also intercut into the opening. This shows a man in a nightshirt being terrified by party costume-style representations of Death and the Devil. The clip itself parodies what Frank Gado describes as 'life's terrors'[24] but, of course, it also parodies Bergman's own obsession with these things. One of the things the young woman, Sara (Bibi Andersson), likes about Isak in *Wild Strawberries* is that he has a sense of self-irony.[25] Clearly these films do focus on the anguish that can be felt in the face of the apparent meaninglessness of life, but some ability to recognize a joke and some sensitivity towards irony, as called for by Lermontov in his preface to *A Hero of Our Time*, is required as part of any analytical approach to Bergman's work. When Tomas ends the opening service in *Winter Light* with the words, 'May the peace of God remain with you always', and then repeats the key word of 'peace' in his final sentence, 'Depart in peace', the irony is heavy with regard to him, but almost brutal with regard to Jonas Persson, who is soon to take his own life and is presented to the viewer with his head bowed and eyes downcast as they have been throughout the service. And when Tomas begins the service that is starting as the film ends, with the words, 'Holy, holy, holy, Lord God of Hosts. Heaven and earth are full of Thy glory,' these ironies are complete.

The in-house joke of featuring Victor Sjöström in a surreal sequence in *Wild Strawberries* (Isak's first dream sequence referred to above) that references his own early film *The Phantom Carriage* has its parallel in *Persona* where the extreme close-up of the sheep's eye in the pre-credits opening reminds us of the eye-slitting sequence at the start of *Un Chien Andalou* (Luis Buñuel and Salvador Dali, 1929, France). Little things like slotting a flash frame of an erect penis in the countdown between '7' and '5' in *Persona* when the Swedish word for '6' is 'sex' just seem mischievous, but other small moments such as having Märta administer medicine to Tomas in *Winter Light*, in an ironic parallel to the Eucharist, potentially carry more weight. The science and rationalism associated with the taking of medicine highlights a key theme for Bergman. If Tomas stands for having belief, or faith, in the irrational, Märta is intellectually positioned as diametrically opposed to this ('God's never spoken because there is no God. It's very simple, really.'). In *Wild Strawberries*, two of the hitchhikers picked up by Isak and his daughter-in-law, Marianne, embody the same polarities: Viktor (Björn Bjelfvenstam) is the rationalist and Anders (Folke Sundquist) the religious believer. 'Modern man is aware of his futility and acknowledges his biological death – that's that,' says Viktor; to which Anders replies, 'Modern man's a figment of your imagination. Man's afraid of a futile death.' And we are back to the central debate for Bergman of whether it is possible to find meaning in life. His rationalists essentially posit the existentialist belief that humans have the freedom to make their own choices and thereby define their own meaning in life. The position those living in Western civilization have been placed in with the decline of Christianity is summed up for Bergman in the passage he has Alma read to Elisabet from a book[26] in *Persona*:

> All the anxiety we bear with us, all our thwarted dreams, the incomprehensible cruelty, our fear of extinction, the painful insight into our earthly

> condition, have slowly eroded our hope of an other-worldly salvation. The howl of our faith and doubt against the darkness and silence is one of the most awful proofs of our abandonment and our terrified, unuttered knowledge.

The one way out Bergman seems to identify is the existentialist method of creating meaning for yourself. Alma gives the example of nurses who have 'lived for their work' and given their whole life to nursing. 'Imagine devoting your life to something,' she says. 'I mean, believing in something, accomplishing something, believing that one's life has a purpose … Sticking to one thing doggedly, irrespective.' Tomas, the pastor in *Winter Light*, has devoted his life to something that has given purpose to his life; but then because his purpose is founded on the premise of there being a God he has come up against 'God's silence'.

The problem is not that the world is full of suffering but that this suffering does not appear to have any meaning. Tomas's lover, Märta, has such bad eczema her hands have to be bandaged. 'If my suffering has meaning, tell me. Then I'll bear it without complaint,' she cries in prayer. Her answer to 'the silence of God' seems to be to live for others, or in her case for one other: Tomas. Somewhat like the nurses in Alma's example, she makes a personal choice as to how to use her life. 'I love you and I live for you. Take me and use me. Behind all false pride and independence I have only one wish: to live for somebody and it's very hard,' she says in her letter to Tomas. She might seem unsure of this choice at times and her choice might be criticized, as it is by the organist, Fredrik, but the point is she is shown by Bergman as wrestling with *the* dilemma for human beings: how to make sense out of life by giving it meaning. At the start of *Wild Strawberries* Isak confidently sets out the various ways he has given shape and meaning to his long life, but all of this is quickly undermined by the events we see, forcing him to re-evaluate. Isak sets out to travel to one of the most prestigious universities in Europe, where he is to be honored for having held his doctorate for 50 years, but all the pageantry of the brief presentation ceremony towards the end of the film, the grand buildings, fanfares, parade of dignitaries and formal use of Latin, is presented in a very cursory, distant and detached cinematic style. Isak's real journey, and the one we follow him on in a much closer, more intense way, is his inner journey to give renewed meaning to his life and, in the process, provide himself with some understanding of his life with which he can be at peace. The literal meaning of *Smultronstället*, the Swedish title of the film, is 'the place where wild strawberries grow', which is a phrase in common parlance carrying the connotation of a special, maybe undervalued, place. It is not the accolades of the world, nor the acclaim of those who have appreciated his work as a doctor, that make sense of the world for Isak, rather it is special moments in childhood places held within memory and to which he can return that bring peace. At the end of the film Isak sets himself the task not of trying to understand life, or his life, but simply of trying to make sense of the single day that we have just witnessed:

> My thoughts turned in the midst of the ceremony back to the events of the day. I decided to try to remember what happened and write it all down. There was, I thought, a remarkable causality in this hopelessly confused chain of events.

The opening image here embodies the nature of the human condition: Isak existing within himself, within his thoughts, as the world goes on around him. The second sentence introduces the whole notion of the questionable nature of memory and carries the connotation of the impossibility of such a task as capturing the 'all' that might be said to have happened to one person. And the final sentence attempts to yoke together, in the way that making sense of personal experience demands, order and chaos. In the face of all this, confronted by the anxiety this causes, Isak turns to his own special *Smultronstället*:

Whenever I feel anxious or worried during the day I usually relax when I recall childhood memories. And I did so this evening.

The nature of the world, its cruelty and suffering, is referred to by Isak's son, Evald. When he finds his wife, Marianne, is pregnant he wants her to opt for an abortion because this is 'an absurd life' only made worse by bringing more 'wretches' into it thinking they will be better off. However, 'real' historical events rarely intrude into these films. Only in *Persona* does the socio-political world encroach; and, even here, although these events take on a very particular force for the individual, this does not constitute any political engagement with the world on the part of Bergman.[27] Early in the film Elisabet is in a very stark hospital room when images appear on a TV screen of a Buddhist monk's self-immolation in 1963 in protest at the persecution of Buddhists by the South Vietnamese government. The low-angled light from the TV screen enables Bergman to illuminate the room, and Elisabet, in a manner reminiscent of a horror movie or film noir. For a minute the film cuts backwards and forwards between images of the monk's burning body and Elisabet's horrified reaction in tightening close-up, until we end with a long shot of her small within the frame having backed into the corner of the room.[28] Later we see Elisabet, in another sequence lasting about a minute, looking at a photograph of Jews captured during the Warsaw Ghetto Uprising of 1943; a group of Jewish men, women and children with their hands in the air is being overseen by armed German soldiers, with one Jewish boy particularly prominent in the foreground.[29] Bergman establishes that what we are seeing is from Elisabet's point of view and then uses a sequence of twelve shots showing different parts of the photograph in extreme close-up, with every shot deepening the intensity with which we are being asked to confront the cruelty of the world.

Thematically, then, there is a strong Bergman stamp being placed on these films. There are differences in the nature of the dramatic narrative, in the age and gender of the protagonists, and in the types of interior settings and locations being employed, but the probing investigation into the nature of the human condition is always present and is always kicking around the same basic ideas. Birgitta Steene suggests:

> Not only is Bergman a film maker rooted in literary traditions; but his greatest contribution to the art of film making may very well be that he has shown that a filmmaker can use his medium to express his Weltanschauung and his feelings about life and death as consistently as composers have used notes and musical instruments and writers have the various literary genres.
>
> (1970, 27)

It is also the case that certain images, or fields of images, recur through these films. Characters are shown looking at each other through a car windscreen, or through the windows of a house that are perhaps curtained, or net-curtained, often suggesting the sense of separation between people. Successions of shots emphasize what are clearly for Bergman crucially important parts of the body. So that, as well as the face, we are repeatedly shown the eyes, the hands, and the back of the head, often through the use of close-ups or extreme close-ups. Sometimes the eyes will be in shadow, or behind dark glasses, or will be shown as requiring glasses to correct poor vision. Mirrors and other reflections recur, suggesting introspection, but also linking to shots of actors performing directly to camera and so looking into the lens and at us, so that the seeing of reflections exists for the actors but potentially also for us as viewers. Sounds, such as those of clocks ticking, bells tolling, water dripping, and wind rustling the leaves of trees, are repeated.

All in all, what we have is a strong case for Bergman being seen as the author of these films. However, it could also be argued there is an increasing confidence in the camerawork and editing to be found in Bergman's films that may stem from the development of his working relationship with Sven Nykvist, cinematographer on a series of films with Bergman from *Jungfrukällan/The Virgin Spring* (1960) onwards.[30] Increasing use, for example, is made of close-ups and extreme close-ups that intensify the relationship between characters placed within the frame and deepen the emphasis placed on hands as well as faces. There is also growing confidence in drawing attention to the filming process and the relationship between the viewer and the film. Running alongside this would be an additional argument that the work prior to 1960, perhaps culminating in *Det sjunde inseglet/The Seventh Seal* (1957) and *Smultronstället/Wild Strawberries*, should be seen as authored not by Bergman but by a combination of Bergman and his cinematographer from that period, Gunnar Fischer.

5

KEY THEMATIC APPROACHES TO EUROPEAN ART CINEMA

ART CINEMA AND CHRISTIAN RELIGIOUS BELIEF

Focus films: *La passion de Jeanne d'Arc/The Passion of Joan of Arc* (Dreyer, 1928, France), *Au hasard Balthazar* (Bresson, 1966, France) and *Ordet* (Dreyer, 1955, Denmark).

Christian religious beliefs have played a major role in shaping European culture, heavily influencing, and in certain periods completely dominating, the artistic and written output of the continent. By the time the film medium emerged in the early twentieth century, the power the Church previously exerted over art through direct patronage and the limitation of permissible ideological perspectives had waned. And yet, even now, a century later, the origins of many of the foundational myths of European culture remain grounded in the Bible. Belief systems and social structures have remained defiantly locked into Christianity. Bergman's *Winter Light* is directly related to the Church, through following a central character who is a pastor and through its concern with the concept of faith. But it is also true that the main character in *Wild Strawberries*, Isak Borg (Victor Sjöström), evaluates his life in largely Christian terms. In *Persona*, Elisabet chooses to follow a trajectory that is essentially that of the monk, or nun, who withdraws from the world into contemplative silence. Bergman's films lend themselves to further investigation in relation to key concepts of Christianity. Here, though, we will consider the Christian tradition, particularly concepts such as the Fall from grace, the presence of sin in the world, the possibility of redemption or salvation, and, crucially, the necessity of faith, in relation to two films directed by Carl Dreyer and one by Robert Bresson.[1]

In *The Passion of Joan of Arc* (1928) Joan's faith is emphasized from the beginning. She is described by the narrator as 'a young girl of faith confronted by a cohort of blind theologians and corrupt lawyers'; in other words, she is facing people of social status and authority who are the very opposite of what they should be. Joan does not have the intellect of these people but sophisticated knowledge counts for nothing in religious terms, where only faith matters. Joan agrees 'these learned doctors' are wiser than she is but adds the rider that 'God is even wiser'. The film emphasizes that because of the simple, direct nature of her religious belief Joan has a moral honesty her accusers, for all their learned sophistication, cannot match. It is the strength of Joan's faith that Dreyer is at pains to highlight and this is also the key concept at stake in his film, *Ordet*, made almost 30 years later. When Inger, who is later to be brought back miraculously from the dead, asks her husband, Mikkel, if he has faith in God he responds, 'Not even faith in faith.' She says she is confident his faith will come and, stroking his hair and staring into the middle distance, adds, 'Just wait and see how warm you'll feel then.' Mikkel's brother, Johannes, who as a result of intense religious reflection has become psychologically disturbed enough to believe he is himself Christ, or a reincarnation of Christ, is continually berating those around him for claiming to have faith but not really believing strongly enough. Dreyer's position on the question of faith may be more complex than all of this might suggest,[2] but what is clear is that faith is identified as of central importance for Christian belief.[3]

In *Ordet*, various people's different definitions of faith are presented as part of what is effectively an ongoing debate about the nature of this crucial concept. Inger, for example, is very clear that Mikkel has something that is as important as faith and without which faith is not enough: 'goodness'. 'Faith is not enough if you are not a good person too,' she says. But Mikkel's atheism is equally important to the debate. The resurrection of Inger as a result, it seems, of faith is handled in a sufficiently skillful way to allow it to 'work' within the context of the film;[4] and yet, on reflection, do we really feel this outweighs the harsh reality of the world contained in Mikkel's reporting of Inger's aborted child 'lying in the bucket in four pieces'? Doesn't the fantasy of the Lazarus moment achieved at the end of the film only serve to underline the inescapable human reality of the extra-cinematic experience as expressed by Mikkel: 'Why should she die? Why should we be torn apart? It's all so meaningless ... What do I know? Only that all I loved and worshipped is to be buried in the earth to rot.'[5]

All three focus films here, *The Passion of Joan of Arc*, *Au hasard Balthazar* and *Ordet*, could be said to revolve around the movement towards death of a central, saintly (if not Christ-like) figure; but, in its culmination in resurrection *Ordet* moves any interest in the transformative powers of religion (and art) to another level. It is not only Inger who returns from the dead but also Johannes who is brought back from madness to life (and reason) and, potentially, characters such as Mikkel and his father, Morten Borgen, who are, through a reawakening of faith, 'resurrected'. What is exposed in all three films is the failure of existing social institutions, religious organizations and philosophies of life to adequately address the ultimate meaninglessness of human existence. The pastor in *Ordet* is condemned by Johannes as 'a man of faith who himself lacks faith'. The patriarch of the family, Morten, admits he has prayed without real faith. The version of Christianity practiced by the church Morten attends is at odds with the more austere approach of Peter Petersen's congregation. ('My faith makes me rejoice in life. Your faith merely makes you long for death,' says Morten to Peter.) The doctor applies scientific reason in aborting Inger's baby in order to save

Fig 5.1 Inger asking Mikkel if he has faith (*Ordet*, 1955).

her life, but then is powerless to prevent her dying. Within a Christian religious framework and taking into account the range of current social practices, the effort made by Dreyer is a version of the effort made by Søren Kierkegaard, that is, to explore the possibilities of what might be a reasonable response to the meaninglessness of existence. In this context, an apparently throwaway line in the film suggesting Johannes has been made mad by reading too much Kierkegaard[6] becomes much more significant for a reading of the film.

In *The Passion of Joan of Arc*, the failure of society and its institutions to offer anything more than repression is emphasized in scene after scene. The nature of the authorities is presented in close-up after close-up of the faces of the male judges interrogating Joan.[7] Their expressions range from mocking condescension, through arrogant self-confidence, to a vicious, spitting anger. The official overseeing all of this (a representation of Richard Beauchamp, Earl of Warwick) is continually associated by Dreyer with the image of a chain and shown ominously overseeing proceedings from a distance. The film focuses on the members of the religious court responsible for arraigning Joan and orchestrating her torture in such a way that the court's lack of 'Christian' compassion is repeatedly demonstrated. However, for the viewer the cold detachment of Warwick may create an even stronger indictment of political institutions, while also highlighting the politicization of religious organizations within the state. In a variety of ways Joan is shown as inescapably trapped. She is found in a series of ever more frighteningly oppressive locations: within the stone-paved court setting where both she and the Bible are chained, within a cell where she is shown to be under various forms of surveillance, in a torture chamber where the images are again of chains but also brutal spikes, and finally being tied to a stake to be burned alive. In various shots early in the film she is shown as surrounded by her accusers who crowd in around her. In the close-ups of Renée Jeanne Falconetti as Joan, for which this film is famous, Joan is again effectively boxed and contained. An old man and a young man who move towards defending her during the court proceedings are easily silenced by the social pressure of their peers. At every point, society and social institutions fail the test of humanity.

The images used in *Au hasard Balthazar* and the positions in which the central 'character' of Balthazar, a donkey, finds himself are similarly utilized to reflect the brutality of human society. Harnesses and chains are used to restrain him and lead him. He is whipped, beaten and kicked. Marie, the only character to show Balthazar kindness, is abused in a similar way to him throughout the film. She sees her childhood, like Balthazar's early days on the farm, as a romantic illusion and chides Jacques for clinging to such a mistaken view of the world. 'We were in an imaginary world, not a real one,' she tells him. 'Reality is something else.' In one episode, Balthazar finds himself working in a circus; Bresson cuts backwards and forwards between shots of Balthazar (in a harness), a tiger in a cage with a chain in the corner, a polar bear in a cage, a chimpanzee with a chain on in a cage, and a close-up of an elephant's eye. Whatever meaning we take from this is clearly heavily influenced by the director's choice of editing and composition of shot, but it is also determined by the fact that in the film we see Balthazar in

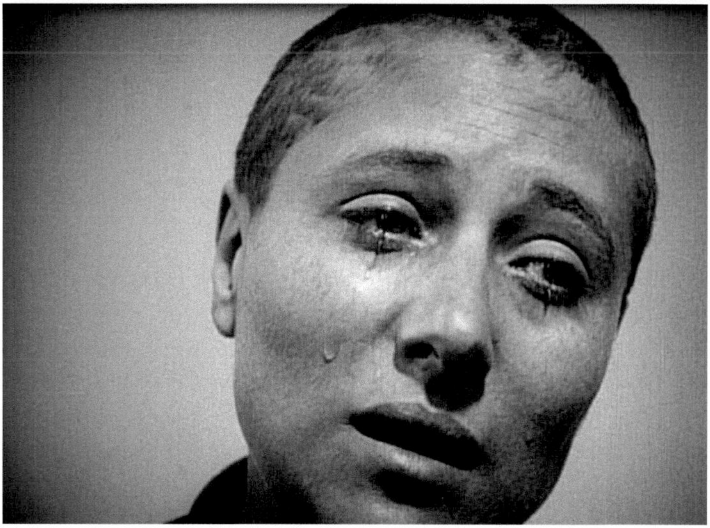

Fig 5.2 Joan boxed and constrained within a close-up (*La passion de Jeanne d'Arc/ The Passion of Joan of Arc*, 1928).

a series of situations in which he is confined and physically abused by his various owners.

The fact that donkeys are associated with Christ and that Balthazar is continually abused has led to straightforward religious interpretations of this film that at base suggest some association between the sufferings of Christ and those of Balthazar.[8] After the brief opening section showing an idyllic existence for Balthazar,[9] he is passed from one abusive or uncaring owner to another in a manner that might be seen to represent Christ's Via Dolorosa, or Way of Sorrows, as he moves towards his crucifixion. It is important to be careful with interpretations that can become too prescriptively simplistic, but we should recognize such suggestive connotative possibilities as these. Certainly, Balthazar is often shown dragging or carrying a burden, he does fall (ill) along the way and meets brief restorative kindnesses, and he does receive a final single wound. James Quandt describes *Au hasard Balthazar* and *Mouchette* (1967), also directed by Bresson, as 'compendiums of cruelty, whose endings have commonly been interpreted as moments of transfiguration, indicating absolution for a humanity that has been shown to be not merely fallen but vile' (2005, n.p.). Such terms might equally be applied to *The Passion of Joan of Arc* in which Joan is frequently shown as Christ-like in her forbearance in the face of suffering but also as intensely human in her desire to escape, if possible, her ultimate fate.

Films such as these cannot be addressed without recourse to the Christian tradition and the various ways in which related religious narratives and images have exerted such a strong influence on Western culture. When the bars on Joan's cell window form the shape of a cross, when the shadow of that cross falls on the cell floor and we are shown the comfort Joan takes from that image, in our interpretation of what we are seeing we have to be able to have recourse to the European religious heritage. When Joan is asked by one of her inquisitors, 'Since you're sure of your salvation, you don't need the Church?', we need to recognize the discussion that lies at the heart of this sentence revolves around the question of whether ordinary people can have some direct path to God that does not involve the intercession of the Church. If we fail to notice this, we are unable to properly contextualize these lines within the script and fail to recognize an element of a continuing debate within the film.

ART CINEMA AND EXISTENTIALISM

Focus films: *À bout de soufflé/Breathless* (Godard, 1959, France) and *Mirror* (Tarkovsky, 1975, USSR).

How can one talk with anything more than awkward uncertainty and anxiety about the inexplicable absurdity of the existence of the 'I'? This is something like the question with which Andrei Tarkovsky immediately confronts the viewer of *Mirror* (1975). A young boy, Ignat (Ignat Daniltsev), who we later find out is the son of the central character in the film, watches black and white footage on TV of a teenage boy who stammers. The teenager stutters his way through some simple sentences that attempt to define who he is in the most elementary way: 'My name is…', 'I come from…' *Mirror* is concerned with the problematic nature of human existence; it is a personal investigation by Tarkovsky that pushes at the boundaries of conventional autobiography. What we have is a stream of the central character's thoughts and memories that, although they have been structured by Tarkovsky, are not designed to give anything approaching a logical narrative. The name of the main character is Alexei rather than Andrei, but much of what is presented as this person's childhood memories seems to be based on Tarkovsky's own experiences. In the film, Alexei's mother not only has the same first name as Tarkovsky's mother, Maria, but as an older woman is also played by Tarkovsky's mother, Maria Vishnyakova. Furthermore, the four poems Tarkovsky uses as an aspect of the narrative voiceover are not only written by his father, Arseny Tarkovsky, but also recited by him. Biographical reality and fictional adaptation play off of each other in such a way as to comment on the constructed nature of both.[10] Generations exist within clearly very different historical contexts and yet in some ways seem to merge into each other in the similarity of their experiences both of the self and the self in relation to others. At the end of the film's prologue, the teenager who has been stammering finds a session with a hypnotherapist, aimed at taking the tension out of his body, has enabled him to speak with clarity. The question for Tarkovsky is whether the fear and anxiety engendered by the experience of the human condition, existential angst, can be controlled in such a way as to enable it to be transcended. As a philosophy, existentialism is often viewed as being gloomy and pessimistic but this is to miss the inherent suggestion that, through personal choice, the individual is given the power to shape their own existence.

In *À bout de soufflé/Breathless*, the question posed most directly around the issue of making choices would seem pretty gloomy. The central female character, Patricia (Jean Seberg), quotes from William Faulkner's novel, *The Wild Palms*, the line: 'Between grief and nothing, I will take grief.' On the other hand, in the face of this literary quote a defiant and highly individual statement of choice is made by the central male character, the gangster, Michel (Jean-Paul Belmondo): 'Grief is idiotic,' is his immediate response. 'I'd choose nothingness. It's not any better, but grief, it's a compromise.' Existentialist philosophy as put forward by Jean-Paul Sartre in *existentialism and humanism* (1948) and *Being and Nothingness* (1956) views human beings not as victims of destiny but as individual embodiments of freedom. The person who defines herself, or himself, as a victim of fate is seen as rendering herself, or himself, an object. Sartre's suggestion is that, 'Man is nothing else but that which he makes of himself' (1982 [1948], 28). He goes on to suggest that, 'Life is nothing until it is lived; but it is yours to make sense of, and the value of it is nothing else but the sense that you choose' (54).[11] Directors such as Jean-Luc Godard and Tarkovsky are not only displaying their interest in such existentialist issues in these films but, through their filmic choices, they are also actively setting about defining the nature of their own individual selves.

> Creativity is the expression of freedom and freedom lies in creating oneself and one's environment unceasingly. Thus the whole structure of human existence revolves around freedom and creativity.
>
> (Ahmad 1991, 75)

In focusing on the last few days in the life of a small-time gangster, Godard adopts certain aspects of mainstream filmmaking relating to plot and genre. The options steadily run out for the central male character as he attempts to elude capture by the police, until finally he finds himself betrayed by a female love-interest. But, along the way, Godard handles cinematography, sound and editing in ways that are distinctly other to what would be expected of a Hollywood studio product. He also ignores the mainstream imperative that dialogue should continually push the narrative forward, so that there is time for Patricia, for example, to close her eyes and muse, 'I'm trying to shut them very hard, so that everything goes black. But I can't manage to. It's never completely black.' New Wave films in France in the early 1960s offered what Geoffrey Nowell-Smith has described as 'a strange mixture of French existentialism and

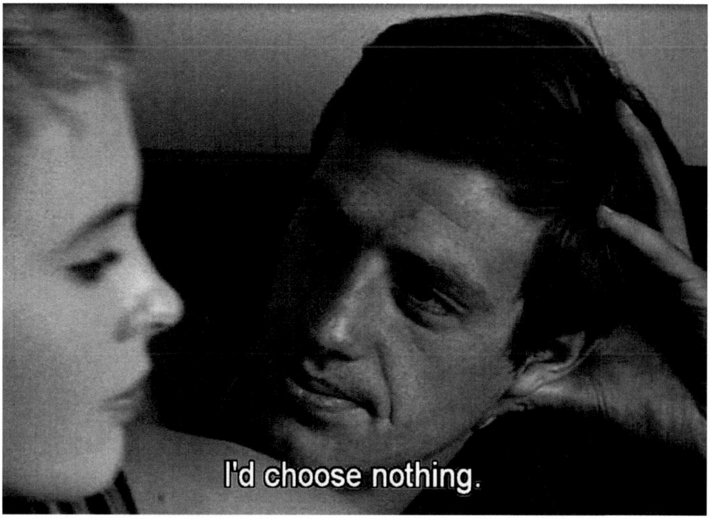

Fig 5.3 Existentialist discussion (*À bout de soufflé/Breathless*, 1959).

the American B-picture' (2010, 121). Patricia, like Sartre and other philosophers linked to existentialism, is wrestling with the concept of consciousness, and the nature of the individual, or personal, experience of consciousness. In *Being and Nothingness*, Sartre describes consciousness as 'a positional consciousness *of* the world' (1992 [1956], 11). He talks about the way in which we are 'conscious of being conscious' (11) and goes on to discuss the concept of nothingness:

> being is prior to nothingness and establishes the ground for it … it is from being that nothingness derives concretely its efficacy. This is what we mean when we say that nothingness haunts being … nothingness, which is not, can have only a borrowed existence, and it gets it from being. Its nothingness of being is encountered only within the limits of being, and the total disappearance of being would not be the advent of the reign of non-being, but on the contrary the concomitant disappearance of nothingness.
>
> (49)

Clearly, this is only to scratch the surface of the philosophical debate around these concepts; but, from our point of view, the crucial thing is to recognize that these issues are being thrown up within films such as *À bout de souffle* and *Mirror*.

The characters in *Mirror* are intensely aware of their consciousness, of their individual existence within the world. When Alexei's mother, as a young woman, meets a doctor early in the film, elements within the setting, the events that take place and the dialogue carry potential depths of connotation. The doctor is uncertain of his route and is seeking directions. Maria, the mother, is sitting on a fence. The doctor has everything he needs in his case but can't open it because he doesn't have the key. The young Alexei's voiceover carries an implied awareness of the possibility of (his father's) death. The possibilities of sadness and, at another extreme, laughter in the face of life are both explored. For the doctor, the problem with people is that, 'We are always running around, fussing about, talking trivialities.' But clearly his opinion is fallible because he can't even distinguish an alder tree from what he vaguely calls a 'nut-tree'. And then, Maria throws into the discussion a mention of Anton Chekhov's short story, *Ward Number Six* (first published 1892). This is the story of Andrei Yefimych Ragin, a doctor who eventually finds himself incarcerated in an asylum which he has been previously running, and who at one point is given these words:

> Life is a miserable trap. As soon as a thinking man reaches maturity and becomes capable of conscious thought, he cannot help feeling that he is in a trap from which there is no escape. When you come to think of it, he has been brought into life from a state of non-existence against his will, by pure chance. What for?
>
> (2010 [1892], 25)

At the end of the story, this character dies. His final thoughts are given and then we are told: 'Then all was gone, and Andrei Yefimych lost consciousness forever.' This section of the film ends with a shot of wind rushing through long grass and foliage. We may recall the second part of the title of Robert Bresson's *Un condamné à mort s'est échappé ou Le vent souffle où il veut/A Man Escaped, or The Wind Bloweth Where It Listeth* (1956), which is a reference to a verse in the Gospel According to St John:

> The winde bloweth where it listeth, and thou hearest the sound thereof, but canst not tel whence it commeth, and whither it goeth: So is euery one that is borne of the Spirit.
>
> (John 3: 8, King James Version, 1611)

And we then move into one of Tarkovsky's father's poems, 'First Meetings', which is about the transforming power of young love but which, in this context, might also be taken as referring to the intensity of the mother-son relationship. It is the mother that gives meaning to life and assuages anxiety, batting away as it were the potential confusions and uncertainties of the individual existence. The boy and/or the lover is able to experience a world in which everything is 'transformed' and given new 'significance', despite the ominous fact held in the poem's last line that Fate continues to track them 'like a madman brandishing a razor'.[12]

One of the other key figures in the debates around existentialism in the period after the Second World War was Albert Camus. In his essay, *Le Mythe de Sisyphe/The Myth of Sisyphus* (1942), Camus attempted to address the issue of the inherent absurdity of life, that is, the way in which human beings find themselves propelled, without any clear purpose, out into a world within which there is no meaning to be found. His interest is in how, given this context, it is possible to go on living. According to Camus this work 'declares that even within the limits of nihilism it is possible to find the means to proceed beyond nihilism' (1955, v). In the opening to the essay itself Camus famously suggested, 'There is but one truly serious philosophical problem and that is suicide. Judging whether life is or is not worth living amounts to answering the fundamental question of philosophy' (3). And so, when Michel in *À bout de soufflé* says he would choose 'nothingness' over 'grief', he is essentially addressing what is for Camus the key question facing

Fig 5.4 The intensity of life/love in the face of Fate (*Mirror*, 1975).

us all. Certainly, the isolation of the individual is made clear in the dialogue between Michel and Patricia: 'I want to know what's behind your face,' says Patricia to Michel; and then, a little later, 'We're looking into each other's eyes and it's useless.'[13] So it is clear that, whether Michel is simply having to face his fate, or whether he is able to make choices and thereby shape his own destiny, he is having to do this alone. 'We have neither behind us, nor before us in a luminous realm of values, any means of justification or excuse. We are left alone, without excuse,' Sartre declares in *existentialism and humanism* (1982 [1948], 34). From the existentialist perspective the question becomes, to what extent Michel has been the victim of fate and, therefore, no more than an object within the world, and to what extent has he used his free will to actively choose his trajectory through life?[14]

What *À bout de soufflé* does not consider, but *Mirror* confronts directly, is the way in which each individual's life must necessarily take place within the context of the broad sweep of history. At one point, people who appear to be refugees from Spain living in Russia are in

Alexei's apartment and their discussions are intercut with footage from (amongst other things) the Spanish Civil War. Later, there is newsreel footage from the Second World War and then from China during the Cultural Revolution showing masses of individuals forming, seemingly homogeneous, chanting crowds. The question thrown up about human existence then becomes, to what extent is the individual's life necessarily shaped by such events and to what extent does it remain a case of making choices within these parameters? The poem recited by Andrei Tarkovsky just before the Second World War images is entitled 'Life, Life'. Some of the lines share something of the sentiment contained in Patricia's words in *À bout de soufflé*, quoted above, about closing her eyes: 'I'm trying to shut them very hard, so that everything goes black. But I can't manage to. It's never completely black.' The lines in Tarkovsky's father's poem have been translated as: 'There's only here and now, and light;/Neither death, nor darkness, exists' (2013, 65). A further implication of this poem is the idea that the time into which you are born does not really matter, since the 'table' at which we sit is 'The same for ancestor and grandson' (65).

ART CINEMA AND THE PRESENCE OF EVIL IN THE WORLD

Focus films: *Nosferatu, Eine Symphonie des Grauens/Nosferatu, a Symphony of Horror* (Murnau, 1922, Weimar Republic) and M (Lang, 1930, Weimar Republic).

What will be apparent by now is the way in which the demarcation of the separate sections within this book is to a certain extent rather arbitrary. In *Mirror*, a key film in the previous section, for example, the central character talks about the desire to use dreams to return to childhood places, much as Izak Borg does in *Wild Strawberries* (Bergman, 1957) in an earlier section. The main character in *Mirror* also mentions at one point that he has not talked to anybody for several days because 'it seemed a good thing to keep silent' and 'words can't express all a person feels'. In other words, he has taken up something of the position adopted by Elisabet in *Persona* (Bergman, 1966), again, as discussed in an earlier section of this book. Small links and connections such as these indicate something of the interlocking tentacles of ideas that can be found across many of these films. Our particular focus here will be on films in which the presence of evil in the world is a central focus. In the first of these films, evil is seen as lurking somewhere just beyond the bounds of civilization from where it threatens to intrude into society, but in the second, it is seen as hidden beneath the apparently benign surface of the individual. Each of these films might be said to represent an investigation into the dark heart of man. In Christian terms, this fascination with evil stems from the notion of man as a creature who, in being cast out from the Garden of Eden, has fallen from a relationship of grace with God. However, the same preoccupation is also apparent within folklore as is demonstrated within *Nosferatu, Eine Symphonie des Grauens/Nosferatu, a Symphony of Horror* (1922). And, as M (1930) demonstrates, that same obsessive interest is found within the 'modern' mass media. One of the marks of culture may be its compulsion to explore the darker aspects of human beings.

In both films the emergence of evil into the world is both unpredictable and uncontrollable. Once Nosferatu, 'the Bird of Death', has 'spread his wings' his progress towards the town of Wisborg is unstoppable. Once the usually hidden, inner expression of his being emerges there is nothing Hans Beckert (Peter Lorre), the central character in M, can do to stop events moving towards their inevitable conclusion.

> Always I have to roam the streets and I always sense that someone is following me. It's me! And I shadow myself! ... Sometimes I feel like I'm hunting myself down. I want to run – run away from me! I can't flee from myself! Must ... must take the path that it is urging me on.

In *Nosferatu*, Hutter (Gustav von Wangenheim) is, depending how generous you are feeling, either an innocent abroad or a complete numbskull. As an estate agent, he travels to a castle in Transylvania to sell a house in his hometown of Wisborg to Count Orlok (Max Schreck), alias Nosferatu. At a coaching inn along the journey the mere mention of 'Count Orlok's castle' leaves the locals aghast. Shortly after this his drivers refuse to go any further. And yet, Hutter continues. Stage by stage he is led further into the realms of darkness. When Orlok meets him just inside the castle he leads Hutter into a black, arched space on the screen into which they both seemingly disappear. The director, Friedrich Wilhelm (F.W.) Murnau, shows Hutter crossing threshold after threshold, over bridges and through gates and doors, as he journeys further into the heart of darkness.[15] When Hutter shows Orlok details of properties in Wisborg it is a portrait miniature of his wife, Ellen (Greta Schröder), that catches the Count's eye. These sorts of paintings were used especially to introduce potential wealthy suitors to each other when they lived some distance apart. Naïve fool that he is, Hutter thinks he is in the middle of a property transaction when he is actually selling his wife to a client. It is the representative of ordinary, everyday man, Hutter (and nobody could be more ordinary and everyday than Hutter), who has opened Pandora's Box, allowing evil into the world. The significant reversal here, of course, is that it is a man who has done this, not a woman as in Greek myth with the first woman, Pandora, nor as in Christian myth with the first woman, Eve. Furthermore, it is the woman, Ellen, who is faced with having to make the ultimate sacrifice to save the world. She is the one who at the start of the film, in a gesture of sensitivity totally beyond Hutter's comprehension, wants to know 'Why did you kill them, the lovely flowers?' when he has picked her a bunch of flowers from the garden. Through his editing of the sequence Murnau shows us that it is Ellen who, across the distance between them, distracts Nosferatu from sucking the blood from Hutter's neck. She is the one who is shown on the balustrade of her bedroom balcony, walking the line between life and death, between saving yourself and sacrificing yourself. Faced with the stupidity of man, it is woman who has to save the situation at such tremendous cost.

Like Cesare (Conrad Veidt) in *Das Cabinet des Dr Caligari/The Cabinet of Dr Caligari* (Robert Wiene, 1920), Nosferatu emerges out of coffins

Fig 5.5 Count Orlok with a miniature of Ellen (*Nosferatu, Eine Symphonie des Grauens/ Nosferatu, a Symphony of Horror*, 1922).

or coffin-like spaces to walk, as if in a trance, towards committing murderous acts. Both may be frighteningly odd but both are recognizably human in form, disturbing representations of something other than what we are but within which we can horrifyingly see ourselves. Cesare might be viewed as representing the way in which ordinary people can be taken over by a figure of authority and power, in his case Dr Caligari (Werner Krauss), and induced to commit acts in a metronomic fashion. But in *Nosferatu*, rather than being linked to German (or Prussian) militarism, Orlok is associated by Murnau with the forces of nature. Professor Bulwer (John Gottowt), we are told, for example, is 'studying the secrets of nature and its basic principles' and Murnau then shows Bulwer with his students looking at a Venus flytrap. A fly is seen in close-up being caught by this plant, and an inter-title informs us that these sorts of things enabled Bulwer's students to catch 'a terrifying glimpse of the deep mysteries of nature'.[16] This approach acknowledges the deadly, frightening, or 'evil' aspects of the natural world as part and parcel of the nature of existence. At the same time, Knock (Alexander Granach), the estate agent who sends Hutter on his journey, is clear that he sees Nosferatu as a leader and a guide, calling him 'the Master', someone people can follow; and he succinctly summarizes Nosferatu's perspective on the world in the repeated slogan, 'Blood is life.'[17] Interpretations of *Nosferatu* can obviously exist on a series of levels, some of which may owe much to the contexts offered by German history in the decades prior to the making of the film. Ellen, when she awaits Hutter's return, not knowing if he will ever make it back, is sitting on a bench-seat looking out to sea, the very incarnation of a war widow. She looks towards a featureless sea and sky surrounded by sand dunes within which iron crosses stand or lean at precarious angles. We are told: 'Ellen was often seen by the sea among the lonely dunes. She yearned for her beloved, her eyes fixed on the distant horizon beyond the waves.'[18]

The anguish of women is also a crucial feature of *M*. The film appears to be about to end with court officials and judges sitting to give, 'in the name of the people', their judgement on the murderer, but before we can hear the verdict the director, Fritz Lang, cuts to three bereaved mothers dressed in black. One is the mother of Elsie Beckmann (Inge Landgut), the young girl whose murder gives the central focus to the narrative, and Lang gives this woman the final words in the film. 'This will not bring back our children,' she says. 'One has to keep a closer watch over the children.' And, as the screen fades to black, she adds, 'All of you!' With the First World War a little over a decade in the past and the Second World War less than a decade into the future, such an ending would seem to deliberately pick up the theme of anti-war artists and activists such as Käthe Kollwitz.[19] The sacrifice made by the women at the end of *M* is not the sacrifice that is made by Ellen at the conclusion of *Nosferatu*, but the issues raised in relation to the German historical context are similar.

A superficial view of *M* might see the film as a demonstration of the way in which evil is to be found hidden within deranged individuals

Fig 5.6 The anguish of women (M, 1930).

who in terms of surface appearance seem quite ordinary. On this reading it is down to the police, helped by the media and the general public, to root out these individuals, put them before the courts and, thereby, improve society. But what the film actually explores is not a degenerate individual but a degenerate society. When the crime underworld organizes beggars to keep watch for the murderer this is easy because there are so many beggars on the streets anyway. The legless and the one-legged down-and-outs we see in the film are a normal, everyday presence on German streets in the period. When we are shown what is described as 'the vagrant population' inside a homeless men's hostel, with two rows of men tightly packed on camp-beds, this could easily be documentary footage from Berlin in 1931. Later, when the murderer, Hans Beckert (Peter Lorre), has been captured by the leaders of the criminal underworld he is taken to an 'abandoned' factory that nobody any longer 'gives a damn about', and what we are given in this snapshot image of German industry is a metaphor for the German economy as a whole. It is not just Beckert that is 'sick' but the whole society. So sick, in fact, that the man who is threatening to take control of the whole crumbling edifice is nothing other than the leather-coated, stick-wielding führer of the criminal underworld, who happens to be an impassioned, fist-clenching, orator ('this monster has no right to survive,' he says of Beckert. 'He must be killed, eliminated, exterminated without mercy or compassion.') When we turn to the police and army in a building elsewhere in the city, as they debate what needs to be done, we are faced with a no less vehement right-wing stance. A uniformed officer suggests with the same grandiloquent, tub-thumping flourishes employed by the leader of the criminal underworld: 'Step up ID checks, comb the entire city, and raids, relentless, ever tougher raids.'

The body politic is shown in M to be at least as 'sick' as the individual murderer the film is ostensibly about. Another official attempting to decide what the response should be to tracking down the murderer is given the lines:

> The idea that each individual is responsible for what happens to the poorest, most anonymous child on the street hasn't even dawned on the public at large.

The ease with which the general public can turn into a baying mob[20] is demonstrated at several points in the film. It is not simply that the masses are easily whipped into a frenzy by (political) oratory and tabloid journalism, but also that there is a very real appetite amongst the public for lurid and disturbing stories. The door-to-door magazine salesman who calls at Frau Beckmann's house while her daughter is elsewhere being approached by the murderer, sells the latest edition of his publication by proclaiming it as offering tales that are 'suspenseful, captivating, sensational'. Lang's point is not only that individuals are too easily subsumed in the mob but also that we are all guilty of morbidly loving shock-horror narratives. Indeed, Lang's ultimate point is that this is exactly why we are watching his film.

6

POLITICAL ASPECTS OF EUROPEAN ART CINEMA

ART CINEMA AND SOCIAL CRITIQUE

Focus films: *La Grande Illusion* (Renoir, 1937, France) and *Die Ehe der Maria Braun/The Marriage of Maria Braun* (Fassbinder, 1979, West Germany).

Speaking around 1960 and looking back to the release of his film *La Règle du jeu/The Rules of the Game* in 1939, Jean Renoir said:

> In no way was it my intention to make a controversial film: it was not at all my intention to shock the bourgeoisie. I wanted to make a movie, even a pleasant movie; but a pleasant movie that would at the same time function as a critique of a society I considered to be rotten to the core and which I still consider rotten to the core.
>
> (2004, n.p.)

This would seem a rather strange position for Renoir to take. If you view a society as 'rotten to the core' and you present your take on this diseased society to an audience that is likely to include those you are attacking, it would seem naïve to expect your work to be easily stomached. At its premiere the reception for the film 'was tumultuous, marked by jeering, damage to seats and even, allegedly, a spectator using a copy of the right-wing nationalist journal *L'Action française* in an attempt to start a fire' (Reader 2010, 18). To some extent, this reaction may have been a product of the historical moment. Political tension was high in Europe: less than two months after *La Règle du jeu* opened Germany invaded Poland, and less than a year later France had been overrun by German forces. At such a time, criticizing French society was unlikely to be easily accepted.

Throughout the interwar period France was alive with political energy. A range of fascist and right-wing organizations was opposed by 'the largest communist party in Europe' (Paxton 2006, 245). But the reception for Renoir's *La Grande Illusion* two years earlier had been much more positive. It was 'an immediate triumph' and 'ended as the highest-grossing film of the year' (Jackson 2009, 7). It dealt with controversial issues, but 'was greeted enthusiastically by critics across the political spectrum – communists and fascists, pacifists and nationalists, anti-racists and anti-Semites' (7). Martin O'Shaughnessy suggests, in part, this enthusiasm may have been due to the way in which *La Grande Illusion* could be interpreted in different ways (2009, 112). Marc Ferro takes the representation of the Jew, Rosenthal (Marcel Dalio), and shows how (despite the fact the film was banned in Germany as too favorable to Jews) this character could be read from diametrically opposed positions: Rosenthal fights alongside his fellow Frenchmen and shares the packages he receives with his comrades, but he is also the only one to receive parcels of special provisions and speaks of defending France in order to safeguard his possessions (1988, 134). It may be that *La Grande Illusion* was open to a variety of readings in a way that *La Règle du jeu* was not.

In his films made in the 1970s, such as *Angst essen Seele auf/Ali: Fear Eats the Soul* (1974) and *Die Ehe der Maria Braun/The Marriage of Maria Braun* (1979), Rainer Werner Fassbinder was similarly interested in critiquing society. And, as with Renoir's work in the late 1930s, the historical context strongly influenced not only the work he created, but also the audience response:

> Fassbinder understood that as a German in the seventies, one had to do real historical work: to recreate not just the images but the mental framework of the past, to not merely acknowledge historical amnesia, but make an effort to understand how and why it manifested itself.
>
> (Jones 2003, n.p.)

There are different views about how Fassbinder's efforts at social criticism should be viewed. Matthias Uecker, for example, discusses the way the character of Maria Braun in *Die Ehe der Maria Braun* can be seen as either the embodiment of West Germany's postwar recovery, or the victim of that so-called 'economic miracle', but he also highlights what he sees as 'the highly selective character' of Fassbinder's portrayal of the postwar period (2001, 45.) Uecker demonstrates how giving more attention to the nature of the marriage in this film would allow greater emphasis to be placed on the husband as also being 'representative of the German experience': 'The German soldier or POW who returns home only to find his wife in bed with another man is one of the central images of the post-war period' (57). In the end, we see the restoration of patriarchal power over Maria, and the reconstruction of the old order in Germany with the agreement of foreign powers: 'Hermann Braun sells three years of his wife's lifetime to a foreign industrialist – and receives as his payment half of the inheritance which should have gone to Maria' (57). Uecker suggests we should not see this film simply as an exposition of how in achieving the 'economic miracle' Maria Braun has lost her soul. If we take into account this 'secret contract', he says, 'a much more complex allegory of post-war Germany emerges than a simple moral vilification of West Germany's new materialism' (58).

Renoir sometimes was, or pretended to be, an innocent regarding political matters. Asked if he was surprised by the poor reception *La Règle du jeu* received, he said he was not expecting it and always tried to make marketable films (1989, 6). Even in making his central political position clear he is restrained in his expression:

> this question of classes is definitely a question to which I have given a great deal of thought … people pretend that there are no more classes,

Fig 6.1 Patriotism and nationalism rather than internationalism? (*La Grande Illusion*, 1937).

> that they've been abolished. In fact, we have a long way to go before abolishing them.
>
> (136)

Some have seen *La Grande Illusion* as confused politically. Colin Crisp suggests although a 'pacifist, internationalist message' runs through much of the film, ultimately the upper-class characters of Boeldieu (Pierre Fresnay) and Rauffenstein (Eric von Stroheim) are redeemed by a certain 'nobility', while the patriotism of the French POWs creates a sense of nationalism rather than internationalism (2015, 185).[1]

Fassbinder seemed clearer about his politics: 'he was convinced that middle-class existence was based on an exploitative capitalist economic structure and an equally exploitative patriarchal social structure' (Rheuban 1991, 5). Joyce Rheuban suggests Fassbinder had a problem with artists whose work effectively supported 'the foundations of the bourgeois world – capitalism, patriarchy, and economic individualism' (7). Fassbinder was interested in the absolute power of those in charge of the system with the capacity to 'predetermine the course of events which secretly governs the lives of others and renders their individual ambitions and actions virtually ineffectual' (16). Wallace Steadman Watson argues Fassbinder's films offer 'a substantial critique of German society, culture, politics, and economic arrangements' but also,

> suggest that the horrors of the Third Reich were not a historical aberration but rather expressions of xenophobic and authoritarian strands in the German character which could also be seen in the materialism, intolerance, and reactionary tendencies of postwar West Germany.
>
> (1996, 2)

However, what Renoir's larger canvas allows him to recognize in *La Grande Illusion* is that the issue is not to do with 'strands' of German, or French, character but with pan-European tendencies, and a pan-European class system. In the interwar period both nationalism and anti-Semitism were rife, not only in Germany but also in many other European countries, including France and Britain. Renoir's film is actually anti-war, anti-nationalist and anti-fascist. The film asserts the world is divided not by frontiers ('Frontiers are made by men: nature doesn't give a damn,' says Rosenthal) and differences of ethnicity and language, but rather by class. The aristocrats, Boeldieu and Rauffenstein, are the old ruling class of Europe. In the castle commanded by Rauffenstein only nettles and ivy grow, and when Boeldieu is dying the last rites are given not just to him but to a whole class and way of life.[2] Maréchal (Jean Gabin) and Rosenthal, by contrast, are the new emerging classes, the middle class and the new rich. Maréchal is well aware there is a difference between himself and Boeldieu despite their shared nationality: 'There is always a sort of wall between us,' he says. Despite the prejudices that surface between Maréchal and Rosenthal after their escape they are able to work through these differences. And, in his relationship with Elsa (Dita Parlo), Maréchal points towards the possibilities for a new Europe: 'When the guards yelled I understood nothing, but I understand her German,' he says.[3]

Since the film takes the phrase as its title, we need to ask what 'the grand illusion' might be. Does this refer to the illusion of Boeldieu and Rauffenstein that war can still be fought on chivalric lines? In other words, are we being asked to face the reality of exactly what war means in the modern world? Is the illusion that of national identity, with the reality being that people are able to identify with each other across borders which only create false boundaries between people? Is the illusion that of nationalism, something with which Maréchal has to come to terms during the course of the film? Is the concept of freedom itself 'the grand illusion' – is freedom really possible? Do Maréchal and Rosenthal (after the First World War, remember) really escape to freedom, or is it an illusion? Was it an illusion that was offered after 1918 that wars could be ended? Or, is what we are being asked to consider here the fact that ordinary people are all 'forced' into war under an illusion that it is in their national interest, when in fact what exists between people are common bonds of humanity? Martin O'Shaughnessy observed that,

> Renoir's films of the period (late 1930s) are not simply shot, as has often been remarked, in 'deep space' (with the full depth of the image being mobilized to bring social groups and contrasting spaces into contact), they are also shot in 'deep time' as the struggles between different socio-historical possibilities are played out across their story space. (2009, 11)

Within the restricted space of Germany, this is the territory marked out for investigation by Fassbinder in *Die Ehe der Maria Braun*. In particular, he sees nationalism as a continuing presence within the German psyche despite the country's recent experience with National Socialism. At one point, Fassbinder counterpoints the sound of German Chancellor, Konrad Adenauer, on the radio proclaiming Germany's right to rearm with an image of Maria Braun vomiting. As Anton Kaes expresses

Fig 6.2 A photographic negative of contemporary German chancellor, Helmut Schmidt (*Die Ehe der Maria Braun/The Marriage of Maria Braun*, 1979).

it: 'The history of the German nation from the end of the war to the so-called economic miracle of the 1950s punctuates and expands the story of Maria Braun' (2001, 179).

For Fassbinder, the people of Germany have been reduced to a position from which, although they may appear to be successful and prosperous, the reality is they are driven by consumerism and materialism. The film opens with an image of Hitler, which is quickly blown up, but it ends with negative photographic images of postwar West German chancellors, Adenauer (1949–1963), Ludwig Erhard (1963–1966), Kurt Georg Kiesinger (1966–1969) and Helmut Schmidt (1974–1982).[4] There is a tragi-comic absurdity about the final sequence in which Maria and Hermann are killed in a massive explosion. The love, romance and hopes of a generation have been destroyed by the inescapable past.

ART CINEMA AND SOCIAL REALISM

Focus films: *Ladri di biciclette/Bicycle Thieves* (De Sica, 1948, Italy), *La Terra Trema* (Visconti, 1948, Italy), *The Loneliness of the Long Distance Runner* (Richardson, 1962, UK) and *Land and Freedom* (Loach, 1995, UK).

Social realist films are films with political attitude. The filmmakers producing these texts set out to engage with the lives of ordinary people and, by exposing what they see as the 'truth' of everyday life, they aim to have a political impact on their audience. Discussing British social realism, Samantha Lay says the intent 'is often reformist, educative or socially purposive in some way, and the choice of issues and the prevalence of certain themes is bound up with a mission or a message' (2002, 13). The intention of both the novelist, Alan Sillitoe, who wrote the short story from which the film was made, and the filmmakers responsible for *The Loneliness of the Long Distance Runner*, directed by Tony Richardson, was to express on screen something of the nature of working-class life for young men in the late 1950s/early 1960s, to expose the way in which borstals were used as places of 'correction' for working-class men, and to express the spirited resistance these young people offered to the restrictions imposed on their lives. Those involved in making *Land and Freedom*, directed by Ken Loach, wished to give their own interpretation of the Spanish Civil War and, in the process, challenge the dominant narrative on offer to the public regarding that conflict. Both these films deal with specific moments in history and aim to address socio-historical issues relating to those moments. The periods looked at are both now 'history' but the central ideas regarding power and inequality remain relevant to successive generations. The lot of the working class in the UK – as intelligent, energetic and witty as any other group in society but consistently unable to expect much, if anything, from their lives – has remained relevant through each successive decade following the making of *The Loneliness of the Long Distance Runner*. The issue of who writes the history we are taught and come to believe and how those people, whoever they might be, angle it to their own ends, remains as politically relevant today as it was when *Land and Freedom* was made, or as it was during and immediately after the Spanish Civil War.

As Lay points out, since these texts explore a specific society at a specific historical moment, it is crucial to be aware of socio-historical context (2002, 13). It is also important, she suggests, to be aware that they remain constructs. Those involved in making these films are not neutral in their stance and attitudes. But social realists would never expect to be impartial in their work. To be disinterested would immediately preclude them from being social realists. Social realism sees itself as relevant to the here-and-now but also, because of its political commitment, of continuing relevance to future audiences. Social realism is about recognizing the world as an inescapably political space and driving into that space in a fully engaged, fully committed way. *Love on the Dole*, the novel by Walter Greenwood published in 1933, was originally proposed as a subject for a film in 1936 but was not seen as suitable material for cinema-goers until it was eventually made and released during the Second World War in 1941. By that time it could be seen as a film calling for a better world to be established after the war, rather than as an attack on the Depression-era society within which ordinary people were condemned, through no fault of their own, to unemployment (White 2008, 36–40).

To take an even earlier British example, *Hindle Wakes* (Maurice Elvey, 1927) openly addressed gender inequality and pointed out the way in which female independence was directly linked to economic independence.[5] The focus of the film is on what Heiða Jóhannsdóttir describes as the central character's 'struggle to break out of conventions of female virtue and domesticity and seek agency in the public sphere' (2012, 181).[6]

'Realism', in terms of the offering of a realistic representation of the world, is a slippery concept. What may be perceived as 'realistic' at one point in history may no longer be seen as such a few years later.[7] The term is similarly problematic when extended across cultures. As a result, the notion of what is meant by 'social realism' may shift over time. The issue is complicated further by the fact that exactly what is meant by realism is open to ongoing debate. Realism as 'a principle of transparent correspondence' between the text and external phenomena, as Darío Villanueva describes it in discussing realism in literature, depends on an implicit assumption of the existence of 'a univocal reality which precedes the text and which is scanned by the author's perceiving consciousness in all its hidden aspects through minute and efficient observation' (1997, 15). In considering painting, Kerstin Stremmel recognizes the same commonplace use of the term. Realism, she says, 'is often used synonymously with naturalism to refer to an attempt at true-to-life reproduction of external reality' (2004, 7). But she goes on to suggest that realistic depiction can also involve 'interpretation and evaluation' (8). Social realism certainly involves these things. According to Julia Hallam and Margaret Marshment, social realist films 'aim to show the effects of environmental factors on the development of character' (2000, 184). They propose that social realism in the late 1980s and early 1990s should be seen as engaging with 'an eclectic range of narrational and visual styles' (196). Further, they suggest in this period: 'filmmakers who wish to engage realism's discursive potential use a range of methods in their attempts to mobilize the social dimension of social realism's project' (196). This is something filmmakers working in the social realist tradition have always done. Jóhannsdóttir, for example, refers to 'the enthusiastic critical reception of the visual realism of *Hindle Wakes*' (2012, 191). This film used sequences that employed multiple superimpositions, shot compositions that involved unusual angles such as looking down on swirling dance floors, and camera movements that embraced the opportunities offered by fairground rides, so that any stereotypical notion of filmic realism was immediately challenged.

The Loneliness of the Long Distance Runner in many ways embodies that classic phrase used in relation to these films in Britain, 'gritty realism'; and yet, it also employs filmmaking that deliberately breaks with the naturalistic portrayals of working-class life that are on offer. David Forrest refers to 'a variety of stylistic motifs which subvert and complicate the staid realist traditions of the British cinema' (2013, 69). One sequence, a montage of shopping scenes showing the Smith family spending insurance money gained from the death of the father, is divided up by the use of a logo associated with the TV broadcasting company from the period, Rediffusion. The jingle-like tune accompanying this sequence and the visual referencing of television advertising is totally appropriate and yet, at the same time, these elements of film construction comment on the narrative events we are shown and ask us to reflect on the nature of consumer culture. In the final scene, a further montage sequence takes us into the thoughts of the central character, Colin. It offers psychological realism but also demonstrates how social realism is prepared to move away from surface realism in order to express ideas seen as more critically important (in this case, the clash between brutalist authority and working-class defiance).[8]

Political ideas are important in social realism. In the middle of *Land and Freedom* there is a twelve-minute scene that shows a group of revolutionaries and villagers in Spain debating the rights and wrongs of the private ownership of land. Just over ten percent of the film is taken up with this discussion. Both camerawork and editing are used entirely in the service of enabling the audience to follow the argument, simply moving us from one speaker to the other. This is an exceptional use of storytelling space within a film and demonstrates the confidence the filmmakers have in their audience; a confidence that would not seem to have been shared by UK distributors or, perhaps, exhibitors. Mike Wayne reports that *Land and Freedom* 'had only a 15 print UK release but 85 in France' (2002, 21). James Chapman says the distributors 'claimed that "it boils down to economics" and averred that multiplex cinemas were reluctant to book the film', but he goes on to record one multiplex chain saying it was the distributors who had prevented customers from seeing the film (2005, 317).

Ladri di biciclette/Bicycle Thieves is seen by Godfrey Cheshire as looking towards 'a cinema of impassioned social conscience' (2007). The approach to filmmaking taken by the Italian Neorealists, says Cheshire, continues 'to represent the struggle for authenticity and political engagement in cinema'. And yet, in aiming for some form of realistic portrayal of (in this case) postwar Italian society, the narrative structure

Fig 6.3 Debating political ideas (*Land and Freedom*, 1995).

of *Ladri di biciclette* is very carefully constructed, not to say, contrived. The form of realism on offer is, as mentioned by Robert Gordon, one in which 'an individual story emerges from and stands for the larger, material condition of a class' (2008, 47). Furthermore, the visual style of this film is often highly conventional. The editing, for example, particularly as the melodrama of the father-son relationship begins to dominate the film, adopts a classical form.[9] Even so, as Millicent Marcus notes, despite such things as the melodrama and classical editing, the social critique put forward by director, Vittorio De Sica, and the writer, Cesare Zavattini, is constantly reinforced:

> In order for the film's social criticism to work … Antonio's plight must not be seen as unique. Accordingly, De Sica and Zavattini offer a series of visual essays on the commonality of Ricci's condition.
>
> (1986, 65–66)

When the central couple pawn their sheets, for example, a shot inside the warehouse-sized space used to keep the items people have left displays shelf after shelf packed high with linen.

Fig 6.4 Social comment within a single shot (*Ladri di biciclette/Bicycle Thieves*, 1948).

The effort to place on screen the reality of ordinary people's lives, but this time in the countryside rather than the city, was approached by Luchino Visconti in *La Terra Trema* (1948).

> The camera never leaves the village, never escapes the strict boundaries delimited on one side by the bus stop and on the other by the oddly shaped rocks (faraglioni) looming out of the sea just offshore. The men leave the village only to serve in the army or to go fishing. The women stay behind, waiting.
>
> (Liehm 1986, 81)

Summing up the stylistic approach to social realism taken by Visconti, André Bazin said:

> If a fisherman rolls a cigarette, he spares us nothing: we see the whole operation; it will not be reduced to its dramatic or symbolic meaning, as

is usual with montage. The shots are often fixed-frame, so people and things may enter the frame and take up position; but Visconti is also in the habit of using a special kind of panning shot which moves very slowly over a very wide arc: this is the only camera movement which he allows himself, for he excludes all tracking shots and, of course, every unusual camera angle.

(2005 [1971], 43)

The use of long takes, location shooting and non-professional actors all contribute to the documentary style given to this dramatization of the conditions of work endured by the poor. No concession is made to the audience. There is no happy ending. The resistant strength of the in-place economic system is emphasized. The sense of entrapment and oppression only intensifies as the film progresses. This is the problem for social realism. If it is going to be truly realistic, it has to show the inescapable web-like nature of life as lived by those born into an environment of limited educational opportunities, dilapidated housing and appalling working conditions: in a word, poverty. And, if it puts these things on screen how is it ever going to attract a mass audience looking to escape these very things. Bazin says of Visconti's approach to *La Terra Trema*: 'his disinclination to sacrifice anything to drama has one obvious and serious consequence: *La Terra Trema* bores the public' (2005 [1971], 45). Of course, it may be the filmmakers concerned are content simply to reach the middle-class audiences who attend art-house cinemas, seeing this as their own, quite profitable, niche market. Talking about *Ladri di biciclette*, Kristin Thompson proposed:

Bicycle Thieves was perfectly calculated for the fast-growing art-cinema market in the United States, or, as *Variety* put it: 'Commercially, the pic is a cinch to clean up in the art houses. It should also find limited bookings in some standard theatres'.

(1988, 215)

ART CINEMA AND POLITICAL COMMITMENT

Focus films: *Mat/Mother* (Pudovkin, 1926, USSR), *Bronenosets Potyomkin/ Battleship Potemkin* (Eisenstein, 1925, USSR) and *Tout va bien* (Godard and Gorin, 1972, France).

If Bazin contends films attempting social realism, such as *La Terra Trema*, 'bore the public', Cesare Zavattini, the neorealist screenwriter and film theorist, sees things altogether differently. He is bored by the films produced by mainstream cinema. In 'Some Ideas on the Cinema' he says:

> I am bored to death with heroes more or less imaginary. I want to meet the real protagonist of everyday life, I want to see how he is made … I am against 'exceptional' personages. The time has come to tell the audience that they are the true protagonists of life. The result will be a constant appeal to the responsibility and dignity of every human being. Otherwise the frequent habit of identifying oneself with fictional characters will become very dangerous. We must identify ourselves with what we are. The world is composed of millions of people thinking of myths.
>
> (2008 [1952], 47)

Bridging the gap between these two positions in some sense, some filmmakers have attempted to harness intense political commitment to methods of film construction other than social realism. These films crank up the level of political pressure beyond that provided by social realism, taking as their sole purpose the endorsement of revolutionary social change. They are films created in support of the total overthrow of capitalism and its replacement by a new way of life based on a set of entirely different economic premises. In order to achieve this end, as with social realist texts, they generally focus on the lives of ordinary people. However, although there may be moments when the reality of working-class lives is put on the screen in minute photographic detail, as in the first days of the workers' strike in *Stachka/Strike* (Sergei Eisenstein, 1925), social realism is not the main aim. Instead, filmmakers working within this field use all manner of filmmaking techniques in an effort to achieve their own version of the dynamism and drama of mainstream cinema.

Herbert Marshall describes seeing screenings of Vsevolod Pudovkin's films *Mat/Mother* (1926) and *Konets Sankt-Peterburga/The End of St. Petersburg* (1927) at the London Film Society.[10] This is not an 'ordinary' audience, but the response of Marshall and those around him does testify to the powerful effect these films had on this particular gathering:

> even those who did not agree in the slightest with the film's politics or its message were quivering with emotion at its artistic impact. This impact helped to swing one in favor of the message. It was a wonderful example of the power of art.
>
> (2014 [1983], 11)

The opening scenes of *Mother* propel us into the middle of a domestic drama. The moment within a father-son relationship when power shifts from the older to the younger man is written on the screen in a succinct sequence of shots in which the dynamics of the mother-father-son triangle is expressed through creative clashes between images. The father, Vlasov (Aleksandr Chistyakov), and son, Pavel Vlasov (Nikolai Batalov), face each other in a physical confrontation from which the father backs down. Prior to the encounter, the father approaches the family home (and, shortly afterwards, leaves it) though a shadowy, expressionist set. When he enters the room he, metaphorically and actually, casts a shadow. The set, one could imagine, pretty faithfully replicates a factory worker's home in Russia in 1905, but the lighting, editing and camerawork demonstrate the preparedness of the filmmakers to use a full range of film techniques to produce a dramatic, narrative construction. For much of the time *Mother* employs simple melodramatic storytelling devices. However, incorporated within this, there is a utilization of film style unrestrained by concepts of social realism. Most obviously, there is a use of Soviet montage that crystallizes political oppositions and expresses the oppressive nature of imperial power in pre-Revolution Russia.[11] Where social realism would generally wish to limit the editing and retain eye-level shots employed in long takes, *Mother* makes considerable use of inter-cut close-ups, not just of faces but also the feet and hands of individual characters and groups, expressing the tension of a clenched fist or the threat of soldiers' feet marching, for example. Significant use is also made of superimpositions. The sequence that shows the audience the factory for the first time takes time out from the narrative for the filmmakers to create aesthetically pleasing, abstract shots from the shapes and forms offered by the chimneys, power lines, buildings, walkways and other frameworks found on a factory site. The sequence that forms a prelude to the trial of the son for being an instigator of strike action uses a similar series of images made up of superimposed, low-angle shots of the stone court building to demonstrate the crushing weight of the judicial system. Montages of superimposed images are used at intense moments throughout the melodrama to convey the emotions of characters, or drama of the moment, as when a series of close-ups show bullets being loaded into rifles when guards begin to fire on political prisoners attempting to escape. Ken Dancyger points out that Pudovkin was employing the basic concept of D.W. Griffith that 'the fragmentation of a scene into shots could create a power far beyond the character of a scene filmed without this type of construction' and taking this a step further, in that the filmmaker was not attempting to 'adapt reality' but to create a 'new reality' (2013, 14). After the striking workers are slaughtered by being fired on by infantry and charged by troops on horseback, in a scene echoing Eisenstein's Odessa Steps sequence from *Bronenosets Potyomkin/Battleship Potemkin* (1925),[12] there is a further sequence of abstract shots of factory machinery, girders, buildings and skylines that merges into similar shots of the Kremlin, before finally settling on the Senate building, the seat of government in the early years after the 1917

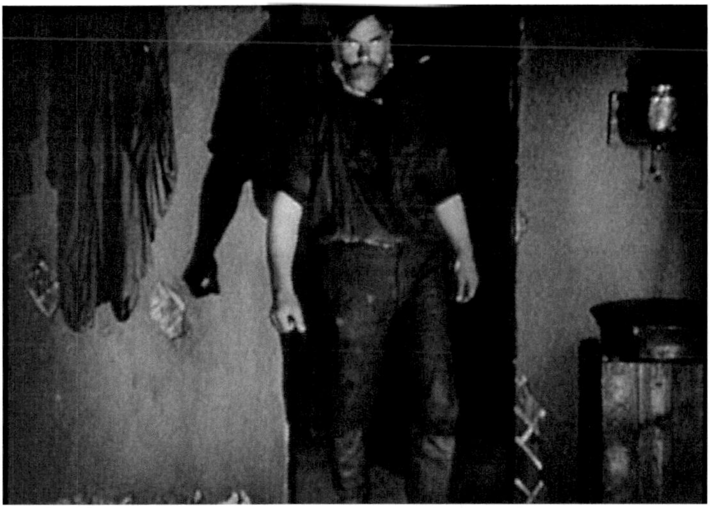

Fig 6.5 The shadow of the threatening father falls across the home (*Mat/Mother*, 1926).

Revolution. In this way, the film takes us beyond the heroic defeat of the 1905 revolutionaries and on to the triumph of 1917 that is seen as belonging in a very real sense to those killed twelve years before. The red flag on top of the Senate symbolically merges into the tattered flag defiantly held moments earlier by the mother.[13] The clear aim is for the audience to be brought to climactic, intellectual and emotional recognition of the revolutionary achievements of the Russian people.

The political commitment shown in *Mother* echoes that of *Battleship Potemkin*. Both films are made during the period in which Josef Stalin is consolidating his grip on the Communist party after the death of Vladimir Lenin. Both are created against a backdrop of intense political debate and social upheaval stretching back to at least the early 1900s. They are knowingly made, carefully propagandistic, works that aim to bolster the revolutionary change that has taken place in Russia. In this sense, *Mother* and *Battleship Potemkin* could never be described as politically innocent but they are films that are made without experience of the Stalinist terror that is to come.[14]

Where Pudovkin uses images of an ice-covered river defrosting in *Mother* to suggest the revolutionary change beginning to emerge in Russia in 1905, Eisenstein opens *Battleship Potemkin* with powerful waves, crashing and breaking on the shore. Where Pudovkin takes aesthetic pleasure in the abstract compositional possibilities offered in filming a factory, Eisenstein creates wonderfully complex shots of sailors in their hammocks within a few minutes of the start of his film in which, because of the swinging motion of hammocks, his shots have the additional possibilities afforded by movement.[15] Immediately after this, Eisenstein continues exploring complexities of composition by using the rails, steps and decks of the superstructure of the ship to divide up the screen space. Movement and alterations in light and shadow catch the eye in all directions. The richness of the framed image that will continue throughout is thus set up from the first couple of scenes. This is attributable to Eisenstein but also to the film's cinematographer, Eduard Tisse. According to Richard Taylor, after she saw some of his work, Nina Agadzhanova-Shutko, who was responsible for scripting this film with Eisenstein, said of Tisse: 'Tisse is not a cameraman – he is God' (2001, 4). After the death of the leader of the uprising onboard the *Potemkin*, Vakulinchuk, his body is shown laying at rest on the Odessa quayside and a series of shots follow showing what the inter-titles describe as 'A mist spread over the sea'. This sequence uses black-and-white cinematography to capture light filtered through mist and reflecting on water in painterly compositions.[16] Afterwards, seemingly endless crowds of people come to pay their respects to this sailor and an inter-title proclaims 'Glory to those who died for the revolution'. This is a sentiment that, because of the horrendous death count after 1917 as supporters of the revolution attempted to defend it against others who wanted it reversed, would have had a resonance that is lost to us.[17]

As with Pudovkin's *Mother*, *Battleship Potemkin* is set in 1905 but everything it has to say refers implicitly to both the moment of the revolution in 1917 and the contemporary moment of 1925 in which the film

Fig 6.6 Eduard Tisse's painterly compositions (*Bronenosets Potyomkin/Battleship Potemkin*, 1925).

is first being screened. So, when one person in the crowd expresses anti-Semitism and shouts 'Kill the Jews!' thinking that in the fervor of the moment when everyone is coming up with slogans like 'Down with tsarism!' he will have an audience, he is immediately set upon by the crowd.[18] In this section of the film Eisenstein uses close-ups of clenched fists to show tension and anger in just the way Pudovkin does in *Mother*. The difference, however, is that Pudovkin's expression of emotion is linked to a character who has been strongly individualized within his narrative, whereas Eisenstein employs the shot as an expression of the collective anger of the crowd. There are individuals we can identify in *Battleship Potemkin*, such as Vakulinchuk who has already been mentioned, but by and large Eisenstein holds to the concept of the collective and collective action. Taylor quotes Eisenstein saying the script needed to have 'an emphasis on the mass, on collective action' (2001, 2). When a flotilla of small boats sets out from Odessa to take provisions to the sailors aboard the *Potemkin* it is a shared, group action that is celebrated. There is individual freedom expressed as the skiffs skip speedily over the water but this is seen as operating within a cooperative bloc. A key question for those such as Eisenstein and Pudovkin, who believed in revolutionary social change was, how should the mass of a counterrevolutionary force be represented in a different way to that of the revolutionary mass in order to show one in a positive light and the other in a negative light? Interestingly, one way this is achieved is through members of the crowd of townspeople from Odessa, who are about to be slaughtered on the Odessa Steps, being carefully individualized. By contrast, the collective group of soldiers marching down the steps firing on the crowd shortly afterwards is de-personalized. They are shown as machine-like marching legs and feet, for example. The soldiers in this famous sequence become 'faceless' (Pramaggiore and Wallis 2005, 191) in a way that the revolutionary mass never does. Marilyn Fabe characterizes the experience of watching the Odessa Steps sequence as: 'shots of masses of people rushing down the steps interspersed with close shots of individuals and shots of the faceless soldiers relentlessly advancing and firing their guns' (2004, 32).

Both *Mother* and *Battleship Potemkin* are very transparently made by filmmakers who are in support of massive social change based on Marxist class struggle. And, the idea that as a filmmaker you need just these sorts of revolutionary aims, in order to produce work with the level of political commitment being discussed here, would seem to be supported by looking at a film such as *Tout va bien* made during a later period of turbulent political upheaval in Europe. It is Jean-Luc Godard's first 'broadly commercial film' (Morrey 2005, 97) since the large-scale civil unrest that occurred in Paris in 1968, an event that forced Godard to evaluate the conservative bourgeois nature of his work to this point. *Tout va bien* explores the possibility of ordinary people taking power and overthrowing the in-place social order. More than that, through its methods of construction, it suggests the necessity of social change being accompanied by an end to mainstream methods of making films. It is 'an attempt to make a political film within the commercial film industry' (98) and the circumstances within which it is made contrast sharply with the context surrounding *Mother* and *Battleship Potemkin*. As a journalist, the character of Suzanne DeWitt (Jane Fonda) stumbles around within her chosen form of expression trying to find new ways of conveying new emerging attitudes, in much the same way Godard and Jean-Pierre Gorin search within the possibilities offered by film. As a filmmaker, Suzanne's partner, Jacques (Yves Montand), seems even less confident about what to do in the face of a changing world. There is 'a constant questioning of how best to represent this situation, the aspirations of the workers and the realities of the political struggle' (101). Certainly, within this film, the Communist Party would not seem to have all the answers and might well be an institution that needs to be challenged along with the conventional trade union hierarchy. The Communist trying to sell his book in the supermarket towards the end of the film is totally unable to explain his position to those who begin to question him. Only the direct action of young people encouraging everybody to see the 'stuff' in the supermarket as 'free' appears to have any impact on the consumers taking their shopping through the tills.[19] Suzanne's question at this point encapsulates Godard and Gorin's question to themselves as well as to their audience: 'To change everything, where do you start?'

Picking up on Bertolt Brecht's ideas around the need to force the audience to detach themselves from immersion in the narrative, Godard and Gorin construct the spectator (or force the spectator to construct him/herself) as a player in the interplay of created, re-created and challenged meanings.[20] They expose the normally hidden techniques of film production that usually allow the spectator to escape into a fantasy world. They reveal film as make-believe with the aim of making it all the more part of the 'real', which as they see it equates to the day-to-day political world. The opening draws immediate attention to the constructed nature and the expense of filmmaking (and, therefore, its complicity with capitalism). This is achieved through a series of simple devices, one of which is to show a succession of cheques being signed. Following Brecht's ideas for the theatre, the actors refuse to allow the audience to identify with them as characters; at certain moments, for example, characters look straight at the camera and address the audience directly, while the set is continually exposed as being precisely that, nothing more than a fabricated space.

Tout va bien even in complying with the narrative love story structure exposes it as a myth and yet reveals, in an even more meaningful way, the importance of relationships with others and, paradoxically, the isolation of the individual. Mainstream (Hollywood) narratives allow viewers to escape the day-to-day world and enter a fantasy within which, through indulging their imagination, they are able to be the heroic central character via identification. Godard and Gorin attempt to cut off this possibility. They also make every effort to prevent the viewer from simply sitting before the screen as a voyeur, or unseen observer. Instead, their effort is to force anybody watching this film to become an active participant. At the same time, continuing the challenge to the audience, they reveal the plurality of reality, producing a series of different perspectives on the same events, while all the time urging the spectator to participate in such a way as to take up their own point of view, or political stance, even if it is necessarily one that is going to shift and change in response to changing experiences of the world.

The use of sub-titles, and mixed English and French dialogue, further disrupts the easy, smooth finish of a classic film narrative, forcing an intensified concentration on what is being said. Further, the dialogue itself refuses the simple (or simplistic) pattern demanded of mainstream films; instead the arguments presented for debate are complicated and intellectually demanding. And, running alongside this, the effort both of the camerawork and editing is to refuse to allow the viewer to identify with any one character. The result is that all the time as a spectator you are being challenged, especially as a viewer more used to prevalent Americanized global screen images. To take one small example: who is the woman who comes in to remove the coffee cups as the central couple are sitting in their flat arguing over their relationship? As viewers we might make up scenarios, wanting her perhaps

Fig 6.7 Who is the woman who enters to remove the coffee cups? (*Tout va bien*, 1972).

to be the maid in order to maintain our constructed fantasy narrative; but because of the nature of this film we have to entertain at least the possibility that she could be part of the catering staff on the set (and, further, consider the potential double bluff that she may be an actor pretending to be a member of the catering corps).

And so, finally, what is the position of Godard and Gorin in relation to this work? Is it the same as that of Eisenstein and Pudovkin with regard to their works? Is the doubt and complexity with which Godard and Gorin seem to be wrestling something Eisenstein and Pudovkin would recognize from the position of the mid-1920s in Russia? Is the expression of their doubt and uncertainty within the film something that is available to Godard and Gorin in a way that it was not to Eisenstein and Pudovkin working within post-revolutionary Russia and confronted, as they were, by the pressing need to consolidate an actual rather than a failed revolutionary moment?

7

EUROPEAN ART CINEMA AND EXPERIMENTAL FILM

Focus films: *Berlin: Die Sinfonie der Großstadt/Berlin: Symphony of a Metropolis* (Ruttmann, 1927, Weimar Republic), *Blue* (Jarman, 1993, UK), *Un chien andalou* (Buñuel and Dali, 1929, France), *Le Sang d'un Poète/The Blood of a Poet* (Cocteau, 1930, France),[1] *Rhythmus 21* (Richter, 1921, Weimar Republic) and *Ballet Mécanique* (Léger, 1923–1924, France).

In general, while they have attempted to explore the possibilities offered by the elements of film construction in more radical ways than mainstream films, the films we have so far considered have held to the mainstream requirement of having a pretty clearly identifiable storyline. Some filmmakers, however, have rejected the dominant need for narrative within cinema and sought other means of utilizing film form to communicate with their audience. A few, while holding to narrative, have pushed the boundaries in such experimental ways as to move their work into an area generally recognized as being part of the avant-garde. *Berlin: Die Sinfonie der Großstadt/Berlin: Symphony of a Metropolis* and *Blue*, two very different films, might be seen in their own ways to fall within this category.

Berlin: Die Sinfonie der Großstadt is the story of a day in the life of a dynamic modern city.[2] It is naturalistic in the sense that one of its key motivations was to take filmmaking out of the studio and on to the streets. It includes recognizable characters and locations. However, its wellspring lies essentially in the editing of Walter Ruttmann who envisions the world of this city as a continuous rhythmic play of form, light and motion. The first stop for anyone wanting to understand where Ruttmann is coming from would be to view his abstract films, *Lichtspiel: Opus I* (1921), *Lichtspiel: Opus II* (1923), *Lichtspiel: Opus III* (1924) and *Lichtspiel: Opus IV* (1925).[3] In *Berlin: Die Sinfonie der Großstadt* lines and shapes flit across the screen, or merge, playing on each other, playing off of each other. People move individually as spots of movement, or collectively as seas of movement, always through architectural spaces dividing up the screen. Machines have a movement and life of their own, mechanical and repetitive, but with each creating its own distinctive rhythmic patterning of screen space. Human action is itself repetitive and ordered, individual, and yet, on a larger social scale, purposeful and coordinated. Although much of what we are shown continues to be edited around a rhythmic play of the abstract shapes found within the machinery and architecture of a city, during sections of Akt III and Akt IV we are given more of a social document, an investigation of the class-driven experience of life with a sense of the wealth and poverty found in Berlin in this period. While classes exist beside each other in the city, the daily lives of some are demonstrated to be much harsher than the leisured comfort experienced by others. Siegfried Kracauer dismisses the links between shots employed by Ruttmann as 'purely decorative and rather obvious' (1997 [1960], 65). But, while to some extent this may be the case, it does not mean the editing cannot create real impact. The screamed repetition of the word 'Geld' ('money, money, money'), which is made to 'fly' off of the page of a newspaper, makes it clear how the filmmakers ultimately feel about this capital-driven, consumerist society. Once again, we have art cinema not only taking society to task but searching for alternatives to the dominance of mainstream cinema. Nora Alter classifies this film as 'an insurgent meditation on the possibilities of an "other cinema",

Fig 7.1 Movement and architectural space dividing up screen space (*Berlin: Die Sinfonie der Großstadt/Berlin: Symphony of a Metropolis*, 1927).

a counter-cinema as it were substituting "real" filmmaking for the standard fare so readily devoured by the masses' (2009, 207).[4]

Derek Jarman's *Blue* is an entirely different piece of work, and yet, it too in the midst of reaching out towards an 'other cinema' retains some residual employment of a narrative structure. The film recounts the movement towards death of a man who is dying as a result of HIV/AIDS. The audience is presented with a simple blue screen and a soundtrack narrating Jarman's meditations around his impending death,[5] still linked to his past and those he has known, still linked to the world and its ongoing events, still having to take part in the matter-of-fact, everyday episodes of life, but with a clear ending, not only of death but of blindness, looming over all of these things. Rowland Wymer shows how *Blue*, while appearing to emerge wholly from Jarman's own life/death, actually had its genesis almost 20 years earlier in an exhibition Jarman had seen in London of work by the French avant-garde artist, Yves Klein. Wymer explains how this connection links Jarman's film to a wider artistic 'protest against the postmodern "cacophony of voices" and "pandemonium of image"' (2005, 171), making the film part of the wider debate about the relationship of art to cinema.

Other films, such as *Un chien andalou* and *Le Sang d'un Poète/The Blood of a Poet*, retain recognizable characters and locations but develop dream-world, or surreal, events that by any measure of everyday experience register as strange, or bizarre. Pierre Sorlin says experimental cinema for Luis Buñuel meant attempting 'to make spectators watch actively and succeed in formulating their own personal reading of the film' (2007, 217). And yet, *Un chien andalou* is highly directive of audience attention and interpretation. The film opens with the inter-title, 'Il était une fois...' ('Once upon a time...'), seemingly announcing itself as a classic fairy story, and goes on to use a series of inter-titles suggestive of time passing, ending with 'au printemps' ('in spring') as we are shown an image of an upright, half-buried, dead couple. According to Buñuel, 'Nothing in the film symbolizes anything' (Buñuel 2006, 102). Yet, simply from considering these basic elements of the opening and ending it is clear this statement by Buñuel is nonsense. The whole concept of storytelling is heavily referenced and played upon, and classic narrative themes of time and death are obviously evoked. As an audience we cannot access a simple linear narrative but it is evident that elements of what we are shown, such as a grown man wearing frilly baby-clothes or the same man being made to stand facing a wall with his hands raised, carry heavily orchestrated connotations. We find ourselves in a strange world within which time and space become discontinuous and dislocated, but we have no trouble recognizing commonplace elements of human relationships and individual psychology. The audience is challenged, as is usual for experimental film, but at the same time the spectator has no difficulty using their knowledge of ordinary narrative strategies as a means of accessing the material. The same would be true of later Buñuel surrealist films such as *Le Charme discret de la bourgeoisie/The Discreet Charm of the Bourgeoisie* (1972, France/Italy/Spain), or *Cet obscur objet du désir/That Obscure Object of Desire* (1977, France/Spain). There may be many instances in these sorts of films in which the precise meaning of an element of symbolism is not entirely clear, or is complex and multilayered, but this is always the nature of imagery. There may also be plenty of imagery that is open to interpretation above and beyond anything that may have been immediately apparent to the author. However, much that is to be found within surrealist texts such as these is present as a result of the knowing and playful involvement of the filmmakers in the creation of meaning. None of which is to deny that 'Buñuel is fascinated less by precise meanings than by mystery and the opaque landscape of the unconscious' (Evans 2007, 39); in other words, by a range of suggestive, half-formed possibilities rather than anything that is circumscribed too absolutely. Raymond Durgnat said of *Un chien andalou*:

> I have seen *Un Chien Andalou* thirteen times, including four viewings in two hours, and each viewing, instead of exhausting the film, has revealed new nuances, new moods. At each viewing the film has transformed itself into a variation on itself.
>
> (1968, 21)

In *Le Sang d'un Poète* (1930) Jean Cocteau opens by relating his film to a poem, emphasizing that in relation to both poems and films there is work to be done by the reader, and reassuring his audience that there is meaning to be found. 'Every poem is a coat of arms. It must be deciphered,' reads the on-screen text. The images are key to Cocteau as they are to Buñuel and Dali.

> In practical terms, a film for Cocteau is a discontinuous series of images. Each image must be set off from another and not flow into the next … Cocteau's primary concern is not to damage what he calls the individual 'relief' of each image, so that the linking and juxtaposing of images in montage is enhanced by the textures of traceable difference.
>
> (Williams 2006, 19–20)

And these images have their origins within Cocteau's own life:[6]

> *The Blood of a Poet*, like so much of what Cocteau created, abounds in autobiographical motifs: the macho Dargelos and the snowball fight, the opium smoker, the poet with his sexual stigmata, and the gunshots that, intentionally or not, echoed his father's suicide long before.
>
> (Peters 1987, 108)

Le Sang d'un Poète is, as Cocteau himself says, 'a descent into oneself, a way of using the mechanism of the dream without sleeping' (2013 [1947], 47). Similarly, the starting point for the images played on by Buñuel and Dali was also, inevitably, their own lives (and dreams). There was disagreement between Cocteau and the Surrealists about how to approach the creation process,[7] but for the viewer the outcome would not seem to be too dissimilar. The images we end up with in both cases are archetypal expressions of eternal human anxieties.[8] Still, this is not easy viewing: James Williams notes, 'the film's extreme, trance-like slowness which Cocteau himself acknowledged as excruciating and which is accentuated by the passages of slow motion and the unremitting sense of claustrophobia created by the enclosed spaces' (2006, 41).[9]

However, because of the richness of the imagery and this slowness there is ample space for the viewer to engage with the film. Beyond this, a strand of thematic (and controversial) interest such as sexuality is further enhanced by placing this film into the context of the period. Féral Benga, who plays a guardian angel in *Le Sang d'un Poète*, was a dancer and artist's model from Senegal who worked in cabaret in Paris from 1925. The sexuality he expressed on stage meant he was quickly viewed in terms of his homoeroticism. Barbette, who makes a guest cameo appearance as an aristocratic lady sitting in a theatre box, was a popular drag artist and high-wire performer working in Paris. As James Smalls expresses it: 'During the interwar Paris years, Barbette and Benga were music-hall performers who became exotic spectacles' (2013, 87).

Fig 7.2 Féral Benga as 'exotic spectacle' (*Le Sang d'un Poète/The Blood of a Poet*, 1930).

Other films, such as *Rhythmus 21*, also *Rhythmus 23* (Richter, 1923) and the series of films by Ruttmann, already mentioned, *Lichtspiel: Opus I*, *Opus II*, *Opus III* and *Opus IV*, leave narrative structures still further behind. Like abstract painting these films take the basic perceptual elements – light, shape/form, movement and colour – and, often through focusing on the rhythmic use of these elements, confront the viewer with pure abstraction.[10]

> Old-fashioned children's kaleidoscopes and various styles of abstract painting serve to remind us of just how fascinated we are by color, shape, light and combined patterns of these elements ... Even within our most usual experience of film (i.e. fictional narratives), it seems likely that this fundamental aspect of cinema, the flashing of shapes and colors before our eyes, is probably an important part of the attraction.
>
> (Benyahia, Gaffney and White 2010, 8)

But within this general concept huge differences can be found within abstract filmmaking. Len Lye's work in the mid-1930s, for example, is much freer in its use of shape and form than either Richter or Ruttmann.[11] Viking Eggeling's *Symphonie Diagonale* (1924) encapsulates abstract film's exploration of the endless variations on a theme that are possible through use of the simple artistic, or graphic, 'mark'.

Ballet Mécanique (Léger, 1923–1924), was a collaborative work made by Fernand Léger with input from the cinematographer, Dudley Murphy, and the photographer and filmmaker, Man Ray.[12] It is neither a narrative film nor an abstract film. Instead, the audience is presented with repeated, often pulsating arrays of disparate images such as a woman's face, a man's face, close-ups of mouths and eyes, mechanical objects in motion, everyday objects, fairground rides, street scenes from unusual angles, a young woman from the leisured classes on a swing, a working-class woman carrying a heavy load up steep steps, an animated Chaplinesque character, and more. There are nods here towards several aspects of Modernist art in the early 1900s; predominantly, perhaps, Dada in its refusal of logic and reason, but also the multiple perspectives of Cubism and the acclaim of the mechanical found in Futurism.

Aaron Sultanik divided experimental filmmakers from the modernist period into two basic groups: those 'influenced by the surrealist-dadaist doctrine that film should function as a visualization of the unconscious' and others who focused much more on 'cinema's power of abstraction' (1986, 55).

> In both cases there is an absence of any realistic or narrative element; their work emphasizes either the surrealist's belief in the erotic, anarchic design of the subconscious or the then prevailing interest in modern painters in the kinetic makeup and interconnectedness of sensation and nature.
>
> (55)

Finally, one of the most interesting aspects of experimental film is that its day-to-day existence disproves the notion that the ordinary, person-on-the-street audience is unable to accept and live in a comfortable relationship with surrealism and abstraction. From the 1920s through to today, experimental filmmakers have found a space to express themselves within the commercial world of advertising. Walter Ruttmann, for example, co-directed *Der Aufstieg* ('the climb')[13] for *The Great Exhibition for Health Care, Social Welfare, and Physical Exercise* held in Dusseldorf in 1926, which was attended by more than seven million visitors (Petropoulos 2014, 263).

8

EUROPEAN ART CINEMA AND HOLLYWOOD

Focus films: *Sunrise: A Song of Two Humans* (Murnau, 1927, US), *Apocalypse Now* (Coppola, 1979, US) and *Seven* (Fincher, 1995, US).

Throughout the history of cinema Hollywood has had an ambivalent relationship with European art cinema. On the one hand, it has been keen to attract talented directors such as Ernst Lubitsch, Michael Curtiz and Fritz Lang, actors such as Greta Garbo, Marlene Dietrich and Ingrid Bergman, cinematographers such as Karl Freund, Boris Kaufman and László Kovács, and other personnel to work in America.[1] On the other hand, it has been less than sure about anything smacking of an avant-garde approach to making films. Hollywood product is classically built around a strong narrative drive, a succinct script, functional storytelling cinematography, continuity editing, naturalistic acting, and recognizable (if stereotypical) sets, locations and costumes. The focus is on a central character who battles through adversity to achieve a clearly defined goal. One way of defining European art cinema is to view it as a body of films that deliberately sets out to challenge precisely these approaches to filmmaking. However, even more fundamental for Hollywood than questions about how films should be made is the issue of profitability. Hollywood is a highly developed business enterprise, defined at base by its emphasis on the commercial aspect of the filmmaking process. In this environment success is seen in terms of the bottom line. In order to achieve profits, Hollywood studio heads and producers have always been intensely aware of themselves as an entertainment industry needing to appeal to the widest possible audience. When the market was more homogeneous in the period up until 1945 this function of the industry was reasonably easily addressed with a one-size-fits-all product. As the cinema market became more dislocated, and as Hollywood found its product increasingly challenged by other forms of entertainment, a piecemeal recognition of the need for the industry to relocate itself within a changed, and changing, marketplace came about. 'Art cinema,' in and of itself, became a brand Hollywood felt it could profitably market. As the old pre-war studio system broke up and the industry reconfigured itself, New Hollywood with its emphasis on moral uncertainty, its tendency to challenge the Establishment, and its willingness to embrace the individual vision of auteurs such as Martin Scorsese and Francis Ford Coppola, became acceptable because of its potential profitability.

The reality is, of course, that any sense of 'art cinema' as not being interested in profits that the approach outlined above might either set up, or reinforce, is neither valid nor, ultimately, useful. Any film being made for cinema exhibition must, because of the technical, personnel and time commitments required, necessarily cost a relatively large sum of money. If the film is to be made, either the patronage of individuals, companies, organizations, or government has to be secured, or investment from those hoping for a return on their money has to be accepted. Furthermore, even if we return to the products of Classical Hollywood before the commercial need to embrace some form of art element within Hollywood was tacitly acknowledged, what we find is individual practitioners using the chance offered by the industry to make films as an opportunity to experiment and push the boundaries towards increasing artistic expression. Charlie Chaplin produced Hollywood product that sold, and Buster Keaton did the same, but they also might be said to have created their own 'art film' and through their efforts inspired those who might more normally have been seen as on the cutting edge of art film, such as the European Surrealists. Setting up binary oppositions between Hollywood and other cinemas can provide useful working positions from which to begin debates around the nature of cinema, although always with the clear proviso that such demarcations are neither clear-cut nor watertight. It might be more productive to see the relationship between actual Hollywood practitioners and those involved in the vast array of possibilities we are lumping together under European art cinema as existing in symbiotic relationship to each other.[2] In 1930, in *Le Sang d'un Poète*, Cocteau may have a surreal scene in which his central character passes through a mirror into another world, but in 1924, in *Sherlock Jr.*, Keaton has already had his comic persona pass through a cinema screen into the film world on the other side.

F.W. Murnau was a director who came to Hollywood in the 1920s and contributed towards cementing within the filmmaking community an awareness of a raft of possible techniques arising from German Expressionism. These approaches eventually became central to American film noir in the 1940s and 1950s. *Sunrise: A Song of Two Humans*, directed by Murnau, revolves around the deadly charms of an alluring woman from the city, essentially the femme fatale of later films. Low-key lighting creates an ominous shadowy world, and distorted, angular set designs tell us all is not well with this world. But other aspects of the more normal Hollywood frame are also re-shaped. As Brian Darr suggests: 'Nearly every shot in the film involves a striking effect, whether from an unusual light source, a superimposition, or a complex camera movement' (2009, n.p.). Mobile camera movements, such as those used in the fairground scenes, owe much to ideas picked up by one of the cinematographers, Charles Rosher, when he was working in Germany; and some of the deep-focus shots employed, as when the Woman from the City (Margaret Livingston) leaves her lodgings, prefigure the work of cinematographers such as Gregg Toland. Within the first few minutes, use is also made of challengingly non-naturalistic editing, with clashing images occupying the two halves of a frame. A superimposed image of a train crossing the screen on a crazy bottom-left to top-right diagonal plays over a simple shot of a train on a track. A steaming ocean liner cruises forward on the left of the screen while an everyday beach scene is shown on the right. Within just a few shots the urgent energy and excitement of holiday-time is succinctly conveyed; but maybe it was not quite what a mainstream audience more used to an escapist romance like *It* (1927) or an epic wartime romance such as *Wings* (1927), both starring Clara Bow, was expecting.[3] *Sunrise* 'failed to recoup its costs' (Fischer 2003, 77). The sheer pleasure that is taken in the cinematic possibilities, as when the Woman from the City tempts the Man (George O'Brien) with the excitement of city life and we have a montage of superimposed shots of nightlife, or when the Man and the Wife rediscover their love for each other in the city and become oblivious to the traffic around them, is technically interesting to filmmakers but does not take the story forward, or add to what we already know. What we end up with is a film that is not financially successful but which wins in two significant categories, 'Best Cinematography' and 'Unique and Artistic Production', at the first Academy Awards ceremony. According to William Parrill, 'Contemporary low-brow critics … regarded *Sunrise* as a European art film, which is, of course, exactly what it is' (2006, 378).

In America, filmmakers often found more freedom to experiment in making B-movies. Joseph H. Lewis, for example, was able to film on location using long takes in *Gun Crazy* (1950), providing a possible source of inspiration for French New Wave director, Jean-Luc Godard.[4] Daniel Eagan says, 'The two most fascinating elements of *Gun Crazy* are its two "real-time" robberies, shot on location, with live sound, the first done in one take' (2010, 433). Francois Truffaut discusses the enthusiasm film critics who were later to become French New Wave directors had for the work of Jules Dassin, most well-known for the documentary-style location shooting of *The Naked City* (1948) and *Night and the City* (1950) (Dixon 1993, 133). These are filmmakers who illustrate the way in which cultural flows have moved both ways across the Atlantic. Even when the films coming out of Hollywood could be seen as nothing other than the standard product of an almost factory-like

Fig 8.1 Distorted, angular set design (*Sunrise: A Song of Two Humans*, 1927).

production process, the influence on European art cinema has continued. It has been the Hollywood 'standard' that has provided 'rules' to be broken and norms of practice to be challenged. There is a sense in which 'art cinema' could not exist without a mainstream, dominant form to counterpoint.[5]

Directors such as Michael Cimino, Francis Ford Coppola, Stanley Kubrick and Martin Scorsese, who emerged in the United States in the late 1960s and the 1970s, were given a certain independence in their filmmaking not previously afforded to Hollywood directors. Their preeminence owed a lot to the relative decline in power of the studios, and the freedom of expression they enjoyed was a result of increasingly liberal attitudes towards the representation of sex and violence. But the way in which they came to be viewed (and to view themselves) as creative artists was in a large measure down to the concept of the auteur, the notion of the director as someone with a personal vision they are able to bring to the screen. This really stems from Europe, from European art cinema, and, in particular, from the self-publicity of the directors of the French New Wave.[6] According to Gene Phillips, 'Coppola himself personally agrees with the fundamental tenets of the auteur theory concerning the pivotal role of the director in the film-making process' (2004, 3). Furthermore, the shooting time afforded to Coppola for *Apocalypse Now*, which ran to 238 days, would certainly suggest he had by this time succeeded in getting everyone around him to see him as an auteur (Phillips and Hill 2004, xviii).

Thomas Elsaesser suggested the brand of auteurs that emerged in America in the 1970s 'drew their self-understanding from identifying with the ideology of the European artist' (2004, 58).[7] Phillips and Rodney Hill quote Coppola as saying the idea for the ending of *Apocalypse Now* stemmed from his reading of the poet, T.S. Eliot, who concludes 'The Hollow Men' with the line, 'Not with a bang but a whimper' (2004, 49). Given that the whole concept of this film arises from a re-interpretation of Joseph Conrad's novella, *Heart of Darkness* (1899), this would certainly seem to be a Hollywood film that is setting itself up as art cinema. In a similar way, in a later period, *Seven* immediately claims art status for itself by the way in which, through references in the script, it claims a heritage that links it back through European cultural expression to Dante Alighieri's *Inferno*; the first part of his early fourteenth-century epic poem, *The Divine Comedy*.

However, in considering *Apocalypse Now* and *Seven*, we are thrown back to the issue of what exactly we might mean by the term 'art cinema'. Are a few references to T.S. Eliot and Joseph Conrad as with the first film, or to Dante, Chaucer's *Canterbury Tales*, and Milton's *Paradise Lost* as with the second, sufficient to confer 'art cinema' status? Or, is the term in danger of becoming a 'catch-all' that hauls in so many disparate films that it becomes essentially meaningless? David Bordwell suggested the art cinema that had emerged in Hollywood in the 1970s picked up on the 'open endings' and 'psychological ambiguity' found in postwar European 'art cinema' in such a way as 'to warp art-cinema conventions in new directions' (2002 [1979], 100). Is this something of what is going on in *Apocalypse Now* and a later film like *Seven*? In this same essay from 1979, Bordwell also pointed out that some filmmakers from the Classical Hollywood period, especially, for him, Alfred Hitchcock, 'had something of the art cinema about them' (100), thereby reinforcing the complex issues at stake in ascribing overarching features to complicated bodies of work that may arise from within certain historical periods and geographical locations.[8]

9

CASE STUDIES

DAS CABINET DES DR CALIGARI/THE CABINET OF DR CALIGARI (1920, WEIMAR REPUBLIC)[1]

[Production Company: Decla-Bioscop AG. Director: Robert Wiene (and Friedrich Feher). Screenwriters: Hans Janowitz and Carl Meyer. Art designers: Hermann Warm, Walter Röhrig and Walter Reimann. Cinematographer: Willy Hameister. Cast: Werner Krauss (Caligari), Conrad Veidt (Cesare), Lil Dagover (Jane), Friedrich Feher (Francis), Hans Heinrich von Twardowski (Alan).]

Synopsis: Francis tells in flashback the story of how he and his friend, Alan, competed for the love of Jane. He recounts how he and Alan saw Dr Caligari and the somnambulist, Cesare, at a carnival in Holstenwall and how Cesare accurately predicted Alan's brutal death. In the story Francis tells, we then see Cesare sent by Caligari to kill Jane. But Cesare, overcome by her beauty, carries Jane off pursued by the townspeople. At a nearby asylum Francis finds the doctor in charge is none other than Caligari, who has been responsible for a series of murders. In a final twist, the extended flashback ends and we find Francis is a patient in an asylum run by a doctor who looks like Caligari.

Watching *The Cabinet of Dr Caligari* the audience, confined in the world of someone classified as insane, sees what the madman sees; distorted perspectives, eerie lights and shadows – an angular world of fears and apprehension. Expressionist sets are used to convey the asylum patient's thoughts, intensify the emotions of characters, and emphasize potential psychological depths behind the action. Holstenwall is a bizarre, nightmare-like place, filled with jagged roads, buildings with pointed rooftops, misshapen windows and doors, and drapes that hang above characters as barely concealed threats. The whole town seems about to fall in on itself and engulf the residents.[2] It is not until the end of the film that we can be sure we are being told this story by someone who has lost touch with reality. This may be a comforting resolution but, given the power of what has preceded this, it may be the images we carry away remain those of both the explicit and implicit horrors of the world evoked by the screened experience.

Made at an early point in film history, *Caligari* can be seen as an attempt to release mainstream cinema from any need to be involved in the straightforward re-creation of reality. *Caligari* 'challenged every rule and convention of Hollywood filmmaking' (Kaes 2006, 41). In its use of staged settings, and in the performance of the actors, this film purposely presents a look that is alien and unreal in order to create a psychological state rather than a physical reality and, perhaps, in doing so, to suggest the 'real' underlying nature of the world is a place of fear and dark forces. The filmmakers are, therefore, both questioning the nature of reality and, through example, suggesting film is a medium that can do things other than simply offering the photographic representation of life. In doing this they raise the issue of what film should be used for, and contribute towards extending the scope of filmic possibilities. When it was screened in New York in 1921, Anton Kaes suggests this 'dark' film 'seemed to challenge the cheerful optimism of the American dream' and as part of 'Expressionism, or the "German style"' contributed to American horror films of the 1930s, film noir of the 1940s and 1950s, and neo-noir of the late twentieth century/early twenty-first century (2006, 42).

Fig 9.1 The attempt at something other than photographic representation (*Das Cabinet des Dr Caligari/The Cabinet of Dr Caligari*, 1920).

The fact that the film was stylistically 'different' may have helped it receive a distribution outside of Germany, and in the process may have assisted other German films to access outside markets. In 1919 German filmmakers were finding it difficult to obtain screen-time for their films in some European markets; the First World War had just ended and both French and British exhibitors were refusing to show German films. However, French film enthusiasts intrigued by its challenging style and content acquired prints of *Caligari* and held their own screenings. Eventually, demand for the film meant the French government lifted its ban and *Caligari* opened in France in 1922.[3]

Some of its appeal may have been the fact that it was one of the first horror films. As such it set some of the plot conventions that would be used and re-used in coming decades: the evil doctor, or mad scientist, who commits murder through a 'monster' who he controls; the mysterious carnival with freakish, peep-show characters that comes to a town bringing terror with it; the monster who falls in love with a beautiful, innocent young girl; and angry townspeople who chase the monster out of their community. Of course, in a wider cultural context each of these narrative features has roots in folk tales found across Europe.

Hans Janowitz claimed the original script he had written with Carl Mayer, without the framing device of Francis telling the story as an inmate of an asylum, amounted to a bleak, pessimistic view of postwar German society. Caligari was evil incarnate and authority was duplicitous, manipulative and, ultimately, murderous. He alleged the framing story 'put our drama into a "box" that obscured its clarity'; essentially, the story could now be seen as nothing more than the wild imaginings of the inmate of an asylum (Budd 1990, 237). According to Janowitz, it was also the screenwriters who suggested settings for the film should be created from bizarrely painted canvases (222), leading to the production company hiring Expressionist designers Hermann Warm, Walter Rohrig and Walter Reimann. Doubt has been cast on both of these claims in the light of an early script being found that was used by Werner Krauss, the actor playing Dr Caligari. This script has its own framing device, with Francis telling his story 20 years later to dinner guests (28). David Robinson suggests the claims of Janowitz in particular, but also others, underplay the contribution to the finished film that resulted from changes to the script introduced by 'Robert Wiene, his crew and the uncredited editor (most likely Wiene himself, in accordance with then current filmmaking practice)' (1997, 25).[4]

Whatever the extent of the contributions from the various creative personnel may have been, in design terms twisted shapes, sharp angles, and a conscious avoiding of verticals and horizontals characterize both the exterior and interior sets. And, it is not just the sets that employ the fantastical style of Expressionism, the costumes, furniture, and even the performances of the actors, are integrated into the whole. Both Werner Krauss (Caligari) and Conrad Veidt (Cesare) move in distinctive ways, suggesting they are part of this strange world. Veidt has a tall, thin, angular body and moves slowly, almost gliding along the walls, while Krauss is hunched and moves by taking short, sharp steps, accentuated by the use of a cane. Repeated use is also made of the penetrating, staring eyes of both actors. Heavy make-up, in particular on Veidt's face, emphasizes the eyes and creates the appearance of something like a mask.[5]

The particular framing story eventually employed, making the story seem to emerge from the mind of a patient in an asylum, which seems to have been added when the film was in production, does on any logical surface evaluation make the film 'safe'.[6] The audience is allowed to escape the film's insane world because in the end it turns out to be the vision of someone who is mad, and not a nightmarish reality. As a result, the filmmakers are able to position themselves so that they are not so directly and obviously critical of German society. From this perspective the sets are simply used to convey the thoughts of Francis and to lay bare this character's emotions. The framing of the central story by the episodes in the asylum becomes reassuring; order has been restored in the sense that the murders and the accompanying evil were all simply figments of the imagination of a madman. Yet, the film still manages to end on a disturbing note: the final shot of Krauss's face is ambiguous and open to interpretation – perhaps Francis was right all along and the doctor is Caligari, the manipulator of Cesare. As Stephen Brockmann suggests, *Das Cabinet des Dr Caligari* 'seems to portray an inherently unstable world in which any viewpoint, including the viewpoint of the supposedly sane Dr Caligari, is thrown into question' (2010, 62).

It would be possible to put forward a scenario suggesting not only those who are murdered, but also Cesare and Francis himself, are victims of Caligari. From this perspective Caligari is seen, firstly, as manipulating Cesare to carry out his wishes,[7] and then, secondly, as having Francis totally within his power at the end. Frustratingly for Francis, if we take this viewpoint he alone knows who is responsible for the murders taking place in the world but is powerless to expose the villain; and, disturbingly for us as an audience, the character with the role of hero is unable to defeat evil and restore order. If we do take Francis as the hero and see the shot of Caligari's face at the end as the triumph of evil, then the film as a story has not performed its ritualistic taming of the horrors of the world, and the restoration of the world as a place of safety has not been achieved.

In this reading, Caligari becomes an embodiment of evil and the film takes on added symbolic power in its ability to talk about the nature of evil within the wider world. In *From Caligari to Hitler*, the film critic, Siegfried Kracauer, suggested films from this period had been able to project forward from the contemporary state of Germany in the 1920s to foretell something of the monstrous nature of events that would unfold in the 1930s and early 1940s. Perhaps, more obviously, it is important to remember that when *The Cabinet of Dr Caligari* was made, the First World War, and the horror of the trenches on the Western Front and starvation at home, had only just ended; and in a powerfully real sense this recent past was still visibly present on an everyday basis in the shape of the physically and psychologically maimed casualties to be found on the streets of German towns and cities. Asylums were full of people who continued to 'live' the full horrors of what human beings were able to inflict on each other. Undeniably, ideas of death and the bringing of death are at the heart of this film, as they are at the centre of other films from the period in Germany, such as *Nosferatu – Eine Symphonie des Grauens/Nosferatu, the Vampire* (F.W. Murnau, 1922). Once we have taken in the dark aspects of *Caligari* we can no longer avoid seeing the simple 'cabinet' of the title as an image of a coffin, and this may be particularly so if we are aware of the way in which this same image is used and re-used in *Nosferatu*.[8]

Logically, with an entranced Jane wandering through the opening scene in *Caligari* and Cesare standing in the asylum at the end, the main story has to be seen as arising from within Francis's crazed imagination. Such aspects of the film are clearly a difficulty for any reading that tends towards attaching insanity to the character of Caligari rather than Francis; and yet, it is not always the most reasoned account of events that we take away with us from a film. The power of some of the central images involving Caligari and Cesare as a fairground attraction (along with the final image of Caligari as the all-powerful director of the asylum) live on in our minds in such a way as to imaginatively carry forward what Janowitz claimed to be the original concept of the writers, to present an examination of omnipotent authority as essentially evil.

Interestingly, the stylistic use of visual distortions continues into the final scenes within the asylum. This clearly raises further questions about how we should interpret the whole film since, even as we realize we have been hearing the story of a (supposed?) madman, we are still being presented with a vision of the world, and therefore seeing the world, as a nightmarish reality. Furthermore, we are also implicated in the labyrinth of possibilities at an additional level: if we identify ourselves with the listener in the opening scene, by the end we find we have been identifying with a person who is insane. We too are in the asylum where we have been listening to a story told by an inmate. Does this mean we too are an inmate of this madhouse? Does this mean we too are insane or, worse, sane but trapped within the insanity of the asylum? And does the asylum then become a metaphor for the world at large?

ZEMLYA/EARTH (1930, SOVIET UNION)

[Production Company: VUFKU. Director and screenwriter: Alexander Dovzhenko. Cinematographer: Daniil Demutsky. Music: Levko Revutsky/Vyacheslav Ovchinnikov (1971 version). Cast: Stepan Shkurat (Opanas), Semyon Svashenko (Vasili 'Basil' Opanas), Yuliya Solntseva (Vasili's sister),[9] Yelena Maksimova (Natalya), Pyotr Masokha (Khoma 'Thomas' Whitehorse), Nikolai Nademsky (Semyon 'Simon' Opanas).]

Synopsis: This is the third part of Dovzhenko's 'Ukrainian trilogy', the first two parts being *Zvenigora* (1928) and *Arsenal* (1929). The central narrative of *Zvenigora* involves a man with two grandsons, one of whom joins the 1917 Russian Revolution while the other opposes the revolution. The story in *Arsenal* revolves around a Bolshevik-led uprising in Kiev in 1918. This focus on revolution continues in *Zemlya*, in which the hero, who with other young communists brings the first tractor to his village, is killed by those who oppose change in the countryside.

Zemlya was made at a critical moment in Russian history when Joseph Stalin was imposing his vision of the future on the only recently formed Union of Soviet Socialist Republics. From the revolutionary perspective, if the communist state established after the 1917 Revolution was to be maintained then agricultural output had to increase. Farming had to be modernized through the introduction of new technology and smallholdings had to be brought together into larger collectives to maximize efficient production. Robert Conquest tells us:

> Between January and March 1930, the number of peasant holdings brought into the collective farms increased from 4 million to 14 million. Over half the total peasant households had been collectivised in five months. And in the countryside the peasants fought back with 'the sawed-off shotgun, the axe, the dagger, the knife'. At the same time, they destroyed their livestock rather than let it fall into the hands of the State.
>
> (1998, 18–19)

All of this can be seen in Dovzhenko's film which acclaims these new ideas for farming and in clear propagandistic terms heralds a new future for agriculture. The central narrative event is the arrival in a peasant village of the first tractor ever seen there. This machine is viewed by the majority in the film as bringing progress, not only ploughing the land at a rate far in excess of the oxen previously used for centuries, but also tearing up fences around land held by local 'rich farmers' to bring it into collective use. These rich farmers, or kulaks, were regarded as the main opposition to collectivization and became a prime target for Stalin as he attempted to impose his agrarian policy by force.[10] In order to change farming practices it was seen as necessary to break the power of this group.[11] Propaganda backing the Party line is clearly found within Dovzhenko's narrative; and the government perspective is further reinforced through a documentary-style montage in the very middle of the film, which shows modern machinery increasing productivity all the way through the process from ploughing the land to baking bread for the people. We cut rapidly between images emphasizing speed, precision, progress and modernity. Just before this sequence the tractor has arrived in the village and been greeted by just about everybody, apart from a few rich farmers, as something akin to a miracle. The hero, Vasili, has addressed the collective mass of the villagers, announcing, 'We'll – prosper – with tractors.' And, Dovzhenko has blazed this message across the screen by giving individual frames to the three parts of this short sentence. But, despite all of this, on its release this film was not well received by the Communist Party. So, what was the problem with the film as far as the existing power base in the Soviet Union was concerned? In the face of a highly contentious policy that was resulting in intense turmoil and violence across the country, Dovzhenko would seem to have hit all the correct notes for a piece of state-authorized propaganda.

Zemlya was rejected by those around Stalin as being too complicit with bourgeoisie ideas of art and not sufficiently in tune with socialist realism.[12] Demyan Bedny, 'one of Stalin's favorite poets' (Liber 2002, 112), was outraged by the film and 'devoted a three-column article in *Izvestia* to denouncing it as "defeatist". This and other attacks resulted in some cuts in the film, and a shortening of its distribution life' (Leyda 1983, 275). Following a special Party Conference on cinema in 1928,

> the film authorities were not bothered with ideas like avant-gardism, formalism, symbolism or experiment, which had no direct relevance to the people. All films were to be comprehensible to and appreciated by the millions, and their one aim was to be the glorification of the emerging Soviet state.
>
> (Furhammer and Isaksson 1971, 20)

Zemlya was deemed too highbrow in its focus on the central eternal experience of the human condition, the cycle of birth and death within the natural world. It opens with images of a cereal crop moving in the wind on a hill beneath low, grey clouds. As we cut closer and the crop continues to ripple in waves, the shadows of clouds pass across the hillside. Both the shadows and the wind in their ephemeral nature are entirely appropriate for the film. The Soviet critics were not incorrect in their assessment of this as filmmaking as art, but the very 'deficiencies' they attacked are, in the eyes of others, qualities to be valued as linking this film to poetry.

At one point, in a series of shots we see plough blades behind a tractor cutting through the soil in close-up, working the land at a new technological pace; but, before this, we are told that 'for 75 years' Vasili's grandfather 'ploughed the earth with oxen'. Dovzhenko insists on having it both ways; he anticipates a future of progress but he acknowledges what he sees as the nobility of generation upon generation of peasants. When Vasili's father is shown using oxen like his father before him to plough the land and, later, when he is seen using a scythe, the camerawork and editing display their admiration for such intimate human connection with the soil and, at the same time, function in such a way as to elevate the physicality of labour. As has frequently been commented, the death of the grandfather, Semyon, in the opening scene is handled so as to make death feel part of the natural order of things, but just as interesting is the response of his friend, Old Peter (Vasiliy Krasenko), to his death. One aspect of this is Peter saying that because of all the hard work he did he would award Semyon 'the Soviet Labour Medal'. The youthful Vasili laughs at Peter's rustic simplicity and responds, 'They don't give medals for using oxen.' As the audience we could smile condescendingly with Vasili at Peter's angry response of, 'Well, what do they give them for?' Or, we could reflect and recognize with Dovzhenko that any progressive movement looking to the future should be built on a firm appreciation for the sacrifices of previous generations. These are things that, correctly from their perspective, troubled the contemporary Soviet authorities about Dovzhenko's work. Adam Bingham is right to say Dovzhenko was a director 'who passionately chronicled the struggles of the peasant class of his native Ukraine' (2004, n.p.).

The triumphant struggle of the communists, led by Vasili's actions in bringing the tractor to the village, to change the ancient ways of

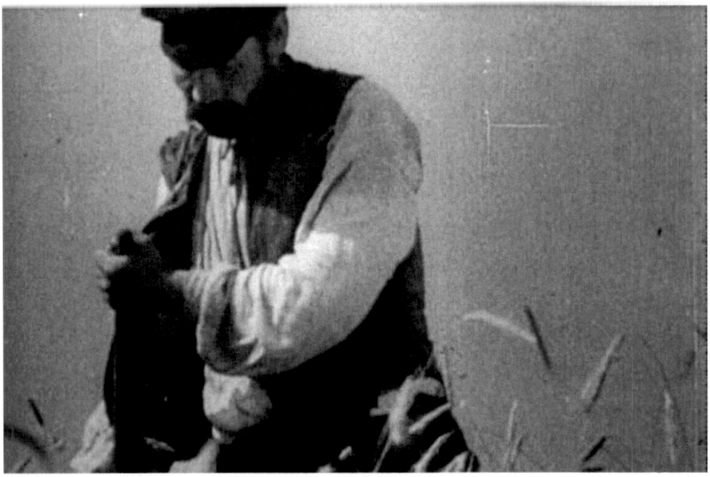

Fig 9.2 Admiration for the physical labour of generations (*Zemlya/Earth*, 1930).

Soviet agriculture is at the forefront of the narrative but, the recurring, ever-underpinning theme is that of the cycle of life. As the grandfather, Semyon, is dying outside beneath an apple tree, surrounded by his family and the bounty of the natural world, sitting playing close by there are two small children, and, as he is dying, we cut back and forth between him and the children. In much the same way, as Vasili is being buried towards the end of the film his mother is giving birth to another child. *Zemlya* celebrates the arrival of change in the countryside but at the same time eulogizes continuity. Generation follows generation. The rupture that occurs in this pattern comes with the death of Vasili, who is killed while he is still young. His murderer, Khoma, who opposes Vasili's ideas of collectivization, is doubly guilty within the internal value system of the film. Not only is he challenging the requirement for change but he is violently intervening in the natural cycle of life. His insanity and his ostracization by the rest of the village is a consequence, not only of going against progress and collective community values, not only of having committed murder, but, more importantly, of having through his actions contravened the natural order of things. There is a series of shots of Khoma in his madness towards the end of the film and one of them shows him running in circles, absolutely minute within the bottom right-hand corner of the frame. But he is not the only person to be framed in this way within the film, that is, to be held within a shot that forcibly presents human insignificance within the vastness of the land and, more importantly, against the immensity of the sky. When the young communists leave to collect the tractor with which to collectively, as Vasili says, 'take the earth away from them', i.e. the rich farmers or kulaks, their group is filmed by Dovzhenko in exactly the same way. Throughout the film, Dovzhenko is in line with government propaganda requirements in that he shows very clearly there is strength in coming together as a group, so that at key moments in the film the peasants take over the frame en masse; but, he is also careful to frame the hundreds of villagers who march together at Vasili's funeral within a long shot that shows them beneath a sky that again takes up more than three-quarters of the screen. As Vasili's body is carried by mourners it brushes past apples that hang plentifully from trees, reminding us of his grandfather's death. It then passes in front of a field of sunflowers that again refer us back to the prominence given to the natural world in the film's opening. But, of course, there is something very different about Vasili's death when compared to his grandfather's: as has been suggested, Vasili dies before reaching maturity, let alone old age. He is young, confident and energetic, through him and others like him change is achieved; but Vasili is also naïve and lacks experience of life. He laughs at the old with the energy of youth but will never grow to enjoy their maturity, will never experience those years that would enable him to reflect on life and the passing of time in the way his father can, and in the way the film does. It is Vasili's father, Opanas, not the young revolutionary hero, who is created by Dovzhenko as the still centre of the film. Opanas is not against the views of the young communist revolutionaries, as his wry comment when they have left his house makes clear, but he understands that radical change will inevitably bring with it confrontation and violence. After Vasili's death, Dovzhenko positions Opanas alone in the frame, seemingly sitting without moving for several days before taking decisive action. First of all he tells the priest, 'There ain't no God,' and then he has his son buried in 'a new way' that allows the people to 'sing new songs of the new life'.[13] But, in Dovzhenko's work, even this politically correct revolutionary denunciation of the Russian Orthodox Church is somewhat ambiguous. The priest stands, silent and unmoved before Opanas. He is not the demented figure of a priest found in Sergei Eisenstein's *Battleship Potemkin*. A little later, as two older women cross themselves as Vasili is carried past to be buried in 'a new way', one says, 'It's all very well if there is no God … but what if there is.'

So, is the past being mourned in *Zemlya*, or is the future being welcomed? It seems for Dovzhenko it is not a case of it having to be either one or the other. His film is about birth *and* death, about the past *and* the present. Renewal and re-birth are natural and normal, the way of the world. Whatever changes may occur in the affairs of man the boundlessness of the sky remains, particularly if you live on the Ukrainian steppes.

UN CONDAMNÉ À MORT S'EST ÉCHAPPÉ OU LE VENT SOUFFLÉ OÙ IL VEUT/A MAN ESCAPED (1956, FRANCE)[14]

[Production companies: Gaumont and Nouvelles Éditions de Films (NEF). Director and screenwriter: Robert Bresson. Cinematographer: Léonce-Henri Burel. Editor: Raymond Lamy. Cast: Francois Leterrier (Fontaine), Charles Le Clainche (Jost), Roland Monod (Le Pasteur), Maurice Beerblock (Blanchet), Jacques Ertaud (Orsini), Jean-Paul Delhumeau (Hebrard), Roger Treherne (Terry).]

Synopsis: A man involved in the French resistance[15] to German occupation during the Second World War, Lieutenant Fontaine, is captured and imprisoned in Fort Montluc in Lyon.[16] He carefully and meticulously plans his escape, seeing the achievement of each stage along his journey towards freedom as a personal victory. When Jost, a young teenage prisoner, arrives in his cell Fontaine is uncertain whether to trust him and take him with him as he tries to escape, or to kill him in order that he cannot raise the alarm. He chooses to take him along and together they succeed in escaping.

In a sense, the title of this film gives away the story. It immediately takes us to the end, sums up what happens, and implies the 98 minutes of screen-time essentially amounts to no more than, 'a man escaped'.[17] As an audience our usual expectations of mainstream narrative film are, therefore, instantly challenged. And yet, when we do reach the end of the film it is not 'a man' but in fact two men that walk away from the prison having scaled the outer wall, and neither of them could have achieved this without the help of the other – 'Had I been alone I might still be there,' says our central character. Cinematically, this is a defiant title in that Bresson seems to eschew mystery, suspense and surprise – we know what is going to happen. However, although he does put aside a particular type of storytelling mystery, the film actually remains highly enigmatic as the French title reveals. '*Un condamné à mort s'est échappé*' tells us this is not going to be just about 'a man' who escapes but about 'a man condemned to death' who escapes; a man, therefore, who escapes death. Or, the French suggests, adding further mystery, we could adopt an alternative title, '*Le vent soufflé où il veut/The wind bloweth where it listeth*'. This, if we do not recognize it for ourselves, the film later tells us, is a quote from the Bible giving Christ's words to Nicodemus (John 3: 8). But it also sounds like a piece of proverbial folk-wisdom. A little reflection on the title means things begin to seem rather more complex than Bresson's initial claim, given before the credits, that, 'This is a true story; I have told it as it happened, without embellishment,' would seem to suggest.[18] John Belton argues, 'The hero, Fontaine, has a universal quality; he represents a larger social type – an everyman-as-prisoner-of-war in occupied France' (2008, 24). The title, Belton explains, refers simply to 'a *man*', 'a man condemned to death (who has escaped)' (24). But this, of course, puts Fontaine way beyond being simply a prisoner of war in wartime France. He is that specific type but he is also an everyman in the larger, all-encompassing sense of that term.

The opening credits are presented against the background of a wall, as is apt for a film that will focus on the idea of a man feeling trapped and wishing to escape. During the film, it is not simply that we know through spending so long with him that Fontaine is held in a small cell; individual shots are frequently composed so as to place Fontaine in an enclosed space within the frame. When he is taken to be questioned, for example, he stands facing the camera but with the blank backs of two German interrogators to either side, so that he is confined in the central section of the shot. Often we see him through the doorway of his cell, so that the wall of his cell and the door take up most of the frame and he is held within a much-reduced vertical space, again, centre screen. When, a third of the way through the film, he manages to get out of his cell by removing a panel in his door, we have a shot from outside the cell as his face emerges through the door but is boxed centre screen in light that casts heavy shadows on his face. When he emerges through the skylight for the first time he is similarly 'trapped' but this time in a diagonal, letterbox-like, opening across the screen. Each movement towards freedom exists within continued entrapment.

When we first see Fontaine he is in the enclosed space of the back of a car, being driven to prison. Immediately, the tension between being in such a space and wishing to get out of it is conveyed as he tries to escape. But before this happens at the very beginning of the film, there is what seems when we first watch the film to be a strange shot that focuses on his hands. Although we only see the hands, Fontaine seems to be turning them over and inspecting them. In the film we will continually return to his hands as he works at making a chisel from a spoon, at chipping away at a door, at levering panels of wood in a door, at making rope, at shaping pieces of metal into hooks, and at other tasks he gives himself. What we are being returned to time and again by Bresson is the idea of work, of not being idle. Hubrard says later in the film, 'You must keep busy. Write to try to stay sane.' This is, as we have been told, 'a true story'. Close-ups of hands might seem to

Fig 9.3 Fontaine boxed and trapped within the frame (*Un condamné à mort s'est échappé/A Man Escaped*, 1956).

be 'embellishments', the very thing we have been told we will not get in this 'true story', but they are not. They give the very essence of the truth of the character of Fontaine (and of André Devigny on whose memoirs the film is based). As Tony Pipolo explains it: 'It is what a fictional figure *does* that creates character; his inner self is revealed by his outward actions and how he performs them. In short, action *is* character' (2013, n.p.). Beyond that, for Bresson, there is some essential truth about the nature of man that is contained within hands as an image carrying a particular weight of connotation for human beings as tool-using creatures. The very specific experiences of a wartime prisoner and the universal (religious) experience of man, again come together and help to focus our attention on what it was that attracted Bresson to Devigny's story.

We are immersed in Fontaine's world. Throughout the film, our focus on him is intense and unrelenting. In the car during the opening sequence there are street sounds but they are made to seem distant, as if we are in Fontaine's mind as he registers things around him and prepares to try to open the car door. Bresson allows nothing to detract from this focus on our central character. For example, the brutality of the German occupation is given but it is expressed through filmic understatement in order to ensure it does not come to occupy the foreground of the film for the viewer; the pistol-whipping Fontaine receives after attempting to escape from the car blurs into a dissolve of him getting out of the car at the prison, and later there is a brief glimpse of a guard picking up a wooden shovel handle to beat him before we cut to Fontaine being carried on a stretcher to his cell.[19] One response Bresson made when he was interviewed about never showing the brutality was to say, 'When you see Fontaine with his bloody face being brought back to the cell, you are forced to imagine the awfulness of the beating – which makes it very powerful' (Samuels 2009 [1972], 100).

These sorts of brief visual glimpses not only invite the viewer to become their own storyteller, padding out the information they are being given through the use of their own imagination, but actually demand that the viewer should do so. Similarly, the dialogue is composed of short, sharp sentences that give the facts and leave room for the viewer's imagination:

> My cell barely measured three meters by two. I soon learnt to communicate with my neighbor. He was waiting to be shot any day now. He was 19 years old.

Bresson's key requirement of us is that we should imaginatively engage with Fontaine's situation. We have to remain alert to clues, as Fontaine has to remain alert to possibilities of escape. When halfway through the film we see Fontaine watching a guard winding a mechanism on a wall, for example, we have to fill in for ourselves that this mechanism is connected to a skylight and that this could form the next stage in Fontaine's escape; we have, in other words, to be in tune with Fontaine's thought processes. Joseph Cunneen suggests Bresson's approach 'forces the spectator to an extra alertness, it is almost as if we have to work out the specifics of the escape for ourselves, facing the same difficulties as Fontaine' (2003, 61). In his *Notes on Cinematography*, Bresson gives the advice that the cinematographer should: 'Accustom the public to divining the whole of which they are given only a part. Make people diviners. Make them desire it' (1977, 54).

If the playing of the Kyrie from Mozart's *Mass in C minor* at the start of the film and the idea of an escape from death were not enough, the religious connotations of the film gradually become clearer.[20] In a sense we have an extended meditation on predestination and free will. When the Pastor says, 'Read and pray. God will save you,' Fontaine's response is, 'He'll only save us if we give him a hand.' This idea of man as capable of actively determining his own fate seems to be further reinforced when Fontaine discusses the position of the men in his prison block. 'We were a hundred unfortunates awaiting our fate. I was under no illusion about my own,' he says. There is a slight pause and because we have come to see him as a condemned man we think we know what is coming next, we expect him to be fatalistic and accepting, but instead he surprises us, concluding that his fate will be 'to escape'. Even this though does not bring us to a conclusion in the debate on predestination: does this confidence mean he simply 'knows' he is predestined to escape, or that he is predestined to escape because he retains this determination and continues to exert his free will in moving towards his goal? Despite at times displaying this sort of certainty, at other times he is beset by doubts.

To begin with in his relationship with the person in the neighbouring cell, Blanchet, he is the one who offers help and reassurance, although he knows this also helps him ('It's a comfort to be looking out for others,' he tells Blanchet). But by the end it seems Blanchet has become the dominant party; they are in their cells next to each other, each speaking to the other without being seen by the other, and like a priest in a confessional box Blanchet says, 'Have faith in your hooks and ropes and in yourself. You have doubts?', and receives Fontaine's response, 'What's hard is taking the plunge.'

As Cunneen suggests: 'Fontaine is acting out a complex dialectic between faith and free will: God is with him, but at the same time he has an obligation to employ all human resources to achieve his own liberation' (2003, 62). Throughout the escape itself Fontaine continues to have doubts and uncertainties. 'I had to act but I couldn't,' he says at one point. The whole thing becomes a series of hesitations followed by sudden leaps of faith as he and Jost succeed in moving stage by stage towards the outer wall of the prison. Along the way Fontaine disturbingly takes on the role of a God-like arbitrator of life and death. Looking down from the height of the roof to a guard patrolling below, and effectively standing between the would-be escapees and their goal, he decides, 'This man had to die.' Perhaps, therefore, in more ways than one, it is fitting that the film ends with the two men walking to freedom to the sound of the opening to Mozart's *Mass*, since in the order of service the Kyrie eleison ('Lord, have mercy') follows the confession of sins.[21]

HIROSHIMA MON AMOUR (1959, FRANCE)[22]

[Production companies: Argos Films, Como Films, Daiei Studios and Pathé Entertainment. Director: Alain Resnais. Screenwriter: Marguerite Duras. Cinematographers: Sacha Vierny and Takahashi Michio. Music: Georges Delerue and Giovanni Fusco. Cast: Emmanuelle Riva (Woman/French actor/'Nevers'), Eiji Okada (Man/Japanese architect/'Hiroshima').]

Synopsis: A Japanese man and a French woman meet and become lovers in Hiroshima in 1959. The woman is in Japan to act in a film aimed at promoting peace. Through the intensity of this brief love affair she re-visits the trauma of her first love at the age of 18 with an occupying German soldier in Nevers in France during the Second World War. Everything that happens occurs explicitly against the backdrop of the dropping of the atomic bomb on Hiroshima in 1945 and implicitly against the tension of the Cold War arms race of the 1950s.

In July 1945 scientists in the United States tested the first atomic bomb in New Mexico. On 6 August, as part of the endgame of the Second World War and with Germany defeated, an atomic bomb was dropped on Hiroshima in Japan. The bomb levelled the city and caused around 80,000 immediate deaths. Three days later an atomic bomb was dropped on Nagasaki causing 40,000 deaths. On 14 August Japan surrendered. In 1952, the United States tested its first hydrogen bomb. Less than a year later, the Soviet Union tested its first hydrogen bomb. The Cold War was fully underway. *Hiroshima mon amour* has to be seen against the background of the Second World War and the Cold War, and more specifically against the backdrop of the emergence of thermonuclear warfare. According to Robert Rosenstone, 'history in the visual media can be a unique way of rendering and interpreting the past' (1995, 4). Referring to *Hiroshima mon amour* amongst other films, Rosenstone argues, 'Their aim is less to entertain an audience or make profits than to understand the legacy of the past' (4).

This film is both an exploration of the nature of human society and an investigation of individual human experience. At the beginning the central female character tells her Japanese lover she has paid four visits to the Hiroshima Peace Memorial Museum.[23] Her recall of this place, along with her testimony to the impact it has had on her, enables the filmmakers to take us on a virtual tour of the museum. The full horror of the brutality of war is brought home to the viewer.[24] Over a shot of exhibits in glass jars, such as might be seen in a laboratory, her voiceover records, 'Human skin, floating loose, still bearing the fresh bloom of suffering.' The poetry of the screenwriter Marguerite Duras's language (here centred in the tension created between the idea of 'fresh bloom' set against the dreadfulness of the rest of the sentence) continually forces us to reflect longer and harder on a subject we might already find distressing enough. One of the questions addressed by the filmmakers is that posited by Michael Roth in *Revisioning History: Film and the Construction of a New Past*: 'What do we mean when we say that we know something historically?' (1995, 91). What he sees at work in *Hiroshima mon amour* and other films directed by Alain

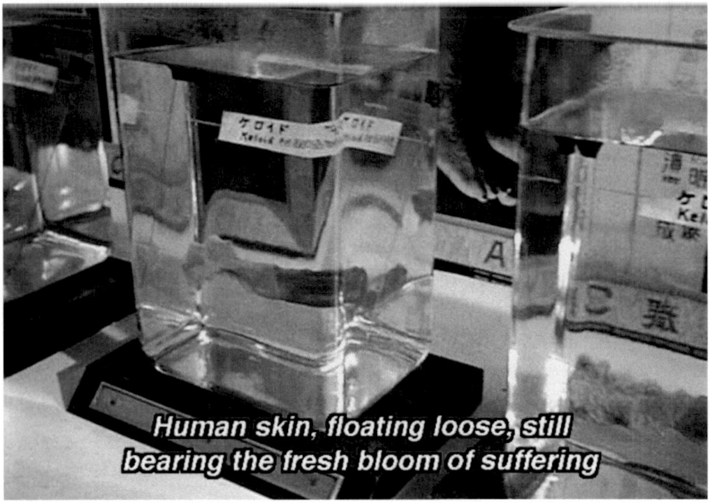

Fig 9.4 The poetry of Marguerite Duras's language (*Hiroshima mon amour*, 1959).

Resnais is 'reflection on the connections between history, memory, and trauma' (91).[25]

But we might also note the strength of political conviction inherent in the words and images we are shown. When, for example, over shots of Japanese protests and demonstrations against nuclear weapons,[26] the woman tells us, 'Anger stirred whole towns,' Duras goes on via her character to tell us who these people were angry with. They were angered, we are told, by the fundamental inequality imposed by some nations on others, by the fundamental inequality imposed by some races on others, and by the fundamental inequality imposed by some classes on others. If this is the view of the woman, it is also the polemical stance of Duras. *Hiroshima mon amour* exists within a strong socio-political context; in part the motivation behind the film is the straightforward desire to document, within a forceful fictional narrative, the obscenity of a thermonuclear attack. In *Revisioning History*, Roth suggests one of the things Resnais explored in making a documentary on the Nazi concentration camps, *Nuit et Bouillard/Night and Fog*, a few years earlier, was 'why documentary knowledge was impossible' (1995, 93). With *Hiroshima mon amour*, Roth argues, Resnais was attempting to go beyond the documentary form to 'explore what other kinds of connection to the past could be established' (93).

Resnais and Duras have chosen not to make a documentary but to employ documentary-style episodes within the dislocations of a tragic love story. They are aware of the problems inherent in making a film about 'Hiroshima': how could a film crew from the West fly to Japan for a few weeks, or months, and hope to create a record of such an experience?[27] In their film, the woman asks at one point: 'What can a tourist do other than weep?' And this highlights the problem: when all is said and done, the filmmakers are 'tourists'.[28] At the same time, the film that is created clearly demonstrates the awareness of Resnais and Duras that neither 'documenting' nor 'fictionalizing' human experience is 'straightforward'. How can the experience of Hiroshima on 6 August 1945 be 'experienced' after and beyond the event itself? Even exhibits in a museum cannot move beyond being 'reconstructions', as the woman frequently acknowledges. And – as the man points out with his question, 'What did Hiroshima mean for you, in France?' – the way(s) in which anyone knows, understands, or remembers an 'event' depends on who they are and where they are positioned in time and space. As Cathy Caruth amplifies, 'For the French, Hiroshima did not signify the beginning of the suffering of the Japanese, but rather precisely the end of their own suffering' (2006, 192). Although, of course, since 'the French' do not exist as a monolithic entity even this recognition of difference in appreciation of a single event is no more than a generalization.

The woman in the film is powerfully aware that, in addition to the impossibility of 'capturing' the past, 'memory' whether of collective history or individual history necessarily exists in tandem with 'forgetting'. Any story we tell about the past, whether of a personal past or a socio-politically shared past, in its shaping of that past is not only inadequate but is also, paradoxically, part of a process of forgetting, or losing, that past. Richard Armstrong says of the presentation of the woman's past in Nevers: 'There is something spare, even stylised, about Resnais's images of Nevers … It is as though the film's visual account of Nevers is already becoming atrophied … by the woman's endless recounting' (2009, 278).

Despite her attempt to recount precisely all she has seen in Hiroshima relating to the bombing, the woman's Japanese lover repeatedly tells her, 'You saw nothing in Hiroshima.' The first time he says this, she responds, 'I saw everything; everything.'[29] There is, of course, a sense in which she did see 'everything', she did see some sort of record of all that man is capable of inflicting on fellow human beings, and she did, therefore, 'see' in a way some sort of definitive statement of all that there is to be said about humanity. In another sense she saw 'nothing' of the real horror of the actual experience of the bomb and its immediate aftermath. And yet, in the deeper, more profound, sense in which the word 'nothing' has often been used in literature, she did see the emptiness, the hollowness, the 'nothingness' of human life and the individual human experience.

In an effort to counter his repeated pronouncement in the first few minutes of the film that she saw nothing, she has her own mantra-like, repeated phrase. 'Four visits to the museum in Hiroshima,' she recites, as if the precision of her documentation ('four times') and the sheer number of visits must mean she has acquired some type of solid, factual knowledge.

Echoing the man's use of 'nothing', the woman sums up her problem, which is also the problem for Resnais and Duras, and the problem for us both as viewers of the film and as people looking back on the dropping of the atomic bomb:

> I saw people walking round. People walking pensively past photographs, reconstructions: since there is nothing else. Photographs, photographs, reconstructions: since there is nothing else. Descriptions, since there is nothing else.

And yet she clings to the attempt to use language and memory and her own 'reconstructions' of events in order to hold on to something rather than nothing. The repetition in the language use here is part of the effort to attempt to provide some sort of solidity and certainty; and it echoes the way in which we repeat remembered narratives of the past in an attempt to hold on to something of that past.

What quickly becomes clear is that beyond the socio-political macro world the filmmakers are intensely interested in the individual human experience.[30] The long opening sequence juxtaposes the naked bodies of the lovers in all their vulnerability with footage of the aftermath of the atomic attack. The whole film might be seen as an examination of the human ability for love and tenderness, set against the equally powerful human ability for hatred and destruction. Time and again we cut back to the lovers, either from some image of physically scarred and maimed bodies or from the traumatized stare of a victim. The juxtaposing of images, and the setting of words against contrasting images, forms a key part of the film technique. As the voiceover describes flowers 'springing re-born from the ashes', we see images of doctors and nurses working on the burns of adults and children.

From the first images, when we see only entwined parts of the bodies of the lovers and are denied an establishing shot, we are constantly challenged to make sense of what we are seeing. If meaning exists, it is to be found somewhere within the complexity and the contradictions. The story of the woman's experiences in Hiroshima is interrupted by flashbacks, which are used to intensify the sense of the character's mental state; and yet, we are never entirely certain if any of this is fantasy rather than memory. 'When you talk, I don't know if you are lying or telling the truth,' says the man, to which he receives the enigmatic response, 'I lie. And I tell the truth.' Of course, for Resnais and Duras, if what constitutes 'knowledge' is problematic and 'memory' is highly questionable, then the whole nature of 'truth' is, to say the least, rather tricky. Furthermore, the uncertainties attaching to communication mean there is always distance between people however close their bodies may be as lovers. Next morning when he is asleep and she is up and on the balcony, she has a brief flashback, a memory of a dead man on the ground, her German lover in the war. She re-enters the room, her Japanese lover wakes, and instantly she asks, 'Coffee?' What is captured is how much both our memories and our minds are our own, and how they operate in parallel with, and are often dislocated from, our day-to-day functioning selves.

The greatest terror for our central female character is the way in which human beings inevitably forget. The immediate pain fades and we forget, both as individuals and collectively as societies. However intense the experience, our memories always fade. 'Like you,' says the woman, 'I am endowed with memory. I know what it is to forget.' The two aspects of human experience, 'memory' and 'forgetting', are yoked together so strongly that they are the same thing: memory is forgetfulness, to remember is to forget. The man's response is, 'No, you are not endowed with memory.' And, of course, he is right. Human beings do not have the ability to remember, they have the talent to forget. Interestingly, she is not really disagreeing with him. Like characters in a Samuel Beckett play they are coming at the same question from different angles, batting it back and forth between them.[31] 'We come to question the relation between memorials and the museum aesthetic of Hiroshima as city of peace and the seeming art of forgetting celebrated in its shiny, rebuilt urban spaces,' says Emma Wilson (2006, 61). 'Listen, I know,' says the woman, 'I know everything; life went on.' And this is the point, she suggests, however horrific the experience may be, however traumatizing, life will go on; after trauma, a woman will move on with her life and a new city will emerge from the ashes. The concept of 'I know' is usually highly problematic in that philosophically we might say it is impossible to 'know' anything; but, on all the evidence, this is one thing we can 'know' the woman goes on to suggest. It should not be possible after the death of a lover for life to go on, but it does; equally, it should not be possible after Hiroshima for another such event to take place, but it will.

'Listen to me. I know this too: it will happen again.'

AGUIRRE, DER ZORN GOTTES/AGUIRRE, WRATH OF GOD (1972, WEST GERMANY)[32]

[Production Company: Werner Herzog Filmproduktion. Director and screenwriter: Werner Herzog. Cinematographer: Thomas Mauch. Music: Popol Vuh. Cast: Klaus Kinski (Don Lope de Aguirre), Ruy Guerra (Don Pedro de Ursua), Del Negro (Brother Gaspar de Carvajal), Helena Rojo (Inez), Cecilia Rivera (Flores), Peter Berling (Don Fernando de Guzman), Daniel Ades (Perucho), Armando Polanah (Armando), Edward Roland (Okello).]

Synopsis: Faced with difficult conditions, an expedition in search of the mythical city of El Dorado under Gonzalo Pizarro in 1560 sends an advanced party down the Amazon on rafts. A power struggle quickly develops between the leader of this group, Ursua, and his second-in-command, Aguirre. Describing himself as 'the wrath of God' and employing a series of increasingly brutal strategies, Aguirre usurps authority and leads the small band on towards total destruction.

Why does Aguirre suggest he should be seen as 'the wrath of God' (and why does Herzog choose this as the title for his film)? The original conquistador this central character is based on did designate himself 'The Wrath of God' but it is Herzog who has chosen to take this as the title for his film. Is it that Aguirre is an agent of God, bringing the anger of an Old Testament God down on his avaricious people? Is it that Aguirre actually becomes a god on earth, not Christ-like and compassionate but violent, a god who brutally enforces his will? ('The earth I walk upon sees me and quakes,' he claims.) Certainly, both the original Aguirre and the film character destroy without mercy those who oppose them and command obedience through fear. In Herzog's film Aguirre journeys towards this vision of himself. Brad Prager says we could view Herzog as both reviling and revering Aguirre's 'unabashed gall, his narcissism, his death drive and his insatiable hunger for power', and he quotes Herzog as saying he was 'fascinated' by the historical character of Lope de Aguirre[33] while, at the same time, recognizing 'he was completely mad' (2007, 26).[34]

For a character commonly seen as mad, the Aguirre we see in the film is more reasoned in his approach than we might expect. From the outset, because he is driven by neither religious fervor nor financial greed, he knows the score: 'No one can get down that river alive.' From the beginning, he is marked out by Herzog as different to the other leaders of the expedition. In two-shots there is always a distance between him and either Ursua, or Pizarro. When they look towards him he looks away. When they stare into the distance and make some grand statement he scrutinizes them with a piercing stare. When they gather the men and make a speech, we cut to Aguirre who is somewhere else both physically and mentally. He knows, and states early on, that 'We're all going to go under.' Later, after he has effectively become leader of the group, he has the priest, Brother Gaspar de Carvajal, read a statement in which he says, 'We have decided to put an end to the quirks of fate.' His decision it seems is to embrace destiny, to throw himself headlong into his fate in such a way that he is no longer at its mercy. As a god he 'despises' mere mortals. 'My men measure riches in gold,' he says. 'It is more. It is power and fame. I despise them for it.' For him (maybe) his journey that others might see as a descent ever further into delusion and madness is a success, a statement of the ability of man to attain transcendence, because for him it has never been about gold but about leaving your mark on history.[35]

On the one hand, Aguirre remains a madman whose delusion defies reason and becomes all the more outrageous as the inevitability of the doom that will engulf the group becomes ever more obvious. On the other hand, he is the ultimate rebel against authority, refusing to accept the power of the leader of the small advanced party, Don Pedro de Ursua, or the leader of the expedition, Pizarro, or, even, the Spanish king, Philip II. As a rebel he is Promethean, even Satanic, a bringer of fire and an embodiment of evil, with echoes of Friedrich Nietzsche's Übermensch, or superman (or, at least, a Nazi version of Nietzsche's concept). For Nietzsche the most basic human drive was the 'will to power', embodied most spectacularly in individuals who transcended common social norms. Aguirre, in this sense, is the tragic

Fig 9.5 Aguirre scrutinizing Pizarro (*Aguirre, der Zorn Gottes/Aguirre, Wrath of God*, 1972).

hero who succeeds in creating meaning out of the meaninglessness of existence. He is not without rationality ('What is a throne but a plank of wood covered with velvet?'), or gentleness (see him with his daughter, Flores[36]), but as Übermensch he exerts power over nobody so strongly as over himself. Nietzsche describes Übermensch as the kind of person who:

> delineates reality *as it is*: he is strong enough for it – he is not estranged from or entranced by it, he is *reality itself*, he still has all that is fearful and questionable in reality in him, *only thus can man possess greatness*...
>
> (1992 [1908], 100–101)

Aguirre sees himself as the essence of treachery: 'I am the great traitor. There can be no greater!' Ironically, although he calls himself the wrath of God, by those who believed in the established order of mid-sixteenth century Christian society, such as Ursua, he would be viewed as Satan-like in his rebellion against God's order. In refusing to accept the authority of the King of Spain he is, in terms of the dominant beliefs of the age, rebelling against God's authority on earth; he is in open revolt against the person who 'truly' is God's agent on earth.[37] And, the levels of irony, paradox and complexity extend still further. Although there was an actual historical figure, Don Lope de Aguirre, who was a conquistador and did seize control of an expedition on the Amazon and did renounce allegiance to the Spanish throne, despite the grandeur of his gesture, the audacity of his rebellion and the scope of his manic vision, this Aguirre was still lost in the mists of the past until Herzog decided to make a film about him.[38] However big your efforts might be to make your mark, to forge a portion of history in your own image, the passage of time will reduce your attempts to nothing. Until that is, perhaps, somebody else with the drive to create meaning out of the meaninglessness of existence comes along and brings about your resurrection.

The film was shot on location in the jungles of Peru, with a cast and crew of 500 working in difficult conditions that might be gauged by the shots of a river in spate shown in some scenes. The drive and determination of Herzog (and Kinski[39]), that might be described as manic, succeeds in bringing the vision into being. In working in dangerous, isolated regions, rejecting not only the studio but also exotic but safe locations, Herzog turns the filming process itself into a physically dangerous journey/quest. According to him, 'Put under extreme pressure, people give you many more insights into their innermost being and tell us about who we really are' (Cronin 2002, 19).

Visually, we are given a beautiful, unsettling and haunting film. The opening sequence, for example, shows in extreme long shot what appears to be simply the imposing grandeur of a mountain scene. Slowly we become aware of the heavily burdened expedition snaking its way step-by-step down the side of this vast mountain. Dana Benelli has spoken about an attempt by Herzog to use 'landscape to articulate a description of "the human condition"' (2014, 90). She also highlights the 'ever-present possibility of being devoured or lost in the landscape' (93).

Man is positioned as minute, ant-like against the vast scale of the natural world. And then, when we move in closer, the handheld camera brings out the full clumsiness of human movement. Maybe from a distance the rivulet flow of a train of people down this majestic mountain has its own beauty, but move closer and the reality of the use and abuse of slaves, for example, becomes unavoidable. At several points the long-handled, double-axe-bladed pike being carried by a soldier sways above the people like a cross; at other moments iron chains on the Indian porters clank heavily across the screen. With a depth of symbolism again reaching into the religious context and the social order, one native porter is shown carrying a massive cannon wheel on his back. And finally, the insanity of it all becomes apparent as we realize there are also two sedan chairs making their precarious passage down this Andean mountainside.

The film may be based on the journal of the real Gaspar de Carvajal who accompanied an expedition to Peru under Gonzalo Pizarro (half-brother of the brutal Francisco Pizarro who conquered the Incas), but it is a fiction conflating the story of the historical Aguirre with de Carvajal's account of a different expedition. Herzog is not constrained by history but uses it as a jumping-off point for his own investigation. Nor is he afraid to draw attention to the fact that this is a reconstruction and thereby invites us to question the status of this particular representation of the past. Cynthia Stone refers to 'the drops of water on the camera lens that call attention to the filmmaking process' and 'the deliberate mixing of historical sources' as elements that have been seen as marking this film as 'postmodern' (2005, 26). On the other hand, the search for a legendary city of gold provides Herzog with the classic narrative structure of the quest, found at the heart of so many stories. In these tales, while the supposed 'El Dorado' proves illusory, the journey is often full of significance in what it suggests about the nature of the human experience.

In one sense, the whole history of expansionist, imperialist Germany, as well as Spain, is here. More precisely, it is possible to read the film as an allegory of what happened to Germany under Hitler and fascism.

Like Hitler, Aguirre announces, 'I don't turn back', and the way he becomes increasingly isolated might at some level recall Hitler's last days. Certainly, for the postwar generation of Germans in the early 1970s dealing with the legacy of the Second World War, the comparisons would have been apparent. But Aguirre identifies himself with other conquerors from the past such as Cortes, so that the whole history of European 'civilization' might be seen to be embodied in this journey. As we move out and away from 'civilization' it is not only the nature of the 'primitive' that comes into view but also the essence of 'civilization'. There is man's determination to conquer (not only others but also the natural world), man's belief in his own god-like strength, the greed of man, the ambition of man, the brutality of man, the treachery of man and, ultimately, the utter madness of man. There is death, disease, murder, execution and the destruction of families. There are also men stranded, trapped, irresistibly carried forward in a direction not necessarily of their choosing (and going round in circles). Some readers may see additional specific connections being made by Herzog. In examining the film in relation to colonialism, Louis Kirk McAuley argues *Aguirre* 'implicitly compares Spain's bloody conquest of the new world with European colonialism in Southeast Asia, and, more specifically, with the political economy of the Vietnam War' (2016, 516).

In the end, to read this film on any single level is to fail to appreciate the depth of the examination of the human condition that is being undertaken. This is an investigation into the heart of man. Brad Prager quotes Herzog as saying the jungle is 'all about our dreams, our deepest emotions, our nightmares. It is not just a location, it is a state of mind' (2010, 94). The physical journey may be down river towards the sea but the psychological journey mirrors Marlow's up river in the novella *The Heart of Darkness*, and Willard's (Martin Sheen) in the film *Apocalypse Now*.[40] Marlow and Willard are narrators who take us on a journey towards a meeting with a character (called Kurtz in both the novella and the film) who has driven himself on into megalomania, but here we follow the Kurtz-like character, Aguirre, more directly. Still, there is a narrator, Brother Gaspar, who is in many ways the classic model of an unreliable narrator. Like Aguirre, Gaspar sees himself as an agent of God on earth but also as something of a god himself. His opening words tell us that on Christmas Day 1560 he read Mass and then 'we descended through the clouds'. Faced by a native who fails to understand the concept of the word of God being contained in a book, Gaspar's response is to run him through with his sword and note in his journal that, 'These savages are hard to convert.' He brings with him it seems, not the love of God but the wrath of God; and when Aguirre takes control, Gaspar makes it clear that the historical position of the Church 'was always on the side of the strong'.

COMRADES (1986, UK)

[Production companies: Skreba Films, National Film Finance Corporation, Film Four International and Curzon Film Distributors. Director and screenwriter: Bill Douglas. Cinematographer: Gale Tattersall. Editing: Mick Audsley. Music: Hans Werner Henze and David Graham. Cast: Robin Soans (George Loveless), Stephen Bateman (Old Stanfield), Philip Davis (Young Stanfield), Jeremy Flynn (Brine), Keith Allen (Hammett), Alex Norton (Lanternist, Sgt Bell, Diorama showman, Laughing Cavalier, Wollaston, Ranger, Tramp, Sea Captain, McCallum, Silhouettist, Mad Photographer).]

Synopsis: During the early 1830s with their wages being reduced a group of agricultural labourers in Tolpuddle, Dorset band together in order to attempt to negotiate improvements. Six of them are arrested under an old law banning secret oaths, found guilty and transported to Australia. A public outcry[41] in England means that after several years they are pardoned and return home to go down in history as the 'Tolpuddle Martyrs'.

On the one hand, *Comrades* is very simple, direct and easy to understand. Throughout its whole three-hour length it is no more and no less than an expression of the words Bill Douglas gives to the wife of one of the agricultural labourers who is to be sent to Botany Bay: 'It's quite simple really, we only have to love one another to know what we must do.' On the other hand, when we take time to consider what is being presented to us we realize nothing is quite as simple as it seems in this film. Every thematic idea has a dual aspect to it, or exists in a yoked binary opposition to a further thematic idea. Douglas has created something that is both simple and complex. It is not the case that one of these positions must be 'wrong', that for the simplicity of the sentiment of 'Love thy neighbour as thyself' to exist then complexity of thought cannot, or vice versa, but that (paradoxically) both exist simultaneously. Furthermore, these two aspects of the film that would seem to be at odds, in fact peacefully co-exist in a supportive partnership.

This combination of simplicity and complexity is thoroughly demonstrated from the outset. Consider the opening 20 minutes of the film. First of all, out in driving rain and mud, the lanternist attempts to generate interest in his show in the village before trying his luck at the local landowner's house. Immediately, 'cottage' is placed in binary linkage to 'mansion', 'poverty' to 'wealth'. The experience of being outside, cold and wet, is positioned against that of being inside, warm and comfortable. A little later, buildings (and human relationships within those buildings) are again placed in opposition to each other. We cut from inside a working family's cottage to inside an Anglican church to inside a Dissenters' meeting hall. Again, the fundamental contrast is between wealth and poverty, but the differences between what occurs within each of these spaces is conveyed through power relationships seen to be at work within each. The authoritarian, dogmatic body language and delivery of his lines employed by Freddie Jones as the vicar, for example, contrasts markedly with the way Robin Soans as George Loveless presents his character. And so, it is a very simple central opposition with which we are faced throughout the opening to the film, that of 'wealth' set against 'poverty'. But, for Douglas, this first level of meaning, the politics of the situation, if you like, is not the heart of the issue. What he presents to the audience is an experience within which those who have very little materially, smile a lot, laugh a lot, and play with children a lot, and, by contrast, those with plenty frown and scowl a lot. The question becomes as much about how we measure 'wealth' and 'poverty' as it is about how financially well-off some people may be in relation to others. For example, over a close-up of a small piece of bread, Old Stanfield (Stephen Bateman) is given the line: 'Give us the goodness of heart to share whatever we have.' And from here we cut, pointedly, to a close-up of the altar in church displaying solid silver candlesticks, salvers and a crucifix on an ornate tablecloth with stained-glass windows behind. But we would be wrong to see this as merely a simplistic contrast between 'poverty' and 'wealth' since, for Douglas, what is embodied in his chosen use of film language is a questioning of what his society means by these words. Just before this, another farm labourer who is to become one of the 'Tolpuddle Martyrs', James Loveless (William Gaminara) says to his wife, 'We are the most beautiful people in the whole world.' It is an unexpected line that seems to relate to nothing that has gone before, but it is entirely in keeping with Douglas's central perspective. The concept of 'beauty' carries with it the accompanying idea of 'ugliness'. Douglas's effort is to question what we mean by these terms. Who is truly 'beautiful'? Who is truly 'ugly'? The vicar takes as his theme for his sermon, Proverbs 14: 23, 'In all labour there is profit.' The key terms here clearly refer to the central Marxist conception of the tension between 'labour' and 'capital', or between the working class and the wealth-owning class. But, for Douglas, who is as interested in exploring religious and moral avenues as he is political, such a use of the term 'profit' necessarily brings to mind Mark, 8: 36, 'For what shall it profit a man, if he shall gain the whole world, and lose his own soul?' The vicar goes on to quote Proverbs 14: 20: 'The poor man is hated even of his own neighbour: but the rich hath many friends.' Douglas might not expect us to know the verses between Proverbs 14: 20 and 14: 23 but he might expect us to look them up: 'He that despiseth his neighbour sinneth: but he that hath mercy on the poor, happy is he. Do they not err that devise evil? But mercy and truth shall be to them that devise good.' What we experience through every nuance of Douglas's film construction is the fact that the real question for him is not so much how to bring about a political redistribution of material wealth, but how to achieve a social re-assessment of the importance of moral and emotional well-being.[42]

Not only is *Comrades* all about illusion, it is itself something of an illusion: on the one hand, it is very easy to understand and, on the other hand, we are dealing with a filmmaker who is fully aware of the intricacies and complexities of filmic representation.[43] If we consider, for example, Douglas's chosen method of getting us from England to Australia in the middle of the film we find we are confronted by a technique that is very simple, even seemingly naïve. A series of painted images, showing places and geographical features along the route taken by ships transporting prisoners to Botany Bay, pass right to left before the camera, forming a panorama that is like something out of a children's picture-book. The daring nature of the director's intervention draws us up short. We are forced, on the one hand, to break with any mainstream cinema illusion of reality and, on the other, to engage intellectually (and imaginatively) with what we see before us. The approach adopted brings into question all the other techniques we have seen used in films for making a transition from one place to another. In its simplicity it forces us to reconsider these similarly placed illusions within films that we must have experienced. We know that for convicts this passage to the farthest reaches of the British Empire must have involved hardships and yet we are faced with these gentle watercolour images.[44] More to the point, we are faced with the disjuncture between our imagined and intellectually known conception of the reality and the lanternist's chosen representation. It is not chance that we find ourselves in this situation. Before presenting us with these picture-book images, Douglas has ensured we are thinking about the trials of the journey to Australia for the convicts by showing us one of the group, George Loveless (Robin Soans), descending through several levels into the deepest hold of a ship through increasing darkness and accompanied by sound effects of wind and rain. Douglas has then cut to George's wife, Betsy Loveless (Imelda Staunton), standing on a cliff-edge looking out at a vast emptiness of ocean. We are pushed along a certain train of thought which is, on the one hand, simple in its expression of the devastation of parting but, on the other, complex in the way in which we are asked to register the contrasting aspects of the same emotion through the confined, boxed spaces of the hold and the cold, blue emptiness of the sea; and only then does Douglas startle us with his use of a colourful pictorial panorama.

There is plenty in *Comrades* that smacks of authenticity: the Dorset landscape of chalk downs, heathland and small fields;[45] the interiors of working people's cottages and landowners' houses; the mud of the lanes and the dirt under the fingernails of the labourers. But the events we see also often operate as symbolic, theatrical set-pieces rather than realistic recreations from the past. The opening scene showing a clash between farmworkers disguised as women and the local militia, for example, gives shorthand expression to the Swing Rebellion of 1830–1831,[46] during which, in response to worsening working conditions for farm labourers after the Napoleonic Wars, machine-breaking occurred across southern England. And, as with scenes, single shots are sometimes similarly used to summarize, or represent an idea in simple, stark terms. This violent opening scene, less than a minute long, begins and ends with two such shots. The first image is a tableau long shot of workers carrying hand-tools that are functional within the scene, but also symbolic of the technological and economic confrontation between machines and labour; and the final image is a close-up of the palm of an open hand with blood running down it. Through these means the context of the period is given succinctly and simply, but we are also challenged as an audience by techniques we are perhaps not used to. Later, when the men are having their wages cut (following the imagery of the bloody hand[47] in the first scene) two hands are thrust even more directly 'into our face' when a worker walks towards the camera and shows us seven fingers in order to express how little he has been paid. As he turns and walks away, unused to characters in films looking straight into the camera, we may feel some sense of relief that we are no longer being 'put on the spot'; but, at that moment, he turns

Fig 9.6 Direct address to the audience (*Comrades*, 1986).

back towards us, strides even closer to the camera than before, and makes the same gesture with re-doubled anger.

It is impossible to ignore the way we are being directly addressed and drawn into the narrative; and this culminates in the moment at the end of the film when George Loveless walks up to the camera, comes into close-up, and delivers a lengthy monologue while looking directly at us. What he expresses, in words taken directly from a pamphlet written by the real George Loveless,[48] is a call for working people to unite and change the world:

> Let every working man come forward ... [and] unite firmly but peaceably together ... then no longer would the interests of the millions be sacrificed for the gain of the few.

Throughout *Comrades* the illusion of reality is repeatedly broken in order to force us into a position of Brechtian distanciation. And yet Douglas is also clearly intensely interested in the magic of fantastical illusion and the pleasure this gives to audiences,[49] particularly young audiences. Again, this is not a contradiction. Storytelling, the construction of representations, the presentation of illusion, can be done for the best of motives or the worst. The actor Alex Norton plays a series of characters in the film and one of the incarnations he adopts is that of Sergeant Bell, who tours a traveling peepshow around West Country towns and villages. This fictional character is from a book by George Mogridge, published in 1839, *Sergeant Bell and His Raree-Show*, and Bell's attitude towards his work in this book is totally in tune with sentiments Douglas would endorse:

> A deal of unkindness in the world; nothing like love and affection! If we loved one another better, the world would go round more merrily than it does.
>
> What! You are laughing at me again, are you? Well! Well! A man may be worse occupied than in making children happy; so I will go on with my show, and you may go on with your laughing.
>
> (11–12)

LE QUATTRO VOLTE (2010, ITALY/ GERMANY/SWITZERLAND)

[Production companies: Invisible Film, Ventura Film, Vivo Film and Essential Filmproduktion GmbH. Director and screenwriter: Michelangelo Frammartino. Cinematographer: Andrea Locatelli. Editing: Maurizio Grillo. Sound: Paulo Benvenuti. Cast: Giuseppe Fuda (old goatherd), Bruno Timpano (charcoal burner), Nazareno Timpano (charcoal burner), Artemio Vellone (charcoal burner), Domenico Cavallo (goatherd).]

Synopsis: An old goatherd takes his goats out from their pen on the edge of a village to pasture on the nearby hillsides each day until the day he dies. A kid is born but later separated from the herd on a mountainside. A tree is felled and dragged from the mountains by villagers for an ancient ceremony. After the ceremony the remains of the tree are converted into charcoal.

This may sound like pretty unpromising, not to say, somewhat disjointed material for a film. However, the director, Michelangelo

Frammartino, has pointed to a deep underlying structure to his film. He has said, for instance, that he did not add titles between the four sections of the film 'in the hope that this film's profound unity may speak louder than its partitions' (2012, 13). Elaborating on this structural integrity he made it clear his interest was in connections between man and nature, between man and 'the animal, vegetable and mineral realms', but also, beyond that, in the way elements are continually transformed into new forms (7). Talking about the charcoal-burners who change wood into charcoal (or carbon), Frammartino has said:

> Their job will be to transform this living, vegetable material into mineral matter. The slow process of mutating the form and state of matter is, in my opinion, one of this film's most intense moments.
>
> (11–13)

And, he has explained that what we are seeing here is 'the triumph of matter over object', so that matter 'does not die but is rather continually transformed' (13).

The apparent disunity and disjointedness demonstrated by the synopsis above in fact hides very deliberate editing and composition of shot that creates a carefully structured film form. In fact, the organization is so strong that the whole thing could be viewed as a film essay with the opening and closing minutes forming an introduction and conclusion, and, in between, the central four stages of an argument moving us through connections between man, animal, vegetable and mineral. Indeed, Frammartino's rationalizations of his work, that frame the film within the context of Pythagorean concepts of the transmigration of souls, only add to the seeming validity of this suggested genre. However, the experience of watching the film is much more like encountering a film poem rather than an essay. The rhythm provides room for the visual images (and sound) to suggest both intense emotions and ideas with layered depths of potential interpretation and reference.

Frammartino has claimed he was only an intermediary, bringing this film into being:

> I gave in to the force of this film the way one would surrender when faced with evidence of an enigma. This film was given to me as a gift; I did not will it through my own pre-existing idea ... I was simply the intermediary between matter and form.
>
> (2012, 10)

He has also said that the viewer, or reader, has a key role in the film: 'A film is a place that the viewer inhabits and brings to life and has a kind of responsibility for creating, a responsibility for telling the story' (2011, n.p.). Certainly, it is the case that space is continually provided for the viewer to bring their own thoughts to bear on what they are seeing. Shots are held for lengthy periods, often with little action taking place within the frame, so that the viewer is placed in the position of having to decide how to take the experience forward for themselves. However, it is also the case that there is an intense effort occurring on the part of the filmmaker(s) to direct the thoughts and emotions of the viewer. From the point of view of film theory, one issue to be considered could be to what extent there can be authorial control over meaning and, beyond that, taking into consideration interviews Frammartino has given, whether there is any such thing as authorial ownership over meaning. Camilo de Marco quotes Frammartino as saying: 'There are those who work in politics and television who are convinced that viewers are children to be led by the hand. I consider *The Four Times* a political film because it gives viewers choices' (2010, n.p.). We may be able to see the point Frammartino is making, but if, as happens in this film, a few minutes after the start we are shown an old man, his eyes downcast, sitting at the base of a tree with goats behind him and the shot is held for half a minute, and then we cut to a close-up from a low angle of the face of the same old man still looking down and the shot is held for about the same length of time, how much 'choice' are we actually given as viewers? Having a static camera allied to long takes provides time for the viewer to interrogate the shot, to investigate it, possibly in a way that is more akin to the approach one might take towards a still photograph, or a painting. However, paradoxically, the slow deliberation of the editing draws attention to the presence of the camera and, as a result, to the presence of the director shaping the composition of the shot, and shaping the experience of the viewer. On the other hand, Monica Seger has given an analysis of Frammartino's approach that is more in line with his stated intended practice, recognizing the way in which the depth of field offered to the viewer in static long shots in *Le Quattro Volte* allow the reader to decide what to look at within the frame and for how long. She contends that 'visually deep space negates the possibility of one clear centre or one dominant truth by exposing multiple points of focus' (2014, 292). Taking this further, she adds that this type of cinematography can also alert us 'to space that extends beyond the confines of the frame, thus challenging us to consider more than the immediately visible' (292–293). Seger's final phrase here is entirely appropriate in that it is not only the framing that challenges us 'to consider more than the immediately visible', but everything about the film.

This is a film that (without ever being as bleak as such a bald statement suggests) is intimately focused on the movement of every living thing towards death. The theme begins just two minutes into the film when we are placed inside the charcoal-burners' mound in utter darkness, with only the muffled sound of the workman's shovel hitting the outside of our place of entombment. Of course, there follows the further necessary aspect to the theme, as Frammartino sees things, when we are immediately taken via a straight cut to an open, green hillside in daylight in a filmic experience of re-birth. Later, when we are placed inside the goatherd's coffin-niche within a cemetery vault and can hear only the deadened sounds of our being sealed in, we know this experience already from the film's prologue. The process of getting the coffin into the niche, which is quite high in the wall of the vault, is documented in all its awkwardness including the dry, rasping sound of the wooden coffin being pushed into place; and it is sound as well as

Fig 9.7 A repeated cinematic pattern of descending darkness (*Le Quattro Volte*, 2010).

visual image that Frammartino uses at this point in order to express the binary duality of death and birth as we cut to the wet, slithering sound of a kid being born. When at the end of the next section of the film this kid, lost and exhausted, settles down in the roots of a tree and the shot gradually darkens until the whiteness of the kid is finally obliterated, we know what we are experiencing is death because the cinematic experience (literally) echoes previous moments in the film.

When later still we are interred by the charcoal-burners in complete blackness with (or, as if we are with) the remains of the once magnificent fir tree, we may reflect that Frammartino is gracing the plant world with precisely the same experience of death as has previously been accorded to man and animal. Maybe our cinematic experience of claustrophobia and fear is less intense by now as we know that what will follow is re-birth. But this is a strange, uncomfortable re-birth. At the end of the charcoal-burning process we study in close-up and extreme close-up (shots often reserved only for parts of the human body in mainstream film) the piles of carbon that emerge. The lifeless, inanimate 'piles' remind of nothing so much as those found in Nazi death camps after their liberation and as documented in Alain Resnais's *Nuit et*

Brouillard/Night and Fog (1955). Only the soundscape of birdsong softens the experience. And, when we return to the village for the end of the film nothing is emphasized as much as the absence of the goatherd; nothing perhaps except for the fact that life goes on. Every shot shows places where we have previously seen him but where now there is only an absence, an empty space on the screen, but an empty space within which we still see him. Is the smoke that rises from the chimney at this point the next stage in the cycle of life, the charcoal transmuted into a reformed expression of matter? Is it the white smoke that emerges from the chimney of the Sistine Chapel to signify that the Pope has been reborn in a new form? Or, is it the smoke of the Auschwitz crematoria? These reflections are, perhaps, illustrative of the space Frammartino allows the viewer for contemplation, or maybe it is the space that is always available to readers but which this director makes us more aware of. We are continually created as observers by Frammartino. For example, in the goatherd's bedroom on several occasions the camera positions us in the same corner of the room with a space in the middle of the room that, particularly when we have already seen at several points Frammartino's technique of setting up a static 'empty' shot into which a character will be 'born', invites our entrance.[50]

> I have tried to avoid having characters enter or exit from the sides of the frame. I wanted them to appear directly from the centre of the shot ... I like the idea of the picture giving birth to characters.
>
> (2012, 13)

But beyond this, minerals rendered as mountains, hillsides, charcoal and the earth itself, vegetation in the form especially of grass, leaves and trees, and animals represented by goats, ants, snails and a dog, all become 'characters' with roles to play within this particular film's idiosyncratic narrative. Frammartino's effort is to re-awaken a link between us and the natural world that the modern world may be in danger of losing, but which some rural communities may have managed to retain. People, goats, ants, trees, leaves, charcoal, birds, dust, smoke: all things merge into one, all things are one. And somewhere around here Frammartino's work links to that of the artist, Mario Merz (Frammartino, 2012, 13). Merz's classic igloo-shaped sculptures not only mirror Frammartino's focus on the charcoal mound, but also mesh with his focus on the relationship between man and the natural world.[51] Discussing Merz, Manfred Schneckenburger says:

> he found the original cell of human and nomadic dwelling in the form of the *Igloo* and went on to create meaningful variations on it in the primordial material clay, applied over thin ribs of glass or sticks ... he sought to counter the 'emptiness of today's technical-mindedness'.
>
> (2000, 558)

Le Quattro Volte is a film that is challenging to mainstream notions of film both in terms of its style and its content. It blurs the line between documentary and fiction, and between the art gallery and commercial cinema experiences. This is a slow, contemplative experience in which, as Seger suggests, 'Frammartino challenges viewers to no longer place the human centre-frame, but rather see it as one form of life among many' (2014, 292). As Joseph Luzzi suggests, this film 'blurs the lines between the human, animal, and mineral' (2014, 154).

SILENCE (2012, IRELAND/UK)

[Production companies: New Wave Films and Harvest Films. Director: Pat Collins. Screenwriters: Pat Collins, Eoghan Mac Giolla Bhríde, Sharon Whooley. Cinematographer: Richard Kendrick. Editing: Tadhg O'Sullivan. Music: Popol Vuh. Cast: Eoghan Mac Giolla Bhríde (Eoghan Mac Suibhne), Hilary O'Shaughnessy (girlfriend).]

Synopsis: Eoghan is a sound recordist working in Berlin. He gets a job that involves traveling to his homeland of Ireland to document the sound found in landscapes free of man-made noise. As he journeys through remote places he is drawn north towards his childhood home on a small island off the coast of Donegal.

What we are and who we are is determined by our origins, by the place of our childhood from which we come and to which we feel inescapably linked. When we are young, both the family home and the surrounding locality can feel like a place of entrapment from which we long to escape. When we are older, these same environments, whether experienced in actuality or in memory, can offer a sense of rootedness that is able to bring with it some form of contentment. These sorts of, perhaps commonplace, observations (that may also represent huge generalizations) seem to provide something like the underpinning impulse behind the creation of *Silence*. Eoghan, the central character in the film, journeys back towards his roots; and his gradual, meditative return to his past is paralleled by the personal journey of the viewer as we begin to appreciate the weight of common human experience invested in the narrative arc of the film. In his notes for journalists offered when the film was released, the director, Pat Collins, said:

> in the way that a reader completes a novel, I think *Silence* has this notion too. We wanted the audience to be included rather than be shut out by an already completed story. Because the script wasn't sealed off from the beginning and it changed as we shot and then it changed as we edited, it is still open to what people can bring to it themselves.
>
> (2012, n.p.)

The actor who plays Eoghan, Eoghan Mac Giolla Bhríde, has echoed this sentiment: '*Silence* is a film that allows the viewer to participate in the story. It doesn't shut you out but rather provides the space for your thoughts and meditation in a way that few films do' (2012, n.p.). As viewers, we end up with something that might be described as a spiritual journey; but, if this tag is appropriate, the 'spirituality' with which we are presented is strongly grounded in very ordinary, everyday experiences. Eoghan meanders his way through Ireland via simple everyday experiences of meeting people and talking to people, and of walking through landscapes and sitting contemplatively within those landscapes. Abbas Kiarostami said he believed in 'a cinema which gives more possibilities and more time to its viewer … an unfinished cinema that is completed by the creative spirit of the viewer' (Rosenbaum 2003, 28–29). Those involved in creating *Silence* leave the completion of the film in the viewer's hands right up to and beyond the end of the screen-time of the film. Eoghan returns to his home locale and to the house he remembers as a child, but as he looks from the bedroom window at the view he (presumably) remembers as a child we know nothing of what he thinks or feels; the imaginative space is left open for us to fill with our own thoughts and feelings.

One of the difficulties with this type of filmmaking is that it does demand so much of the viewer. Ira Jaffe contends that 'even mature audiences prefer to avoid the understated emotional pain in this cinema' (2014, 9). Slow movies, she says, 'bring to the fore cheerless aspects of existence that are likely to worsen if ignored, but drape them in stillness, blankness, emptiness and silence' (9). Initially, these words might seem to effectively describe the experience of watching *Silence*. But one term in particular does not seem to do justice to the film: 'emptiness'. This is a work that is full rather than empty. For one thing it is full of sound: an array of birdsong; a range of water, wind and wave sounds from the gentle to the dramatic; a variety of songs and musical genres; and a diversity of voices from both the past and the present. The device of having Eoghan meet people along his journey stems from Collins's experience working on documentaries. Each resulting voice adds to the fullness, or richness, of the experience of contemplation. A young person, an old person, an academic, a writer, 'ordinary' people, are all placed on an equal footing and each contribute to stimulating the viewer's thoughts and imagination. The device of having Eoghan move through a variety of landscapes functions in a parallel way, with each new space, as with each new person, further prompting our engagement with ideas. David Ingram has argued that: 'A slow-paced art film can be an invitation to take pleasure in looking and in the contemplation of ideas, in a way that can have ecological implications' (2013,

58). And, in part, this is what happens when Eoghan is seen recording sound on the Burren, a karst landscape in County Clare formed out of sediments laid down beneath the sea something like 350 million years ago. Human engagement with this landscape goes back at least until the clearance of the Burren's forests by Neolithic farmers (Gibson 2012, 24). At this point in the film, in a static long shot, Eoghan is shown as a small human figure moving across this vast, seemingly sculpted, limestone landscape. We then cut to a shot of the landscape but without any human figure, so that we are initially disorientated, unsure of the scale of what we are seeing, deprived of anything against which to measure this immensity. The camera pans right to left (a movement often seen as 'backwards' in cinematic terms) over this countryside for a full 40 seconds before we cut to Eoghan, who is again placed as a minute figure within a massive space. The possibilities of what we might contemplate within the space for thought provided for us as viewers as we watch this sequence may be endless but must, in part, stem from the focused awareness of a human being within a certain immense space that has been given to us by the particulars of framing and composition that have taken place. Thoughts related to the concept of human size set within the scale of the natural world, and against a backdrop of geological time, must surely necessarily be part of any contemplative engagement. In the final analysis, the extent to which 'the contemplation of ideas' takes place at all clearly depends on exactly what each individual brings to the viewing experience; but, the central truth embodied in the filmmaking itself is that 'the invitation' to embrace reflective consideration is definitely there. As Collins has said: 'The meditative journey is more important than the narrative destination' (Whyte 2013, n.p.).

Towards the end of the film, when he has returned to his home on Tory Island off the coast of Donegal, Eoghan is again viewed as small within the frame. In a long tracking shot he is shown becoming smaller and smaller as he walks along the cliff-edge between land and sea. Like Antoine Doinel in François Truffaut's *Les Quatre Cents Coups/The 400 Blows* (1959), who is famously shown trapped within a tracking shot before coming up against

Fig 9.8 A small figure within a vast landscape (*Silence*, 2012).

the barrier of the sea, Eoghan seems unable to escape out of the 'end' of the shot that is always ahead of him, always just out of reach. But instead of coming up like Antoine against the sea, Eoghan reaches the end of a headland with only the edge of the cliff falling away before him, at which point there is a sudden cut to an extreme long shot showing Eoghan as not just small but absolutely minute within the frame.[52] How you respond to this, emotionally and intellectually, as a viewer is again to some extent down to you but also to some extent determined by the particular sequence of shots that has been employed.

This concept of a film that urges the viewer to become actively engaged in a contemplative (and creative) process is carried through into the use of sound, according to Marion Leonard and Robert Strachan. They point out only a third of *Silence*'s duration is given over to dialogue while the rest is 'soundscape and music', with soundscape predominating. This weighting, they say,

> invites the audience to be active listeners, responsive not just to dialogue but also to the other sonic elements. The very fact that sections without dialogue are long (and frequent) by normative cinematic standards engenders an experience in which the environmental soundscape is inescapable.
>
> (2015, 170)

The end of Mahler's Ninth Symphony used on the soundtrack has been described by Tom Service as 'a moment in which the music slowly, achingly, bridges the existential gap between sound and silence, presence and absence, life and death' (2014, n.p.). Such things would seem to be important for Collins's film. Sitting in his family home discussing his roots with Eoghan, the writer Michael Harding says: 'When you push yourself into existence it's like the first note of a song. It comes out of silence. And your last breath will be followed by silence.' Pondering similar issues, the song on which the film ends is Sandy Denny's 'Who Knows Where the Time Goes'; and earlier, as Eoghan begins his journey back from Berlin to Donegal, we hear Rory Gallagher's 'I Fall Apart' containing lines such as, 'Till the end of time/You'll be on my mind'. The course of a human life, and the accompanying experience of the feeling of the passage of time, form a constant thread through visuals, sounds, dialogue and narrative arc. As Eoghan prepares to leave Berlin at the start of the film, his girlfriend quotes lines from Friedrich Hölderlin's poem, 'Lebenslauf'/'The Course of Life': 'So durchlauf ich des Lebens/Bogen und kehre, woher ich kam.' ('And so, I follow the arc of life/and return to my starting place.') As Eoghan, the central character, journeys back to his roots, one of the voices that haunts him is a female singer delivering the song, 'The Breeze and I', which includes the lines, 'The breeze and I are saying with a sigh/That you no longer care.' And, at this point, an additional layer of complexity is introduced in that the singer turns out to be the actor, Eoghan Mac Giolla Bhríde's mother, Nellie Nic Giolla Bhríde.

Visual and sound images of wind and water recur throughout the film. Talking about waves breaking on the seashore, Tim Robinson, a cartographer, says the sound is:

> almost like, as if you were listening to the sound of the past, not really of history which has definite sort of structures to it, but all the bits of the past that don't get into history, all the voices that are forgotten, that have never been heard, never expressed themselves, all telling their stories.

In a sense this sounds like a quite positive take on the past and the brevity of human existence, but Robinson then adds, 'And those stories, in a way, all cancelling each other out in a sort of voiceless confusion.' The whole of *Silence* is a steady musing on existence, with each articulation of contemplative thought accompanied by the doubt and uncertainty contained in the proviso offered by Harding after his poetic expression of life as a movement between two silences: 'I think: I don't know.' We are given a series of possible ways of imaginatively and intellectually looking at this, but in the end we are left with unavoidable uncertainty. Hamlet's final words in the play of that name by William Shakespeare are, 'The rest is silence.'[53] This communicates something about the moment of death, but it is also an acknowledgement that there is no knowable answer to the existential questions Hamlet and Shakespeare have been posing in this play.[54]

10

CONCLUSIONS

After we have defined and redefined 'art cinema', outlined some of the key movements, and explored a range of sample films associated with the concept, our key terms of 'European art cinema' and 'European art film' remain both problematic and contentious. We have been able to do no more than glimpse a few European films, filmmakers, and film movements that have been seen by critics and film theorists as linked in some way to the idea of 'art cinema', but however far we were to extend our survey these difficulties would remain. We have considered a diverse body of films that could be argued to sit uncomfortably rather than comfortably with each other.

Nevertheless, despite these reservations, 'European art cinema' exists as a recognizable phenomenon. Filmmakers have consistently produced a stream of European films seen by both critics and the public as sufficiently different from mainstream fare to be placed in a special category distinguished as art cinema. For much of the time, the film industry has branded and marketed these products as art cinema. It is important to understand the nature of the canon that has been produced as a result, and to appreciate why it has come to be seen to all intents and purposes as *the* European canon. Only from that position can we begin, if we wish, to question the premises of the critical pillars on which this list of all that is 'best' rests.

Concepts that have always been of interest to the arbiters of taste in art – memory, consciousness, death, the nature of individual self and the nature of society – are at the heart of film as a medium. Film seems to defy, even to overcome, death more powerfully than the statue, or the portrait. It seems able to present the experiences of memory and dreams in previously unimaginable, strikingly visual ways. It seems to embody distant places in a way that is (perhaps) superior to landscape art. It seems able to explore the inner world of consciousness at least as effectively as the novel. It seems capable of examining the nature of human relationships within society as perceptively as drama. It seems able to employ its language with the subtle sophistication of poetry. Given such possibilities it is inevitable film has come to be seen by many, employed by many, and analyzed by many, as an art.

This 'art cinema' has presented itself in a variety of guises over the past 100-plus years: some espousing high culture, some rejecting high culture, some ideologically conservative, and some ideologically radical. Generally, it has been critically acclaimed. Usually, it has reached only niche markets. Always, it has struggled to accommodate cultural aspirations to commercial demands. In part, it has been defined by its difference to the mainstream and its challenge to the mainstream (but this is also a feature of some other films, particularly 'cult movies', which might not be deemed 'art cinema'). Occasionally, it has disregarded film's narrative possibilities in order to explore opportunities offered by the medium for abstraction or surrealism. More often, it has employed narrative in a much less plot-driven form than the mainstream norm. Repeatedly, through its construction it has asserted its belief in the contribution cultural activity can make to human society. Commonly, it has refused to rest contented with current levels of technical or ideational cinematic exploration. Invariably, it has requested, and expected to obtain, the audience's thoughtful intellectual engagement. Art cinema may offer the audience deep emotional experience but, either at the moment of its screening or afterwards, it demands the viewer's reflective exploration of conceptual possibilities located within the text. Though, even here, we have to be careful. All of this is up for debate. Andrei Tarkovsky claimed Eisenstein made thought into 'a despot' and said, by contrast, he wanted to make films that were 'the occasion for a deeply intimate *experience*' (2005 [1986], 183), although he also said he saw it as his 'duty' to 'stimulate *reflection* on what is essentially human and eternal in each individual soul' (200) (my italics).

In studying European art cinema (to be fair, in studying film as a whole) contexts are all-important. These contexts – social, historical, cultural, political, economic, religious, philosophical – are multiple and exist not only in relation to the film product but also in relation to filmmakers and audiences. The Christian tradition, for example, as we have seen, provides an inescapable context for European art films. To quote Tarkovsky again, he said he was 'staggered' by artists who assumed they were able to 'freely create'. He added that it was 'the lot of the artist to accept that he is created by his time and the people amongst whom he lives' (181).

Engaging with European art films involves the viewer taking up a position, intellectually and politically, in relation to the material on offer and the existence of that material within unavoidable contexts. This engagement will necessarily reveal as much about the viewer as it does about the film under discussion. Films do not exist in any absolute, finished, framed and contained sense, and certainly do not have any absolute status as 'art'. They are subject to re-evaluation at each and every occasion of viewer-text interaction.

The films looked at here have either been made with the intention of attaining acceptance as art, or have been seen by critics and audiences as achieving the sophistication of art. Again, it has to be agreed, we are dealing with elitism. 'Attaining acceptance as art' implies the existence of an established group within society that is qualified to determine 'artistic achievement'. 'Achieving the sophistication of art' implies any films produced can be classified according to whether they measure up to agreed levels of technical and/or intellectual prowess. We face the unavoidable scenario that for film to be art it has to meet some body's, or somebody's, definition of art and then succeed in fulfilling that definition for some audience, or some spectator, that subscribes to that definition. Certainly (although these things remain subject to revision), an elite body of interpreters seems to have to come up with a pretty consistent interpretation of the history of European cinema as regards what qualifies as 'art cinema'.

And so, we are left sitting in a field of problematic and contentious issues within which we have to be content to debate and discuss possibilities. As we survey these films, or interrogate them more closely, we naturally need to recall that every film is an individual piece of work, that every film 'movement' in reality contains highly individual creative personnel producing highly individual pieces of work. Maybe, in the end, the term 'European art cinema' is too loose, too diverse, too undefined. Certainly, in studying it we need to continually see it anew and come at it again. Seen in this context, it remains an enlightening concept to be examined, discussed and contested. Art cinema, continually, sets out to address the mysteries of human existence, pushes us towards pondering the absurdities and the possibilities of it all, asks us to consider inconsequential human existence as a matter of chance or design, scientific fact or religious/philosophical conundrum.

NOTES

CHAPTER 2: OUTLINING THE THEORETICAL LANDSCAPE

1 Much has been written about creativity as being linked to escaping rational thought. See, for example, Arthur Koestler (1964) *The Act of Creation*, New York: Arkana.

2 For some indication of the political complexity of the conversation that might ensue between the beholder and the creator, regarding Théodore Géricault's *The Raft of the Medusa*, see Albert Boime (2004, 115–149).

3 Canudo later added dance to this list, making cinema the seventh art.

4 In response, one might argue that all film, not just 'art cinema', demands creative and intellectual engagement; perhaps, even, that in fact the most banal Hollywood product demands greater intellectual engagement than the most challenging avant-garde film. That, in the face of commercial film's encouragement of easy viewing and unthinking acceptance of the status quo, the most intensely aware form of spectatorship is demanded.

5 Exactly what might be said to be the 'norms' of such a divergent body of work as 'Hollywood', and exactly what might be seen to be the 'expectations'

of a 'mainstream audience' (to say nothing of how we might define a 'main stream audience') would offer further problematic debates.

6 We might note that it is the harking back to ancient Greece and Rome that gives the traditional foundation to the conceptualization of 'art' and 'high art'.

CHAPTER 3: A BRIEF HISTORICAL OVERVIEW OF EUROPEAN ART CINEMA

1 There are slight pans to left and right at certain points, but this film is marked out by its set design. Frequently the screen is divided into a series of spaces (both across the flat screen and into the 'depth' of the shot) within which characters are able, through their actions, to comment on the central events of the scene. These design features, allied to the size of the cast and the use of location filming, mark this out as a quality production when compared to the earlier *La Naissance, la vie et la mort de Notre-Seigneur Jésus-Christ* (Lucien Nonguet and Ferdinand Zecca, 1903), despite the fact this earlier film employs colour through a stencil-based tinting process.

2 The film also contributes towards bringing high art into the cinema through the use of a score by Camille Saint-Saëns, in his early seventies by this time.

3 A series of paintings and engravings of the meeting of Henri III and the duc de Guise and the assassination were also made. The most well-known may be *The Assassination of the duc de Guise at Blois* by Paul Delaroche, exhibited at the Paris Salon in 1835.

4 Perhaps, having used Delaroche's painting (see above) as the impetus for his film version of that attack, he also used Delaroche's *Les Enfants d'Édouard/The Children of Edward* (1831) as the starting point for his film of that name in 1909.

5 Experienced stage actors were used in these films; Paul Mounet, for example, took the title roles in both *Macbeth* and *Le Retour d'Ulysse*.

6 The film starred one of the most famous stage and screen actors of the time, Sarah Bernhardt. The leading man was Lou Tellegen who, as a French actor acclaimed in America, may have been an inspiration behind the main character in *The Artist* (Michel Hazanavicius, 2011).

7 The film is announced as 'a new work of experimentation by Kino-Eye', a group that included Vertov's brother, Mikhail Kaufman, and his wife, Elisaveta Svilova.

8 Of course, this also raises issues about the relationship between documentaries and art cinema that we do not have room to explore here. What is clear is that this period of Soviet film history demonstrates the way in which there is always a dynamic at work between the two forms. Esfir Shub's work, for example, most famously *The Fall of the Romanov Dynasty* (1927), shows this inter-relationship at work. Her found footage of pre-revolutionary Russian factory owners indicates that Eisenstein's characterization in *Strike* (1925) was not merely satirical but was, in fact, heavily based on reality. Similarly, her use of shots of battleship guns reveals how these images were used before the Revolution, and before *Battleship Potemkin* (1925), as an expression of naval and, by extension, Russian government power. At the same time, her choice of images could be seen as potentially influenced by these Eisenstein films.

9 It is more complex for one thing because the famine of 1921–1922 'when an estimated five million died' (Goodwin 1993, 99) occurred before Stalin came to power and well before the famine of 1932–1933. And, this is an implied parallel further complicated by the overwhelming necessity for the Bolsheviks of fighting the Russian Civil War from 1917 to 1922.

10 Debates over exactly what is meant by 'socialist realism' (not employed formally as a term until 1932) have been extensive but agree on the fundamental requirements of communicating with ordinary people and promoting communism. (Eisenstein's phrase, 'positivist realism', implies some sense that society can be analyzed from a scientific perspective, but can be taken to mean essentially the same thing.)

11 The *Sozialdemokratische Partei* was known just after the war as the *Mehrheitssozialdemokratische Partei* (The Majority Social Democratic Party).

12 How we define 'politics' is obviously crucial to such a discussion but is too far-reaching for us to go into here. Harold Lasswell in *Politics: Who Gets What, When, How* is sometimes seen as offering a starting point through the title of his book but also via comments such as, 'The study of politics is the study of influence and the influential' (1936, 3).

13 'They were little, ghost-like skeletons, covered with faded rags and smocks. They had colourless hair and colourless eyes. They walked on emaciated bare feet ... Their leader was a girl. The austere countenance of the Virgin. The sweet countenance of the mother' (von Harbou 2007, 13). This is from the novel by von Harbou from which she wrote the script with her husband, Fritz Lang.

14 Regardless of whether the film itself displays anti-Semitism (and this has been much discussed), the narrative revolves around the issue of a disaster predicted to be about to hit a city's Jewish population.

15 'Across the globe, as the magnitude of anti-Semitic incidents grew exponentially during the 1930s, few public protests against the mistreatment of European Jewry occurred' (Brustein 2003, 3).

16 There has been some dispute over who was responsible for freeing the camera in this film, Murnau or Freund. Most likely it was a joint venture that also involved the input of scriptwriter, Carl Mayer. 'Film histories generally overlook the care Mayer took to write for the camera, describing in detail perspectives, positions, and movements' (Silberman 1995, 25).

17 This desire to link the form to music can be seen in the references to composers such as Claude Debussy in films from the period and in the theoretical impulse during the period to view film as in some way related to the musical expression achieved in the symphony.

18 Three paintings from the series, each undertaken from the same position but under different conditions of light, are held in the Musée d'Orsay in Paris.

19 The film, in its own melodramatic way, also looks at the lot of women in a patriarchal society where they struggle to be able to secure their future for themselves.

20 See Dorothee Binder (2005) for a range of designs from *L'Inhumaine* together with stills from the film.

21 *Finis Terræ*, from the Latin, 'End of the Earth', was made eight years before Michael Powell's more well-known *The Edge of the World*.

22 See Katherine Groo (2014, 458–462).

23 See, for instance, Fernand Léger's enthusiasm for the film recorded in, for example, Michael Witt and Michael Temple (2004: 59), and Malcolm Turvey (2011, 48–49).

24 See Ian Aitken (2013, 762–763) for a succinct introduction to the film.

25 The film is divided into five acts rather than the usual four movements of a symphony, suggesting the structure of a play.

26 Tendencies towards left-wing political analysis to be found in *Rien que les heures* and *Berlin: Die Sinfonie der Großstadt* are made more explicit by Vigo, who said: 'by showing certain basic aspects of a city, a way of life is put on trial … the last gasps of a society so lost in its escapism that it sickens you and makes you sympathetic to a revolutionary solution' (Salles Gomes 1971, 68).

27 The rooftops that are such a key image for this film and which provide the German Expressionist style of the opening to Clair's next film, *Le Million*, are perhaps referenced by Jean Vigo in the ending to his *Zéro de conduit/Zero for Conduct* (1933).

28 The idea of the penniless bohemian who unexpectedly comes into money perhaps feeds into Éric Rohmer's early film *Le Signe du lion/The Sign of Leo* (1959) written by Paul Gégauff.

29 An image and associated concept François Truffaut will take up in *Les Quatre Cents Coups/The 400 Blows* (1959).

30 *The New York Times*.

31 'One of the major differences between Carné and Feyder had been their political viewpoints. Despite the left-wing sympathies apparent in many of his films (like *Les Nouveaux Messieurs*) there were certain ambiguities in Feyder's politics, as witnessed by *La Kermesse héroïque*, a film which provoked controversy in left-wing circles for its reactionary spirit and principles' (Blakeway 1990, 98).

32 Susan Hayward says Duvivier 'dedicated *La Bandera* (1935) to Franco, a film based on the Spanish Legion in which some troops were Franco's soldiers' (2006, 125).

33 Feyder worked with Charles Spaak on *Le Grand Jeu*, *Pension Mimosas* and *La Kermesse héroïque*. Spaak also worked with Duvivier on *La Bandera* and *La belle équipe*. Other key players also appear and re-appear in the credits for these films: actors like Gabin and Arletty, cinematographer Jules Kruger, production designers such as Alexandre Trauner and Lazare Meerson, and composer Maurice Jaubert.

34 The fluid two-minute crane shot of the people singing the anthem, 'La Marseillaise', is a tour de force.

35 Renoir was also heavily involved in putting together a documentary for the Communist Party of France in 1936 called *La vie est à nous/Life Belongs to Us*.

36 Lantier has a supposed hereditary madness that leads to the desire to kill.

37 At the start of his film, Renoir references Pierre Beaumarchais's play *La Folle Journée, ou Le Mariage de Figaro* (1784). Figaro has a speech, in the play, in which he essentially asks the aristocracy what they think they have done to deserve their rank and wealth. It is, Charles Drazin suggests, an 'unmistakable attack on the class system' and was seen as a 'subversive work that helped pave the way for the French Revolution' (2011, 183). Renoir's attack on contemporary 1930s French society would seem clear, particularly in the year of the 150th anniversary of the Revolution, when the country might be measuring itself against the original aims of that social reformation.

38 Stylistically, Renoir's filmmaking is built around long takes and depth of field, so that when montage editing is employed, as in the hunting scene, a particularly strong effect is achieved.

39 Zavattini was a screenwriter on *Sciuscià/Shoeshine* (1946), *Ladri di biciclette/Bicycle Thieves* (1948) and *Umberto D.* (1952).

40 'The use of non-professional performers had been a feature of Soviet cinema in the 1920s, and of dramatized and staged "documentaries" in the United States and the United Kingdom in the 1930s' (Wagstaff 2007, 31).

41 Christopher Wagstaff identifies Giuseppe De Santis, for example, as someone who 'stands out as a figure incorporating popular cultural forms into his neorealist films – peasant culture, popular song, consumerism, comic-book literature and Hollywood narrative genres – but all in the service of left-wing ideological orthodoxy' (2007, 22).

42 For a more in-depth consideration of what we might mean by neorealism in this context, see 'Realism and Neorealism' (Haaland 2012, 33–61).

43 See Asbjørn Grønstad and Henrik Gustafsson (2012, 194–197).

44 The life and death of another priest, Giuseppe Morosini, was also important in providing details for the character of the priest (Brunette 1996, 364).

45 For a sense of this period in Rome, see Robert Katz (2004), in particular pp.209–265.

46 Italy continues to wrestle with the difficulties of reconciling itself with events surrounding the Ardeatine Massacre, and so Rossellini's film is of continuing interest in this respect. See Rebecca Clifford (2013). Also, Alessandro Portelli (2005) 'The massacre at the Fosse Ardeatine: history, myth, ritual and symbol'.

47 See, for example, how the father's reflection on the past draws him into a position of standing for all Germans: 'Everything was taken away. My money was taken by inflation. My children were taken by Hitler. I should have rebelled but I was not strong enough.' Or, see the scene in which his son plays a gramophone record of a speech by Hitler amongst the ruins of the Reich Chancellery. (For a discussion of this, see Noa Steimatsky (2008, 57–61).)

48 'After Romano's death, all of Rossellini's films, to some extent, will attempt to confront death' (Gallagher 1998, 247. See also p.211).

49 For a short discussion of the ending, see Peter Brunette (1996, 85–86).

50 Andreotti eventually became Italy's prime minister in the early 1970s and was a prominent but controversial figure in Italian politics throughout the 1980s and 1990s.

51 A film magazine founded by André Bazin in 1951.

52 The complexities of this aspect of the New Wave are dealt with by Geneviève Sellier (2008). She describes, for example, Jean-Luc Godard as putting his central female character in *À bout de soufflé* (1960), Patricia (Jean Seberg), 'back in the traditional place allocated to women in Western culture … the object of the male subject's love and/or hatred' (2008, 16).

53 Alexandre Astruc, 'Naissance d'une nouvelle avant-garde: la caméra-stylo,' *L'Écran français*, 144 (30 March 1948). Also, Alexandre Astruc, 'The birth of a new avant-garde: La caméra-stylo,' in Graham, P. (ed.), *The New Wave: Critical Landmarks*, Garden City, NY: Doubleday, pp.17–23.

54 This is commonly associated with the American film critic, Andrew Sarris. For a more nuanced appreciation of this, see John Caughie (2001 [1981]), especially pp.61–62.

55 See Truffaut's reference to his work with Marcel Moussy on the script (Neupert 2007, 179).

56 In a sense this is no more than a truism about all film movements, and an aspect of the sweeping generalizations we describe as history.

57 Rouch's *Chronique d'un été/Chronicle of a Summer* (1961), although a documentary, can be viewed as strongly related in conceptual and thematic terms to the French New Wave.

58 In an article written in 1954, Anderson described Jennings as 'the only real poet the British cinema has yet produced' (Anderson 2004, 366).

59 Locations in Halifax and Derby were used in these films, although some scenes for *Look Back in Anger* were filmed in London.

60 Although we do tend to be given 'a set of familiar, repeated and therefore expected locations; the pub, the back street, the dance-hall, the interior of the working-class terraced house' (Lacey 2002, 169).

61 Richard W. McCormick explains that for these feminist critics 'it is especially troubling that the story of the Third Reich and World War II is told in such a way that a non-Jewish German woman appears to be its primary victim'; but, he suggests, although a valid reading, this is based on an inaccurate view of the film. Lene is not a victim of the war, 'if anything she thrives during the war. Rather she is a victim of the postwar era and its restoration of traditional gender roles' (2000, 251).

62 While Brad Prager says Herzog 'has said on numerous occasions that he never had any intention to create a metaphor for Hitler through Aguirre' (2007, 28), at some level the connection (and a strong one, at that) clearly exists.

63 An interesting dimension to Herzog's forays into the rainforests of South America is the idea that the making of, in particular, *Fitzcarraldo* 'participates in the contemporary re-enactment of the colonialist drama'. Herzog is accused of 'neocolonialist impulses' and indulging in 'cultural colonialism' (Schindler and Koeprick 2007, 119).

64 When, having been away for five years, Karin (Hanna Schygulla) says to Petra in *Die bitteren Tränen der Petra von Kant*, 'Nothing's changed much,' Petra's response is, 'Things stay the way they are in Germany'.

65 According to Jeremy Varon, who looks at left-wing violence in both the United States and West Germany in the period, 'armed struggle was an extreme expression of ideologies, attitudes, and sensibilities deeply

embedded in both the American and West German New Left movements' (2004, 3).

66 Fernando Solanas and Octavio Getino (1969), 'Hacia un tercer cine' ('Towards a Third Cinema'), *Tricontinental* 14, October 1969, 107–132.

67 In response to a political move to the Right in Denmark, Trier has said he 'will not make a political film, even though I might touch upon some political topics' (Stevenson 2002, 187). However, in 1996 he spoke out against a Danish law making it illegal for single women or lesbians to choose to have children through artificial insemination, seeing this as 'a punishment action against women who choose not to live in the traditional nuclear family' (114).

68 In particular, Horeck and Kendall reference Trier's *Antichrist* (2009).

69 Horeck and Kendall see 'new extremism' as a 'trend or tendency' in a range of recent European films rather than 'the collective label for a new "genre" or "movement"' (2011, 5).

70 Karen Bach, known as Karen Lancaume in the porn business, took her own life in 2005 (Huffer 2013, 169–171).

71 'In real life, Despentes writes in *King Kong Theory*, she and a friend were gang-raped in 1986, by a carload of three men, while hitching a lift across Paris: "While it's going on, they pretend not to know exactly what's happening. Because we're wearing miniskirts, and one of us has green hair and the other orange, we must 'fuck like rabbits', and so the rape they are carrying out is not actually a rape. As with most rapes. I imagine. I don't imagine that any of those three guys now considers himself a rapist"' (Turner 2013, 35–37).

72 'Right wing and religious groups in France rallied against the film upon its release, leading the government to place its first ban on a film in the country since 1973' (Heller-Nicholas 2011, 164).

73 See 'Raffaëla Anderson and the French Porno Industry'. Accessed 9 June 2015. https://againstpornography.org/raffaelaanderson.html.

CHAPTER 4: KEY CRITICAL APPROACHES TO EUROPEAN ART CINEMA

1 Semiotics, or semiology: the study of meaning inscribed within individual 'signs' as they operate within coded systems and conventions.

2 'human culture is made up of signs, each of which stands for something other than itself, and the people inhabiting culture busy themselves making sense of those signs' (Bal and Bryson 1991, 174, quoted in Rose 2007, 75).

3 Barthes's classic example of how he saw 'the photographic message' as working records his response to an image on the cover of *Paris Match*: 'a copy of *Paris Match* is offered to me. On the cover, a young Negro in a French uniform is saluting, with his eyes uplifted, probably fixed on the fold of the tricolor. All this is the meaning of the picture. But, whether naively or not, I see very well what it signifies to me: that France is a great Empire, that all her sons, without color discrimination, faithfully serve under the flag, and that there is no better answer to the detractors of an alleged colonialism than the zeal shown by this Negro in serving his so-called oppressors' (Barthes 1972, 125–126).

4 'surely it is to the BBC, forbidden by the regime' says Paul Julian Smith (2006, n.p.), but there seems no evidence for this.

5 RNE started in 1937, with its first transmitter being a gift from Hitler to Franco. From 1939, a year before this film is set, news bulletins were broadcast in the early afternoon and last thing at night.

6 See Robert Stam's 'The Birth of the Spectator' (2000, 229–234) for an overview of the emergence of the concept of spectatorship in the 1970s.

7 One of the leaders, Juan Bravo, was from Segovia, and was eventually beheaded.

8 Should this be Spanish society, European society, or Western society; and, should this be the society of 1940 when the film is set, of 1973 when the film is made, or of now when the film is viewed?

9 It is in this scene that Fernando looks to the mountains and tells the children their grandfather called the mountain, 'the mushroom garden'. This is, he says, where the best mushrooms, chanterelles, are to be found. Across Spain small bands of Republicans retreated to the mountains, with some holding out for up to ten years. In 1948, for example, the 200 or so residents of El Acebuchal were ordered to leave their village in Andalucia, accused of supporting Republicans in the nearby mountains. (See David Baird 2008.)

10 The words of '*Oh, Señora mía. Oh, Madre mi.*' are: '*Oh, my lady. / Oh, my mother. / I offer myself entirely to you / As proof of my filial affection. / I consecrate this day, / My*

eyes, my ears, my tongue, my heart, / In a word, all my being. / Since I am all yours, / O mother of goodness, / Guard and defend me / As your thing and possession. Amen.'

11 Here signs may be seen to act through absence as well as presence: there are two maps of Spain but none of the rest of the world, or even the rest of Europe. In a film very much about isolation and being alone (see the characters of Fernando, Teresa, Ana and Isabel), Spain too is cut off, and has cut itself off.

12 The photographic image of Franco seems to be reversed.

13 St. Jerome, patron saint of translators, librarians, students and schoolchildren, cut himself off in the wilderness in order to contemplate death. He is also the character who, according to legend, removed a thorn from the lion's paw and so tamed the monster.

14 Linking back to *The Spirit of the Beehive*, he also ordered a people's radio to be produced, the Volksempfänger.

15 Until 1945 the city was called Stadt des KdF-Wagens bei Fallersleben. During the war military vehicles and equipment were produced here using forced labour. After the war, using migrant workers, the city joined the postwar German 'economic miracle'.

16 Andrew Sarris is generally credited with promoting the concept of the auteur into a theory that became central to film studies (2005 [1962], 99–107).

17 This points towards the importance of the nature of children and childhood experience for Bergman.

18 Effectively, they have performed one dimension of the multidimensional dance of relationships continually rehearsed by Bergman, all aspects of which encapsulate some sense of the distance that remains even in closeness between couples.

19 The area around the altar is, in Christian terms, divided off as a sacred space containing the presence of God during the Eucharist.

20 This points towards the importance of religion and, above all, the silence of God, for Bergman.

21 That is, for virtually the whole film.

22 In *The Phantom Carriage/Körkarlen* (1921), a silent film directed by Sjöström, Death's carriage arrives to collect the soul of unrepentant sinner, David Holm, played by Sjöström.

23 As shocking as this is, the added detail of another hand holding the hand in place might be seen as more troubling in what it says about the human condition.

24 See Frank Gado (1986, 79).

25 On the other hand, Philip Mosley says that although Bergman 'didn't lack humour' he was 'totally without a sense of self-irony' (1981, 33).

26 This book seems not to be any book in existence and the 'extract' seems to have been made up by Bergman.

27 The Spanish Civil War is mentioned by the pastor, Tomas, in *Winter Light* but only from a personal perspective centred within his own angst: 'During the Spanish Civil War I refused to be aware. I refused to accept reality. My God and I lived in a world where everything fitted in.'

28 The first and most famous monk to commit this act in Vietnam in 1963 was Thích Quảng Đức in early June in Saigon, but he was followed by others across the country. 'Nguyen Hoan, only twenty-one, burned himself to death in the fishing port of Phan Thiet. A seventeen-year-old novice priest in Hue wrapped himself in a Buddhist flag soaked with kerosene, lit a match, and went up in flames. A Buddhist nun, also in her teens, sat down in a Catholic school playground in the village of Ninh Hoa and ignited herself. In most cases the searing images were captured on film and broadcast in the United States' (Jacobs 2006, 150).

29 The image is the most well-known one from the report, *The Jewish Quarter of Warsaw is No More!* (*Es gibt keinen jüdischen Wohnbezirk in Warschau mehr!*), written by the SS general in charge of suppressing the uprising, Jürgen Stroop. (Photographs and extracts available at: http://www.auschwitz.dk/Stroop.htm. Accessed 4 August 2015.)

30 'it was not until the 1960 film *Jungfrukällan* (*The Virgin Spring*) that Bergman and Nykvist more or less became an inseparable team' (Sundholm et al. 2012, 296).

CHAPTER 5: KEY THEMATIC APPROACHES TO EUROPEAN ART CINEMA

1 Chapter 9 offers a reading of Bresson's *Un condamné à mort s'est échappé ou Le vent soufflé où il veut/A Man Escaped* (1956) that draws heavily on Christian interpretative possibilities.

2 See Eric Ziolkowski (2011, 293–310) for an investigation of the relationship between Kaj Munk's play, *Ordet* (1932), Dreyer's film and Kierkegaard's philosophy.

3 In the context of Kierkegaard's philosophy, the claim by Johannes to have regained his reason at this point is significant since Kierkegaard might be seen to suggest there is a certain reasonableness attaching to the concept of faith, in that, given the human condition faith would not seem an unreasonable position to continually attempt to gain and regain. See, for example, M. Jamie Ferreira (1998, 207–234) 'Faith and the Kierkegaardian Leap' for a discussion of the concept of 'a leap to faith'. See also Howard Hong and Edna Hong (2000, ix–x) for a useful brief account of the complexities facing the reader of Kierkegaard's work.

4 We might consider potential references to similar resurrections in William Shakespeare's *The Winter's Tale*, *Much Ado About Nothing* and a series of other plays. See Sean Benson (2009).

5 Mikkel's position is in some aspects similar to that of Laertes and Hamlet on the death of the virtuous Ophelia in Shakespeare's play, *Hamlet*. At the end of Shakespeare's *The Winter's Tale* a statue of the guiltless Hermione is restored to life. Interestingly, paralleling the situation with Inger's aborted child, in *The Winter's Tale* we must reconcile the on-the-face-of-it happy ending with a seemingly 'meaningless' death, in this case that of the young child, Mamillius.

6 The reasons for Johannes declining into madness are explained more fully in Munk's original play.

7 After a series of French victories against the English in 1429, attributed by some to Joan's iconic leadership, she was captured by a French nobleman who supported the English and eventually handed her to the English. She was tried and executed in 1431. See the introduction to Daniel Hobbins's (2007, 1–32) *The Trial of Joan of Arc* for an account of the circumstances surrounding the trial.

8 In the gospels of Matthew (21: 1–7) and John (12: 14–16) Jesus enters Jerusalem on a donkey and reference is made to what is suggested to be a related Old Testament prophesy: 'Behold, your King is coming to you. He is just and having salvation, lowly and riding on a donkey, a colt, the foal of a donkey!' (Zechariah 9: 9).

9 Although, even in this short six-minute opening, the inescapable reality of death is felt through the presence of Jacques's sister whose death ends this idyll.

10 Margarita Terekhova plays both the mother, Maria, as a younger woman in scenes set in the 1930s/1940s and Alexei's estranged wife, Natalia, in scenes set in the contemporary period. Ignat Daniltsev plays both the young Alexei in the 1930s/1940s and the older Alexei's son, Ignat, in the 1970s.

11 See John White (2015, 10).

12 You will come across different English sub-titles depending on which version of the film you are watching and further different translations of the poems again in Arseny Tarkovsky (2013) *Life, Life: Selected Poems*.

13 'to look at the Other's look is to posit oneself in one's own freedom and to attempt on the ground of this freedom to confront the Other's freedom ... But this intention must be immediately disappointed, for by the sole fact that I assert myself in my freedom confronting the Other, I make the Other a transcendence-transcended – that is, an object' (Sartre 1992 [1956], 494).

14 The main character in Camus's *L'Étranger/The Outsider* (1942), Meursault, who has committed a murder says at the end of his life: 'I'd lived in a certain way and I could just as well have lived in a different way. I'd done this and I hadn't done that. I hadn't done one thing whereas I had done another. So what?' (2000 [1942], 115).

15 The inn is like a portal to another world. At this point Murnau inserts an image of a striped hyena, a creature not found in Europe but one that is largely nocturnal. The hyena also has a reputation for a hideous 'laugh' and terrifying night-time cries, is believed to disturb shallow graves, is said to have been found with the remains of human skulls in its lairs, and in folklore is described as attacking and killing people. The species is actually connected with North Africa and south-west Asia, something that could be seen to fit with the geographical placement of the origins of evil within the film.

16 The ship that brings Nosferatu to Wisborg is the *Empusa*. This may refer to the Greek demigoddess who seduced young men as they slept and drank their blood, offering a female equivalent of Nosferatu, and/or it may

reference the mantis-like insect that catches and grips its prey in a lightning quick movement.

17 This is a truism as regards animal existence but may also echo concepts embodied in, and subsequently surrounding, German Chancellor Otto von Bismarck's 'Blut und Eisen' ('blood and iron') speech of 1862: 'Not through speeches and majority decisions will the great questions of the day be decided – that was the great mistake of 1848 and 1849 – but by blood and iron' (Steinberg 2011, 180–181).

18 Nosferatu could represent the threat of the Other coming from the East. Orlok's castle (filmed on location at Orava Castle, Slovakia) is in the Carpathian Mountains and the plague is said to have started in Black Sea ports. Not only do the Carpathians contain some of the most remote and inaccessible areas in Europe, but the Transylvanian/Black Sea region could be considered to be on an ebbing and flowing political, historical and cultural fault-line between East and West. Another possibility might be to see the film as containing a right-wing ideology within which Nosferatu is the hook-nosed manifestation of the threat to Europe offered by Judaism.

19 Probably Kollwitz's most well-known image summarizing this attitude is 'Seed for the Planting Must not be Ground' (1942) showing a mother wrapping her arms around three terrified children to protect them from some unseen threat, but there are plenty of others including the almost equally famous posters, 'Survivors – Make War on War' and 'Never Again War! – Make War on War' (both 1924). 'As the woman who "saw the suffering of the world", she used the arsenal of her art, forged in Wilhelminian Germany, to protest and plead for the dispossessed of not just the Weimar Republic but of all postwar Europe' (Prelinger, Comini and Bachert 1992, 111).

20 The mob, of course, also pursues Knock in *Nosferatu* and Cesare in *Das Kabinett des Dr Caligari*.

CHAPTER 6: POLITICAL ASPECTS OF EUROPEAN ART CINEMA

1 Although this is to some extent true, if we are to see Maréchal as journeying towards some better understanding of nationalist sentiments it is

important to initially see him expressing nationalism. When he is in solitary confinement it is specifically French voices he longs to hear and the point at which we really begin to identify him as the central character is when he announces the capture of Douaumont and instigates the singing of the 'La Marseillaise'. Given this type of contextualization the final section of the film then truly expresses some sense of character development.

2 Interestingly, we only see the signs and symbols of the altar being packed away rather than the actual delivery of the sacrament, but what we also see in the process is play being made on the symbol of the cross (as a Christian cross, an Iron Cross and a Red Cross).

3 The study of the use of language throughout the film would reveal a key area of interest for Renoir around communication and lack of communication, particularly within classes and between classes. For example, in demonstrating the trans-European nature of this ruling class Rauffenstein and Boeldieu use English to speak to each other, but prior to this the English officer cannot understand Maréchal when he attempts to tell him about the escape tunnel.

4 Willy Brandt (1969–74) is omitted from Fassbinder's 'rogues' gallery'.

5 The words of Fanny Hawthorn as she leaves the small-minded local community are: 'Don't worry, lad. I'm a Lancashire lass and so long as there are spinning mills in Lancashire I can earn enough to keep myself respectable.' Words given additional resonance by the Wall Street Crash being just two years away, and words that lead directly into the subject matter of *Love on the Dole* (1941).

6 The play on which the film was based attracted controversy when first performed in 1912. According to George Rowell: 'It is difficult … to conceive the reactions, both approving and hostile, which *Hindle Wakes* provoked, feelings reminiscent of those aroused by *Ghosts* twenty years earlier and as influential as the reception of *Look Back in Anger* forty years later' (Rowell and Jackson 1984, 45).

7 What she describes as 'the historical nature of perceptions of realism' (1988, 202) is considered by Kristin Thompson.

8 Some of the montage sequences have frequently been described as 'heavy-handed' (Murphy 1992, 23). William L. Horne sums up this attitude claiming, 'the director clearly misjudges some of his sequences' (1999, 116).

9 The psychological depth of this father son relationship and the way it is carefully embedded within the narrative is explained succinctly by Millicent Marcus (1986, 58–64).

10 'Access to the new Soviet films had been frustrated by censorship bans everywhere since 1926, reinforced by political intervention, with Germany the only country where *Potemkin* could be seen publicly, albeit in a censored form. In Britain, Pudovkin's *The Mother* [Matj] (1926) and *The End of St Petersburg* [Konets Sankt-Peterburga] (1927) were shown in October 1928 and February 1929 respectively, at the members-only Film Society, and *Potemkin* finally had its premiere, also at the Film Society, in November 1929' (Christie 2014, 154).

11 For Pudovkin, editing was key to the storytelling possibilities available to the filmmaker via moving images. In *Film Technique*, published in Russia in 1926, he set down what he saw as the central principles of editing (Braudy and Cohen 2004 [1974], 7–12).

12 For differences between Pudovkin and Eisenstein on editing and montage, in particular Pudovkin's advocacy of linkage between images and Eisenstein's emphasis on 'collision', see Yuri Tsivian (2015, 314–321).

13 'Although no woman appears among the fathers – Marx, Engels, Lenin – as in *Mother* the maternal myth was appropriated by the Soviet regime to connect the nation on an affective level, and the party itself assumed a maternal guise' (Hubbs 1993, 234).

14 This is not to say ruthless suppression of political opposition had not already taken place under Lenin. The rights and wrongs, interpretation and re-interpretations of Russian history is not a debate this book can begin to address.

15 An extra dimension is added to Eisenstein's images through the pleasure taken in displaying athletic male bodies. Discussing Part II of *Ivan the Terrible* (1958), Al LaValley argues that, 'Throughout all the films the presence of naked male bodies has threatened to disrupt the narratives that contain them and to become iconographic gay male images in their own extradiegetic right' (2001, 61).

16 The shots are reminiscent of work by artists such as J.M.W. Turner and James Abbott McNeill Whistler, or, more interestingly, Ivan Aivazovsky, in paintings such as 'The Black Sea at Night' (1879).

17 Jonathan Smele notes that 'a plethora of multifaceted wars swept across and beyond the Russian Empire as it collapsed at the end of the First World War and was then refashioned as the Union of Soviet Socialist Republics' (2015, 1). He estimates total deaths as a result of the Russian Civil Wars (1917–1921) as 'at least 10,500,000' (2). This figure is broken down in a footnote into 'fatalities in action', 'deaths due to terror' and 'deaths due to famine and disease' (63). See Chapter 3, '*Battleship Potemkin*: Pathos and Politics' in Goodwin, J. (1993) *Eisenstein, Cinema, and History* for an outline of the relationship of the historical events of 1905 to Eisenstein's version of things.

18 John D. Klier begins the opening chapter to *Pogroms: Anti-Jewish Violence in Modern Russian History* with the simple sentence: 'In the early months of 1881, the Jews of the Russian Empire were poised on the verge of four decades of pogrom violence' (2004, 3). According to *Antisemitism: A Historical Encyclopedia of Prejudice and Persecution, Vol 1*: 'The Black Sea port of Odessa was the most pogrom-ridden city in the Russian Empire, with serious anti-Jewish riots occurring in 1821, 1859, 1871, and 1905 and smaller disturbances in 1849 and 1881' (Levy et al. 2005, 519). The entry offers a stark contrast to the camaraderie of Eisenstein's film: 'Amid a setting of revolutionary disorder and counterrevolutionary violence, at least 400 Jews were killed between 18 and 22 October 1905, and over 1,600 Jewish properties were ransacked or destroyed' (519). See also Robert Weinberg (1993).

19 'The events in the supermarket sequence really happened. One week before we shot the supermarket sequence the CP was selling its program in the very same supermarket. Three months before we shot the sequence the leftists looted a very fashionable store and distributed the goods in the suburbs of Paris.' Jean-Pierre Gorin in David Sterritt (1998, 61).

20 See Ian Stone on the Brechtian use of a prologue, for example (2013, 138–139).

CHAPTER 7: EUROPEAN ART CINEMA AND EXPERIMENTAL FILM

1 *Le Sang d'un Poète* is the first film in what eventually became, with *Orphée* (Cocteau, 1930, France) and *Testament of Orpheus* (Cocteau, 1960, France), a trilogy relating to the myth of Orpheus.

2 This film is often considered alongside *Rien que les heures/Nothing But Time* (Alberto Cavacanti, 1926, France), which looks at a day in the life of Paris, and *Man With a Movie Camera* (Dziga Vertov, 1929, Soviet Union), which takes a composite look at a series of Soviet cities.

3 'Lightshow' would be one translation of Lichtspiel but the concept of 'play of light' carries more of the sense of what is going on here.

4 Despite the implied criticism of 'the masses' it is not so clear that this group is being targeted by Ruttmann. His concern was more with the way in which, because of commercial concerns, the film industry effectively worked to prevent artistic expression in the medium. Malte Hagener quotes Ruttmann searching for a way forward on this matter in *Der isolierte Künstler/The Isolated Artist*: 'It might be possible to reach the reconciliation and equilibrium between art and commerce through an exterior power: for example, through patronage or the state' (2007, 47). Ruttmann was later to work with Leni Riefenstahl on *Triumph des Willens/Triumph of the Will* (1935) and to die from wounds received while working as a war photographer.

5 'Jarman and three friends and former collaborators – John Quentin, Nigel Terry, and Tilda Swinton – recite the text over a continuous blue screen' (Pencak 2002, 157).

6 See James Williams (2006, 38–40) for a succinct summary of the 'events' of the film.

7 'At the time of *The Blood of a Poet*, I was the only one of this minority to avoid the deliberate manifestations of the unconscious in favour of a kind of half-sleep through which I wandered as though in a labyrinth' (Cocteau 1985, n.p.). The 'minority' to which Cocteau refers is that of avant-garde artists.

8 Although, it would seem Cocteau has more surface interest in the question of the role of the poet in society as a figure set apart from others. A key theme in *Le Sang d'un Poète* is the necessity of repeated deaths on the part of the poet moving towards fulfilling his destiny. We might note that the pentagram we see in close-up on the poet's back alongside an old scar was a symbol once used to denote the five wounds of Christ.

9 Cocteau refers to 'an almost sickening slowness' (1985).

10 See Michael O'Pray (2003) for a much fuller examination of this.

11 See *A Colour Box* (1935) and *Kaleidoscope* (1935). Lye's technique involved drawing directly on to film.
12 'While the film clearly bears the imprint of Léger's predominantly machine aesthetic in the first half of the 1920s, it also contains Man Ray's distinctive treatment of people in his photographs and other films' (Freeman, 1996, 32).
13 A film with an amazingly succinct animated expression of the effect of the First World War on Germany.

CHAPTER 8: EUROPEAN ART CINEMA AND HOLLYWOOD

1 To say nothing of studio heads such as Carl Laemmle, Adolph Zukor, William Fox, Louis B. Mayer and Sam Goldwyn. See Larry Langman (2000) for an overview of the influence of Europeans on Hollywood.
2 In biology 'symbiotic' can refer to a parasitical relationship.
3 Or, perhaps, Fox Film Corporation made a mistake releasing *Sunrise: A Song of Two Humans* sandwiched between the re-release of their own *Seventh Heaven* with an added soundtrack and the release by Warner Brothers of *The Jazz Singer*. According to Allen and Gomery, '*Sunrise* had no chance at the box office' (1985, 91).
4 See Dudley Andrew (1987, 14).
5 There are also always those who are working within the standards offered by Hollywood to challenge social norms and values even within the most stereotypical of studio-produced fare.
6 We should be careful not to get too carried away with such ideas: 'Hollywood remains, above all, a business' (King 2007, 2).
7 See Thomas Elsaesser, Alexander Horwath and Noel King (2004) for an examination of American cinema in the 1970s.
8 Bordwell's essay is also a useful starting point for considering postwar European 'art cinema', in relation to what he sees at its precursors in film *d'art*, German Expressionism and French Impressionism, in relation to his category of 'modernist cinema', and, in relation to what he describes in a footnote as, 'More radical avant-garde movements, such as Soviet montage filmmaking, Surrealism, and *cinéma Pur*' (2002 [1979], 101).

CHAPTER 9: CASE STUDIES

1 An earlier version of this essay can be found in *Routledge Encyclopedia of Films* (2015).

2 Expressionism had an impact in particular on art and theatre in Europe (and, perhaps, especially in Germany) during the early twentieth century. Expressionism aimed to give a subjective view of the world, expressing emotions and feelings rather than presenting a supposed objective view of reality. In theatre, stylized staging and lighting was employed to intensify the emotional impact on the audience. The dark cynicism of German Expressionism after the First World War, *Die Neue Sachlichkeit* (*The New Objectivity*), seen in the work of Otto Dix and George Grosz where the subject is often rendered as a distorted caricature, might also be relevant here.

3 David Robinson explains how overseas markets were closed to German films after the First World War but how using the 'art film' tag enabled *Caligari* and other German products to access those markets (Robinson 1997, 42–43).

4 For a well-argued exploration of Wiene's contribution to the film and how it was downplayed, in particular by Janowitz and the critic, Siegfried Kracauer (1947), see Uli Jung and Walter Schatzberg (1999, 51–76).

5 For some contextualization of Caligari and Cesare within the fairground freak show tradition, see Paul Dobryden (2012, 80–85).

6 We open with Francis about to tell his story to an inmate in an asylum and end with him still confined within the asylum, surrounded by characters resembling figures from his dark imaginings.

7 Cesare, we might note, is not only put into a state where he will not question orders but is also trained to kill to order.

8 There is, for example, an image of Orlok (Max Schreck) entering Hutter's (Gustav von Wangenheim) room at night in which the door opens like the lid of a coffin.

9 Solntseva formed a 'lifelong collaborative partnership' with Dovzhenko after their marriage in 1929, working as co-director on all his films (Foster 1995, 344).

10 'Most kulaks employed nobody, and even the most prosperous peasant in 1927 had no more than three cows and three working animals, with about 10 hectares of sowing area to support an average family of seven ... By 1928, 97.3 per cent of the total sown area was still being farmed by individual peasants' (Sakwa 1998, 36). Robert Conquest suggests, however we might try to define this group, 'the kulak was, as an economic class, no more than a Party construct' (1986, 74).

11 How coherent a group this ever was (see above), and how many members of farming communities at other levels also opposed collectivization, are matters for intense historical debate; but, although the resulting number of victims is similarly debated, what is not in doubt is that the policy of collectivization was violently opposed and even more ruthlessly enforced, and that the resulting upheavals led to famine on a massive scale. Sakwa (1998, 37) supports a figure of 'about 5 million' for those who died from famine in 1932–1933, but also suggests '15 million were left homeless by collectivisation, a million of whom were sent to labour camps and some 10 million deported to Siberia, a large proportion of whom perished' (36–37).

12 The term 'socialist realism' was not yet officially in use but its central ideal of representing everyday life in traditional 'realistic' ways that could be understood by ordinary people was very much used to oppose artists who expected revolutionary, avant-garde change in the arts as much as in any other area of life.

13 Doubt would seem to be cast on how liberated this 'new life' under Communism would be by the fact that the film was censored in 1930 for supposed obscenity – at one point the workers urinate into the tractor's radiator when it runs out of water, and then during Vasili's funeral his fiancée, Natalya, displays her anguish by tearing at her body, crying out, and beating the pillows on her bed while naked (Celli 2011, 124).

14 An earlier version of this essay can be found in *Routledge Encyclopedia of Films* (2015).

15 Vesna Drapac sees this film as a useful corrective to the concept of resistance as having to be 'active' in the sense of militarily confronting the enemy, and as a valuable expression of the predominant reality of actual resistance (2013, 376–397).

16 Lyon, the third largest city in France, was a key centre for the French Resistance, or Maquis, within Vichy France during the Second World War. In 1942 Fort Montluc was requisitioned by occupying German forces and used to imprison around 7,700 people, mainly Jews and resistance fighters, through until the summer of 1944. After the Allied Normandy landings in June 1944 several massacres of prisoners took place. This film was based on the memoirs of André Devigny, who escaped from Montluc in 1943. (See Ministère de la Défense (2015). 'The Memorial Montluc Prison (Rhône)', Ministère de la Défense. Accessed 31 January 2016. www.defense.gouv.fr/actualites/memoire-et-culture/le-memorial-de-la-prison-de-montluc-rhone and images at Mémorial National de la Prison de Montluc 'Le Mémorial' (n.d.) Mémorial National de la Prison de Montluc. Accessed 31 January 2016. www.memorial-montluc.fr/home.)

17 'What is perhaps most striking about *A Man Escaped* is that it manages to create an atmosphere of almost unbearable suspense despite the fact that the title gives the basic narrative arc of the film away' (Foster 2012, n.p.).

18 The way Bresson's 'soundscape' embellishes the story and creates meaning would form a study in itself, as might elements of homage such as that to Jean Vigo's *Zero de Conduite* (1933) as Fontaine and Jost scramble across the prison roof.

19 Torture at Montluc 'included bathtubs filled with boiling and freezing water, branding irons, whips, electric prods, clubs, and hypodermic needles' (McFarren and Iglesias 2013, 70).

20 Shots throughout the film of Fontaine looking up – towards the ceiling of his cell, towards the skylight, towards Jost on the roof – may reference Psalm 121 ('I will lift up mine eyes') for Bresson.

21 When Devigny and the person who escaped with him in real life, Gimenez, were recaptured, Devigny abandoned Gimenez (Pipolo 2010, 104); so, the cool calculation Fontaine demonstrates is perhaps absolutely in tune with the (necessary) outlook of the person on whom his character was based.

22 An earlier version of this essay can be found in *Routledge Encyclopedia of Films* (2015).

23 The Hiroshima Peace Memorial Museum was opened in the Peace Memorial Park with its Memorial Cenotaph just four years before *Hiroshima mon amour* was filmed.

24 'Awakening in the morning, the women found their hair had fallen out,' says the woman in voiceover, and the mere mention of 'hair' alongside images of women with apparently shaven heads creates a reference not only to newsreel footage of Holocaust death camps but also to Resnais's earlier film, *Nuit et Brouillard/Night and Fog* (1955).

25 Among Resnais's other work Roth cites in particular *Nuit et Brouillard/Night and Fog* (1955) in which he says, despite the documented horrors, 'we are ceaselessly reminded that we are seeing nothing of the reality of the camps' (1995, 93).

26 In 1954, the United States exploded a 15-megaton nuclear bomb in the Marshall Islands. The radioactive fallout was immense and dusted a Japanese boat, the *Lucky Dragon*, tuna fishing 160km from the test site.

27 'The power relationships in the film are complex, since the narrative is centred in a Western character visiting Japan, yet that character is a woman, inverting a gendered hierarchy of unequal cultural relationships' (Nygren 2007, 187).

28 This is a particularly intense example of the problem with all forms of knowledge and what it means to 'know'. When the man says he cannot imagine Nevers, she responds, 'Nevers. 40,000 inhabitants. Built as a country seat,' as if encyclopaedic knowledge really helps someone to 'know' something.

29 Her response is given over a black screen.

30 For an exploration of individual memory and collective memory, and the relationship between memory and history, in relation to concepts of bearing witness and understanding trauma, see *Witness and Memory: The Discourse of Trauma* (2003) edited by Ana Douglass and Thomas Vogler, which includes a chapter by Kyo Maclear, 'The Limits of Vision: *Hiroshima Mon Amour* and the Subversion of Representation,' 233–248.

31 'One must avoid thinking of the difficulties this world presents, otherwise it would be unbearable,' for example, could come from any dramatist working within what Martin Esslin (2014 [1961]) classified as the 'Theatre of the Absurd'.

32 An earlier version of this essay can be found in *Routledge Encyclopedia of Films* (2015).

33 Cynthia Stone tells us, 'Lope de Aguirre, the leader of a rebellion of some 300 Spaniards against the authority of Felipe II during an expedition down the Amazon to conquer the mythical El Dorado was decapitated and quartered in 1561.' The early accounts of the rebellion are 'unanimous in their condemnation of Aguirre,' she adds (2005, 24).

34 Stone examines the different versions of events surrounding Aguirre's revolt against the Spanish Crown and the ways subsequent readers have interpreted these stories in line with their own ideological ends. So that, for example, 'many left-wing Spanish American and Basque intellectuals, from the nineteenth century to the present, have tended to see the aspersions cast on Aguirre as part of a larger strategy to silence dissenting voices during the colonial period' (2005, 28).

35 See Gregory A. Waller (1981, 55–69).

36 At one point he offers Flores a slow loris he has found. The scene seems odd and unrelated to the narrative, unless we consider how he describes this creature to his daughter: 'This animal sleeps its whole life away. It is never really awake.'

37 The power and authority of the Catholic Church and the Crown in relation to subjects and in relation to each other were much disputed physically and intellectually at the time. See Ellen Meiksins Wood's *Liberty and Property: A Social History of Western Political Thought from Renaissance to Enlightenment* (2012), which includes a chapter on the Spanish Empire.

38 In relation to *Aguirre* and the nature of history and truth, and the creation of narratives of the past, see Luisela Alvaray (1995, 35–44).

39 Gilberto Perez (2000, 185–194) sees the director and the actor as 'two versions of the same madness, barely under control' (193).

40 See Beate West-Leuer (2009, 1157–1168).

41 'mass politics reached a new, more sophisticated and effective level by 1832' (LoPatin 1999, 9).

42 Which is not to say any full appraisal of this film would not need to consider both the historical context of the period in which the film is set and the political climate in the UK during the 1970s and 1980s.

43 And somebody who, despite their emphasis on film as a visual language, is also acutely aware of the nuances of written and spoken language.

44 'When a ship leaves England with prisoners, she generally takes in as many as possible, men of all ages, stowing them down together in a prison, with about twelve square inches for each man to eat, drink, and sleep: at least, so it was in the ship that took me out' (Loveless 1838, 19).

45 For a valuable starting point on the representation of rural landscape in this film, see Newland, P. (2015) 'We Come, Our Country's Rights to Save: English Rural Landscape and Leftist Aesthetics in *Comrades*', *Visual Culture in Britain*, 16 (3). Accessed 4 March 2016. www.tandfonline.com/doi/full/10.1080/14714787.2015.1078257

46 An article by Stuart MacDonald gives interesting background information on the introduction of threshing machines in Great Britain. MacDonald, S. (1975) 'The Progress of the Early Threshing Machine,' *The Agricultural Historical Review*, 13 (1): 63–77. Accessed 2 March 2016. www.bahs.org.uk/AGHR/ARTICLES/23n1a4.pdf

47 Shots of hands form a strand of imagery through the whole film.

48 See Loveless, G. (1838) 'The victims of Whiggery: a statement of the persecutions experienced by the Dorchester labourers'.

49 For details of all the pre-cinema references in the film, see Douglas, B. (1987) 'A Lanternist and his Comrades', The Bill Douglas Cinema Museum. Accessed 3 March 2016. www.bdcmuseum.org.uk/about/bill-douglas-a-lanternist-and-his-comrades/. Originally printed in *The New Magic Lantern Journal*, 5.2, August 1987.

50 The shot is not actually 'empty' when we realize that our observer's role invites us to scan the space and contemplate each element of the composition.

51 The Arte Povera movement that began in the 1960s, and within which Merz was a key figure, aimed (and this may be relevant to Frammartino) to utilize materials commonly regarded as worthless and in the process to challenge the commercialization of the art world.

52 The drama of the transition mirrors that of Truffaut's transition to a freeze-frame as Antoine turns back from the sea towards the camera.

53 *Hamlet*: Act 5, Scene 2, l.356.

51 In focusing on the universal, the reading offered here ignores the specificity of the locations. Collins said he wanted 'to explore Irishness using a modern cinematic language – and for it to be universal while still being distinctively Irish. What's the point of me making films as if I were from some other country? I might as well give up if I can't bring something distinctive – from my upbringing, the influences that shaped me or the place I come from' (McAuliffe 2014, n.p.). Emphasising the Irish connection Dara Waldron has focused on language use in the film and Lacan's concept of the Real – that natural state of being lost to us at the point at which we acquire language. 'Crucially,' she says, 'Eoghan, as a native speaker, returns to where his native tongue is spoken. Yet his journey home, which requires speaking his native language at intermittent intervals, can also be found to involve an acceptance of language *per se* in its limitations (as silence)' (2014, 202).

BIBLIOGRAPHY

Abel, R. 1998. *The Ciné Goes to Town: French Cinema, 1896–1914*. Oakland, CA: University of California Press.

Ahmad, S.M. 1991. *Existential Aesthetics: A Study of Jean-Paul Sartre's Theory of Art and Literature*. New Delhi: Atlantic Publishers.

Aitken, I. 2001. *European Film Theory and Cinema: A Critical Introduction*. Bloomington: Indiana University Press.

Aitken, I. 2013. *The Concise Routledge Encyclopedia of the Documentary Film*. London and New York: Routledge.

Albright, D. 2000. *Untwisting the Serpent: Modernism in Music, Literature, and Other Arts*. Chicago: University of Chicago Press.

Allen, R.C. and D. Gomery. 1985. *Film History: Theory and Practice*. New York: McGraw-Hill.

Alter, N.M. 2009. '*Berlin, Symphony of a Great City* (1927): City, Image, Sound.' In N.W. Isenberg, ed. *Weimar Cinema: An Essential Guide to Classic Films of the Era*. New York: Columbia University Press.

Alvaray, L. 1995. 'Filming the Discovery of America: How and Whose History is Being Told.' *Film-Historia* 5 (1): 35–44.

Anderson, L. 2004. Edited by P. Ryan. *Never Apologise: The Collected Writings*. London: Plexus.

Andrew, D. 1987. *Breathless: Jean-Luc Godard, director*. New Brunswick, NJ and London: Rutgers University Press.

Andrew, D. 1995. *Mists of Regret: Culture and Sensibility in Classic French Film*. Princeton, NJ: Princeton University Press.

Andrew, D. 2004. 'Adapting Cinema to History: A Revolution in the Making.' In R. Stam and A. Raengo, eds. *A Companion to Literature and Film*. Malden, MA: Blackwell.

Andrews, D. 2013. *Theorizing Art Cinemas: Foreign, Cult, Avant-Garde, and Beyond*. Austin: University of Texas Press.

Armes, R. 1974. *Film and Reality: An Historical Survey*. London: Penguin.

Armstrong, R. 2009. '"'Nevers' … is just a word like any other": The Failure of Words and the Wandering Woman in *Hiroshima mon amour*.' In P. Collier, Elsner, A.M., and O. Smith, eds. *Anamnesia: Private and Public Memory in French Culture*. Oxford: Peter Lang.

Arnheim, R. 2006. *Film as Art*. Oakland: University of California Press.

Astruc, A. 1967. 'The Birth of a New Avant-Garde: La Camera-Stylo.' In P. Graham, ed. *The New Wave*. Garden City: Doubleday.

Aufderheide, P. 2007. *Documentary Film: A Very Short Introduction*. Oxford and New York: Oxford University Press.

Baer, E.R. 2012. *The Golem Redux: From Prague to Post-Holocaust Fiction*. Detroit, MI: Wayne State University Press.

Bainbridge, C. 2007. *The Cinema of Lars von Trier: Authenticity and Artifice*. London: Wallflower Press.

Baird, D. 2008. *Between Two Fires: Guerrilla War in the Spanish Sierras*. Frigiliana: Maroma Press.

Bal, M. and N. Bryson. 1991. 'Semiotics and Art History.' *Art Bulletin* 73 (2): 174.

Balderston, T. 2002. *Economics and Politics in the Weimar Republic*. Cambridge: Cambridge University Press.

Barthes, R. 1972 [1957]. *Mythologies*. Translated by A. Lavers. London: Cape.

Bazin, A. 2004 [1954]. 'The Italian Scene (Cinema 53 à travers le monde, 1954).' In B. Cardullo, ed. *Bazin on Global Cinema, 1948–1958*. Austin: University of Texas Press.

Bazin, A. 2005 [1971]. *What Is Cinema? Volume 2*. Berkeley and Los Angeles: University of California Press.

Belton, J. 2008. 'The Phenomenology of Film Sound: Robert Bresson's A Man Escaped.' In J. Beck and T. Grajeda, eds. *Lowering the Boom: Critical Studies in Film Sound*. Urbana and Chicago: University of Illinois Press.

Benelli, D. 2014. 'The cosmos and its discontents.' In T. Corrigan, ed. *The Films of Werner Herzog: Between Mirage and History*. London and New York, Routledge.

Benson, S. 2009. *Shakespearean Resurrection: the Art of Almost Raising the Dead*. Pittsburgh, PA: Duquesne University Press.

Benyahia, S.C., F. Gaffney and J. White. 2010. *A2 Film Studies: The Essential Introduction*. London and New York: Routledge.

Betz, M. 2009. *Beyond the Subtitle: Remapping European Art Cinema*. Minneapolis: University of Minnesota Press.

Beugnet, M. 2004. *Claire Denis*. Manchester and New York: Manchester University Press.

Binder, D. 2005. 'Der Film L'Inhumaine und sein Verhältnis zu Kunst und Architektur der zwanziger Jahre.' *History and the Arts* 29. Accessed 18 March 2015. http://epub.ub.uni-muenchen.de/10635/

Bingham, A. 2004. 'Poetry in Motion: Dovzhenko's *Earth*.' *Senses of Cinema* 31. Accessed 26 January 2016. http://sensesofcinema.com/2004/cteq/earth/

Blakeway, C. 1990. *Jacques Prévert: Popular French Theatre and Cinema*. Cranbury, NJ: Associated University Presses.

Boime, A. 2004. *Art in an Age of Counterrevolution, 1815–1848*. Chicago: University of Chicago Press.

Bordwell, D. 2002 [1979]. 'The Art Cinema as a Mode of Film Practice.' In C. Fowler, ed. *The European Cinema Reader*. New York and London: Routledge.

Bordwell, D. 2005. *Figures Traced in Light: On Cinematic Staging*. Oakland: University of California Press.

Bradford, R. 2008. 'Introduction to the Fiftieth Anniversary Edition.' In A. Sillitoe. *Saturday Night and Sunday Morning*. London: Harper Perennial.

Brady, M. and J. Leal. 2011. *Wim Wenders and Peter Handke: Collaboration, Adaptation, Recomposition*. Amsterdam: Rodopi.

Braudy, L. and M. Cohen. 2004 [1974]. *Film Theory and Criticism: Introductory Readings*. 6th ed. Oxford and New York: Oxford University Press.

Bresson, R. 1977. *Notes on Cinematography*. Translated by J. Griffin. New York: Urizen Books.

Brockmann, S. 2010. *A Critical History of German Film*. Rochester, NY: Camden House.

Brunette, P. 1996. *Roberto Rossellini*. Berkeley and Los Angeles: University of California Press.

Brustein, W.I. 2003. *Roots of Hate: Anti-Semitism in Europe before the Holocaust*. Cambridge: Cambridge University Press.

Buchanan, J.R. 2014. *Shakespeare on Film*. New York and London: Routledge.

Budd, M., ed. 1990. *The Cabinet of Dr. Caligari: Texts, Contexts, Histories*. New Brunswick and London: Rutgers University Press.

Buñuel, L. 2006. 'Notes on the Making of Un Chien Andalou.' In S. MacDonald, ed. *Art in Cinema: Documents Toward a History of the Film Society*. Philadelphia, PA: Temple University Press.

Butler, M. 2004. *Film and Community in Britain and France: From La Règle du jeu to Room at the Top*. London and New York: I.B.Tauris.

Camus, A. 1955 [1942]. *The Myth of Sisyphus and Other Essays*. New York: Vintage.

Camus, A. 2000 [1942]. *L'Étranger/The Outsider*. Translated by J. Laredo. London: Penguin.

Canudo, R. 1993 [1911]. 'The Birth of the Sixth Art.' In R. Abel, ed. *French Film Theory and Criticism, 1907–1929: A History/Anthology*. Princeton, NJ: Princeton University Press.

Cardullo, B. 1987. *Indelible Images: New Perspectives on Classic Films*. Lanham, MD: University Press of America.

Cardullo, B., ed. 2011. *André Bazin and Italian Neorealism*. New York and London: Continuum.

Caruth, C. 2006. 'Literature and the Enactment of Memory (Duras, Resnais, *Hiroshima mon amour*).' In L. Saltzman and E. Rosenberg, eds. *Trauma and Visuality in Modernity*. Lebanon, NH: University Press of New England.

Caughie, J., ed. 2001 [1981]. *Theories of Authorship*. London and New York: Routledge.

Celli, C. 2011. *National Identity in Global Cinema: How Movies Explain the World*. New York and London: Palgrave Macmillan.

Chapman, J. 2005. *Past and Present: National Identity and the British Historical Film*. London and New York: I.B.Tauris.

Checkel, J.T. and P.J. Katzenstein, eds. 2009. *European Identity*. Cambridge: Cambridge University Press.

Chekhov, A. 2010 [1892]. *Ward Six and Other Short Stories*. Translated by A. Dunnigan. New Brunswick, NJ: Transaction.

Cheshire, G. 2007. '*Bicycle Thieves*: A Passionate Commitment to the Real.' *The Criterion Collection*. Accessed 28 November 2015. https://www.criterion.com/current/posts/467-bicycle-thieves-a-passionate-commitment-to-the-real

Christie, I. 2014. 'Eastern Avatars: Russian Influence on European Avant-Gardes.' In Hagener, M., ed. *The Emergence of Film Culture: Knowledge Production, Institution Building, and the Fate of the Avant-Garde in Europe, 1919–1945*. New York and Oxford: Berghahn Books.

Ciment, M. 2003. 'Michel Ciment: The State of Cinema.' San Francisco Film Society. Accessed 13 June 2015. http://web.archive.org/web/20040325130014/http://www.sfiff.org/fest03/special/state.html

Clifford, R. 2013. *Commemorating the Holocaust: The Dilemmas of Remembrance in France and Italy*. Oxford: Oxford University Press.

Cocteau, J. 1985. Preface to *Two Screenplays: The Blood of a Poet and The Testament of Orpheus*. *The Criterion Collection*. Accessed 16 December 2015. https://www.criterion.com/current/posts/16-the-blood-of-a-poet

Cocteau, J. 2013 [1947]. *The Difficulty of Being*. Translated by E. Sprigge. Brooklyn, NY and London: Melville House Publishing.

Cohen, J.-L. 1995. *Scenes of the World to Come: European Architecture and the American Challenge, 1893–1960*. Paris: Flammarion.

Collins, P. 2012. '*Silence* Pressbook.' New Wave Films. Accessed 5 February 2016. www.newwavefilms.co.uk/assets/872/Silence_Pressbook.pdf

Conquest, R. 1986. *The Harvest of Sorrow: Soviet Collectivization and the Terror-Famine*. New York and Oxford: Oxford University Press.

Conquest, R. 1998. *The Great Terror: A Reassessment*. London: Pimlico.

Cook, R.F. and G. Gemünden, eds. 1997. *The Cinema of Wim Wenders: Image, Narrative, and the Postmodern Condition*. Detroit, MI: Wayne State University Press.

Crisp, C. 2015. *French Cinema: A Critical Filmography, Volume 1, 1929–1939*. Bloomington: Indiana University Press.

Cronin, P. 2002. *Herzog on Herzog*. London: Macmillan.

Cunneen, J. 2003. *Robert Bresson: A Spiritual Style in Film*. London and New York: Continuum.

Dale, R.C. 1972. *Cinema Yesterday and Today*. Translated by S. Appelbaum. New York: Dover Publications.

Dancyger, K. 2013. *The Technique of Film and Video Editing: History, Theory, and Practice*. 5th ed. Burlington, MA: Focal Press.

Darr, B. 2009. '*Sunrise: A Song of Two Humans*.' San Francisco Silent Film Festival. Accessed 22 December 2015. http://www.silentfilm.org/archive/sunrise-2009

Despentes, V. 2009. *King Kong Theory*. London: Serpent's Tail.

Dixon, W.W. 1993. *The Early Film Criticism of François Truffaut*. Bloomington: Indiana University Press.

Dixon, W.W. 1997. *The Films of Jean-Luc Godard*. Albany: State University of New York Press.

Dobryden, P. 2012. '23 May 1920: Das Cabinet des Dr. Caligari Brings Aesthetic Modernism to the Fairground.' In J.M. Kapczynski and M.D. Richardson, eds. *A New History of German Cinema*. Rochester, NY: Camden House.

Douglass, A. and T.A. Vogler, eds. 2003. *Witness and Memory: The Discourse of Trauma*. New York and London: Routledge.

Drapac, V. 2013. 'Recasting the heroic resistance ideal: Robert Bresson's *Un condamné à mort s'est échappé*.' *French Cultural Studies* 24 (4): 376–397.

Drazin, C. 2011. *The Faber Book of French Cinema*. London: Faber and Faber.

Durgnat, R. 1968. *Luis Bunuel*. Berkeley: University of California Press.

Durgnat, R. 1974. *Jean Renoir*. Berkeley and Los Angeles, CA: University of California Press.

Eagan, D. 2010. *America's Legacy: The Authoritative Guide to the Landmark Movies in the National Registry*. New York and London: Continuum.

Ede, L.N. 2010. *British Film Design: A History*. London and New York: I.B.Tauris.

Elder, R.B. 2013. *Dada, Surrealism, and the Cinematic Effect*. Waterloo, Ontario: Wilfrid Laurier University Press.

Elsaesser, T. 1996. *Fassbinder's Germany: History, Identity, Subject*. Amsterdam: Amsterdam University Press.

Elsaesser, T. 2004. 'American Auteur Cinema: The Last – or First – Great Picture Show.' In T. Elsaesser, A. Horwath and N. King, eds. *The Last Great American Picture Show: New Hollywood Cinema in the 1970s*. Amsterdam: Amsterdam University Press.

Elsaesser, T. 2011. 'Stop/Motion.' In E. Røssaak, ed. *Between Stillness and Motion: Film, Photography, Algorithms*. Amsterdam: Amsterdam University Press.

Elsaesser, T., A. Horwath and N. King, eds. 2004. *The Last Great American Picture Show: New Hollywood Cinema in the 1970s*. Amsterdam: Amsterdam University Press.

Esslin, M. 2014. [1961]. *The Theatre of the Absurd*. London and New York: Bloomsbury

Evans, P.W. 2007. 'An Amour Still Fou: Late Buñuel.' In G. Harper and R. Stone, eds. *The Unsilvered Screen: Surrealism on Film*. London and New York: Wallflower Press.

Fabe, M. 2004. *Closely Watched Films: An Introduction to the Art of Narrative Film Technique*. Berkeley and Los Angeles: University of California Press.

Ferreira, M.J. 1998. 'Faith and the Kierkegaardian Leap.' In A. Hannay and G.D. Marino, eds. *The Cambridge Companion to Kierkegaard*. Cambridge: Cambridge University Press.

Ferro, M. 1988. *Cinema and History*. Translated by N. Greene. Detroit, MI: Wayne State University Press.

Fischer, L. 2003. 'Sunrise: A Song of Two Humans.' In R. White and E. Buscombe, eds. *British Film Institute Film Classics, Volume 1*. London and New York: Taylor & Francis.

Fiske, J. and J. Hartley. 1978. *Reading Television*, London: Methuen.

Flitterman-Lewis, S. 1996. 'The Image and the Spark: Dulac and Artaud Reviewed.' In R.E. Kuenzli, ed. *Dada and Surrealist Film*. Cambridge, MA: MIT Press.

Forrest, D. 2013. *Social Realism: Art, Nationhood and Politics*. Newcastle upon Tyne: Cambridge Scholars Publishing.

Foster, G.A. 1995. *Women Film Directors: An International Bio-critical Dictionary*. Westport, CT: Greenwood Press.

Foster, G.A. 2012. 'A Man Escaped.' *Senses of Cinema* 62. Accessed 31 January 2016. http://sensesofcinema.com/2012/cteq/a-man-escaped/

Fowler, J. 2005. *Unleashing Britain: Theatre gets real, 1955–64*. London: V&A.

Fox, A., M. Marie, R. Moine and H. Radner. 2015. *A Companion to Contemporary French Cinema*. Hoboken, NJ: Wiley Blackwell.

Frammartino, M. 2011. Interview with Jonathan Romney. *Le Quattro Volte*. DVD. New Wave Films.

Frammartino, M. 2012. '*Le Quattro Volte* a film by Michelangelo Frammartino.' Pressbook. Accessed 19 February 2016. http://coproductionoffice.eu/catalogue/downloads-films/37/LQV.pdf

Franklin, J. 1986. *New German Cinema*. Bromley, Kent: Columbus Books.

Freeman, J. 1996. 'Léger's Ballet Mécanique.' In R.E. Kuenzli, ed. *Dada and Surrealist Film*, Cambridge, MA and London: MIT Press.

Freeze, G.L. 2009. *Russia: A History*. 3rd ed. Oxford: Oxford University Press.

French, P. 2011. '*Le Quattro Volte* – review.' *The Observer*, 29 May 2011. Accessed 12 June 2015. www.theguardian.com/film/2011/may/29/le-quattro-volte-michelangelo-frammartino

Furhammer, L. and F. Isaksson. 1971. *Politics and Film*. Translated by K. French. London: Studio Vista.

Gado, F. 1986. *The Passion of Ingmar Bergman*. Durham, NC: Duke University Press.

Gaffney, F. 2015. '*Ladri di biciclette/Bicycle Thieves* (1948).' In S. Haenni, S. Barrow and J. White, eds. *The Routledge Encyclopedia of Films*. London and New York: Routledge.

Gallagher, T. 1998. *The Adventures of Roberto Rossellini*. Boston, MA: Da Capo Press.

Galt, R. and K. Schoonover, eds. 2010. *Global Art Cinema: New Theories and Histories*. Oxford and New York: Oxford University Press.

Gibson, D.B. 2012. *From Chiefdom to State in Early Ireland*. Cambridge and New York: Cambridge University Press.

Giovacchini, S. and R. Sklar. 2013. *Global Neorealism: The Transnational History of a Film Style*. Jackson: University Press of Mississippi.

Goodwin, J. 1993. *Eisenstein, Cinema, and History*. Champaign: University of Illinois Press.

Gordon, R.S.C. 2008. *Bicycle Thieves*. London: BFI.

Graf, A. 2002. *The Cinema of Wim Wenders: the Celluloid Highway*. London: Wallflower Press.

Greene, N. 2007. *The French New Wave: A New Look*. London: Wallflower Press.

Griffiths, K. 2009. *Emile Zola and the Artistry of Adaptation*. London: Modern Humanities Research Association.

Grønstad, A. and H. Gustafsson, eds. 2012. *Ethics and Images of Pain*. London and New York: Routledge.

Groo, K. 2014. '*La Roue/The Wheel* (1923).' In S. Haenni, S. Barrow and J. White, eds. *The Routledge Encyclopedia of Films*. London and New York: Routledge.

Haaland, T. 2012. *Italian Neorealist Cinema*. Edinburgh: Edinburgh University Press.

Hagener, M. 2007. *Moving Forward, Looking Back: The European Avant-garde and the Invention of Film Culture, 1919–1939*. Amsterdam: Amsterdam University Press.

Hake, S. 2013. *German National Cinema*. 2nd ed. New York and London: Routledge.

Hall, S. 1973. 'The determination of news photographs.' In S. Cohen and J. Young, eds. *The Manufacture of News*. London: Constable.

Hallam, J. and M. Marshment. 2000. *Realism and Popular Cinema*. Manchester and New York: Manchester University Press.

Harbou, T. von. 2007. *Metropolis*. Rockville, MD: Wildside Press.

Hayward, S. 2006. *French National Cinema*. London and New York: Routledge.

Hayward, S. 2013. *Cinema Studies: The Key Concepts*. 4th ed. Abingdon and New York: Routledge.

Heller-Nicholas, A. 2011. *Rape-Revenge Films: A Critical Study*. Jefferson, NC: McFarland.

Higgins, S. 2006. *Still Moving: The Film and Media Collections of The Museum of Modern Art*. New York: The Museum of Modern Art.

Hjort, M. and S. MacKenzie, eds. 2003. *Purity and Provocation: Dogma 95*. London: BFI.

Hobbins, D., ed. 2007. *The Trial of Joan of Arc*. Cambridge, MA: Harvard University Press.

Hong, H.V. and E.H. Hong, eds. 2000. *The Essential Kierkegaard*. Princeton, NJ: Princeton University Press.

Horeck, T. and T. Kendall, eds. 2011. *The New Extremism in Cinema: From France to Europe*. Edinburgh: Edinburgh University Press.

Horne, W.L. 1999. '"Greatest Pleasures": *A Taste of Honey* (1961) and *The Loneliness of the Long Distance Runner* (1962).' In J.M. Welsh and J.C. Tibbetts, eds. *The Cinema of Tony Richardson: Essays and Interviews*. Albany: State University of New York Press.

Hubbs, J. 1993. *Mother Russia: The Feminine Myth in Russian Culture*. Bloomington: Indiana University Press.

Huffer, L. 2013. *Are the Lips a Grave? A Queer Feminist on the Ethics of Sex*. New York: Columbia University Press.

Ingram, D. 2013. 'The Aesthetics and Ethics of Eco-film Criticism.' In S. Rust, S. Monani and S. Cubitt, eds. *Ecocinema Theory and Practice*. New York and London: Routledge.

Isenberg, N. 2009. *Weimar Cinema: An Essential Guide to Classic Films of the Era*. New York: Columbia University Press.

Jackson, J. 2009. *La Grande Illusion*. London and New York: Palgrave Macmillan.

Jacobs, S. 2006. *Cold War Mandarin: Ngo Dinh Diem and the Origins of America's War in Vietnam, 1950–1963*. Lanham, MD: Rowman & Littlefield.

Jaffe, I. 2014. *Slow Movies: Countering the Cinema of Action*. New York and Chichester: Wallflower Press.

Jaggar, A. 1983. *Feminist Politics and Human Nature*. Totowak, NJ: Rowman & Allanheld.

Jelavich, P. 2006. *Berlin Alexanderplatz: Radio, Film, and the Death of Weimar Culture*. Berkeley and Los Angeles: University of California Press.

Jóhannsdóttir, H. 2012. 'The Inflected Text: Hindle Wakes and its Film Adaptations.' In G. Ipsen, T. Mathews and D. Obradović, eds. *Provocation and Negotiation: Essays in Comparative Criticism*. Amsterdam and New York: Rodopi.

Jones, K. 2003. 'Heartbreak House: Fassbinder's BRD Trilogy.' *The Criterion Collection*. Accessed 19 October 2015. www.criterion.com/current/posts/1046-heartbreak-house-fassbinder-s-brd-trilogy

Joyce, M. 2012. 'The Soviet montage cinema of the 1920s.' In J. Nelmes, ed. *Introduction to Film Studies*. New York and London: Routledge.

Jung, U. and W. Schatzberg. 1999. *Beyond Caligari: the Films of Robert Wiene*. New York and Oxford: Berghahn Books.

Kaes, A. 2001. 'The Presence of the Past: Rainer Werner Fassbinder's The Marriage of Maria Braun.' In M. Landy, ed. *The Historical Film: History and Memory in Media*. London: Athlone Press.

Kaes, A. 2006. 'The Cabinet of Dr Caligari: Expressionism and Cinema.' In T. Perry, ed. *Masterpieces of Modernist Cinema*. Bloomington: Indiana University Press.

Katz, R. 2004. *The Battle for Rome: The Germans, the Allies, the Partisans, and the Pope, September 1943–June 1944*. New York: Simon & Schuster.

Kennedy-Karpat, C. 2013. *Rogues, Romance, and Exoticism in French Cinema of the 1930s*. Madison, NJ: Fairleigh Dickinson University Press.

King, G. 2007. *New Hollywood Cinema: An Introduction*. London and New York: I.B.Tauris.

Klier, J.D. and S. Lambroza, eds. 2004. *Pogroms: Anti-Jewish Violence in Modern Russian History*. Cambridge and New York: Cambridge University Press.

Kline, T.J. 2010. *Unraveling French Cinema: From L'Atalante to Cach*. Malden, MA and Oxford: Wiley-Blackwell.

Klinowski, J. and A. Garbicz. 2012. *Feature Cinema in the 20th Century: a Comprehensive Guide: Volume One: 1913–1950*. Planet RGB.

Kolb, E. 2008. *The Weimar Republic*. Translated by P.S. Falla. London and New York: Routledge.

Kosta, B. 1994. *Recasting Autobiography: Women's Counterfictions in Contemporary German Literature and Film*. Ithaca, NY: Cornell University Press.

Kovács, A.B. 2013. *The Cinema of Béla Tarr: The Circle Closes*. New York: Columbia University Press.

Kracauer, S. 1966 [1947]. *From Caligari to Hitler: A Psychological History of the German Film*. Princeton, NJ and Oxford: Princeton University Press.

Kracauer, S. 1997 [1960]. *Theory of Film: The Redemption of Physical Reality*. Princeton, NJ: Princeton University Press.

Lacey, S. 2002. *British Realist Theatre: The New Wave in its Context, 1956–1965*. London and New York: Routledge.

Landy, M. 2000. *Italian Film*. Cambridge: Cambridge University Press.

Langman, L. 2000. *Destination Hollywood: The Influence of Europeans on American Filmmaking*. Jefferson, NC: McFarland.

Lasswell, H.D. 1936. *Politics: Who Gets What, When, How*. New York: Whittlesey House.

LaValley, A. 2001. 'Maintaining, Blurring, and Transcending Gender Lines in Eisenstein.' In A. LaValley and B.P. Scherr, eds. *Eisenstein at 100: A Reconsideration*. New Brunswick, NJ and London: Rutgers University Press.

Lay, S. 2002. *British Social Realism: From Documentary to Brit-grit*. London: Wallflower.

Lenin, V.I. 1971 [1922]. *Collected Works Volume 42*. Moscow: Progress Publishers. Accessed 16 February 2015. www.marxists.org/archive/lenin/works/1922/jan/17.htm

Leonard, M. and R. Strachan. 2015. 'More Than Background: Ambience and Sound Design in Contemporary Art Documentary Film.' In H. Rogers, ed. *Music and Sound in Documentary Film*. New York and London: Routledge.

Lermontov, M. 2006 [1841]. *A Hero of Our Time*. Translated by J.H. Wisdom and M. Murray. New York: Dover Publications.

Levy, R.S., ed. 2005. *Antisemitism: A Historical Encyclopedia of Prejudice and Persecution Volume 1*. Santa Barbara, CA: ABC-CLIO.

Leyda, J. 1983. *Kino: A History of the Russian and Soviet Film*. Princeton, NJ: Princeton University Press.

Liber, G.O. 2002. *Alexander Dovzhenko: A Life in Soviet Film*. London: BFI.

Liehm, M. 1986. *Passion and Defiance: Film in Italy from 1942 to the Present*. Berkeley: University of California Press.

Lindgren, E. 1970 [1948]. *The Art of the Film*. New York: Collier Books.

LoPatin, N.D. 1999. *Political Unions, Popular Politics and the Great Reform Act of 1832*. London and New York: Palgrave Macmillan.

Loveless, G. 1838. 'The victims of Whiggery: a statement of the persecutions experienced by the Dorchester labourers: with a report of their trial: also a description of Van Dieman's land, and reflections upon the system of transportation.' *Bristol Selected Pamphlets* 28. Accessed 20 February 2016. www.jstor.org/stable/60246686

Luzzi, J. 2014. *A Cinema of Poetry: Aesthetics of the Italian Art Film*. Baltimore, MD: John Hopkins University Press.

Mac Giolla Bhríde, E. 2012. 'Irish Playwrights and Screenwriters Guild: Eoghan Mac Giolla Bhríde.' *Film Ireland* 140. Accessed 8 February 2016. http://filmireland.net/2012/08/02/issue-140-spring-2012-irish-playwrights-screenwriters-guild-eoghan-mac-giolla-bhride/

Manvell, R. 1955. *The Film and the Public*. Harmondsworth: Penguin.

Marco, C.D. 2010. 'Michelangelo Frammartino, director.' *Cineuropa*. 19 May 2010. Accessed 19 February 2016. http://cineuropa.org/it.aspx?t=interview&l=en&did=145628

Marcus, M. 1986. *Italian Film in the Light of Neorealism*. Princeton, NJ: Princeton University Press.

Markowitz, S.J. 1994. 'The Distinction between Art and Craft.' *Journal of Aesthetic Education* 28 (1): 55–70.

Marshall, H. 2014 [1983]. *Masters of Soviet Cinema: Crippled Creative Biographies*. London and New York: Routledge.

Martin, B.F. 2006. *France in 1938*. Baton Rouge: Louisiana State University Press.

Martin, S. 2011. *Andrei Tarkovsky*. Harpenden: Kamera Books.

McAuley, L.K. 2016. '"What's Love Got to Do with It?": Sympathy, Antipathy and the Unsettling of Colonial American History in Film.' In R.A. Rosenstone and C. Parvulescu, eds. *A Companion to the Historical Film*. Malden, MA and Oxford: Wiley Blackwell.

McAuliffe, C. 2014. 'Back to the land: Pat Collins on *Silence*.' *Sight & Sound*. 14 February 2014. Accessed 9 February 2016. www.bfi.org.uk/news-opinion/sight-sound-magazine/interviews/back-land-pat-collins-silence

McCann, B. 2014. *Le Jour Se Lève: French Film Guide*. London and New York: I.B.Tauris.

McCormick, R.W. 2000. 'Gender, Film, and German History: Filmmaking by German Women Directors from Weimar to the Present.' In E.P. Frederiksen and M.K. Wallach, eds. *Facing Fascism and Confronting the Past: German Women Writers from Weimar to the Present*. Albany: State University of New York Press.

McDonald, T.J. 2010. *Virgin Territory: Representing Sexual Inexperience in Film*. Detroit, MI: Wayne State University Press.

McFarren, P. and F. Iglesias. 2013. *The Devil's Agent: Life, Times and Crimes of Nazi Klaus Barbie*. Bloomington, IN: Xlibris.

McLane, B.A. 2012. *A New History of Documentary Film*. 2nd ed. New York and London: Continuum.

Meiksins Wood, E. 2012. *Liberty and Property: A Social History of Western Political Thought from Renaissance to Enlightenment*. London and New York: Verso.

Mikaberidze, A., ed. 2013. *Atrocities, Massacres, and War Crimes: An Encyclopedia*. Santa Barbara, CA: ABC-CLIO, LLC.

Moeller, H-B. and G. Lellis. 2012. *Volker Schlöndorff's Cinema: Adaptation, Politics, and the 'Movie-Appropriate'*. Carbondale: Southern Illinois University Press.

Mogridge, G. (as Peter Parley) 1839. *Sergeant Bell and His Raree-Show*. London: Thomas Tegg.

Monaco, J. 2004 [1976]. *The New Wave; Truffaut, Godard, Chabrol, Rohmer, Rivette*. New York: Harbor.

Morrey, D. 2005. *Jean-Luc Godard*. Manchester and New York: Manchester University Press.

Mosley, P. 1981. *Ingmar Bergman: The Cinema as Mistress*. London: Marion Boyars.

Murphy, A.B., T.G. Jordan-Bychkov and B. Bychkova Jordan. 2014. *The European Culture Area: A Systematic Geography*. 6th ed. Lanham, MD: Rowman & Littlefield.

Murphy, R. 1992. *Sixties British Cinema*. London: BFI.

Murray, B. 2010. *Film and the German Left in the Weimar Republic: From Caligari to Kuhle Wampe*. Austin: University of Texas Press.

Neupert, R. 2006. 'The French New Wave: New stories, styles and auteurs.' In L. Badley, R.B. Palmer and S.J. Schneider, eds. *Traditions in World Cinema*. New Brunswick, NJ: Rutgers University Press.

Neupert, R. 2007. *A History of the French New Wave*. 2nd ed. Madison: University of Wisconsin Press.

Nietzsche, F. 1992 [1908]. *Ecce Homo: How One Becomes What One Is*. Translated by R.J. Hollingdale. London and New York: Penguin.

Nolley, K.S. 1999. 'Reflections on Class: *Tom Jones* (1963) and *Joseph Andrews* (1977).' In J.M. Welsh and J.C. Tibbetts, eds. *The Cinema of Tony Richardson: Essays and Interviews*. Albany: State University of New York Press.

Nowell-Smith, G. 2010. 'The Reception of the Nouvelle Vague in Britain.' In L. Mazdon and C. Wheatley, eds. *Je t'aime … moi non plus: Franco-British cinematic relations*. New York and Oxford: Berghahn Books.

Nygren, S. 2007. *Time Frames: Japanese Cinema and the Unfolding of History*. Minneapolis: University of Minnesota Press.

O'Pray, M. 2003. *Avant-Garde Film: Forms, Themes and Passions*. New York and London: Wallflower Press.

O'Shaughnessy, M. 2009. *La Grande Illusion*. London and New York: I.B.Tauris.

Orpen, V. 2007. *Cléo de 5 À 7*. Champaign: University of Illinois Press.

Paci, V. 2006. 'The Attraction of the Intelligent Eye: Obsessions with the Vision Machine in Early Film Theories.' In W. Strauven, ed. *The Cinema of Attractions Reloaded*. Amsterdam: Amsterdam University Press.

Parkinson, D. 1995. *History of Film*. London and New York: Thames and Hudson.

Parrill, W.B. 2006. *European Silent Films on Video: A Critical Guide*. Jefferson, NC and London: McFarland.

Paxton, R.O. 2006. 'France.' In C.P. Blamires and P. Jackson, eds. *World Fascism: A Historical Encyclopedia, Volume 1*. Santa Barbara, CA: ABC-CLIO.

Pencak, W. 2002. *The Films of Derek Jarman*. Jefferson, NC and London: McFarland.

Perez, G. 2000. 'Film in Review: Bad Boys – Klaus Kinski and Werner Herzog.' *The Yale Review* 88 (2): 185–194.

Perry, T., ed. 2006. *Masterpieces of Modernist Cinema*. Bloomington: Indiana University Press.

Persson, H-A. and B. Stråth, eds. 2007. *Reflections on Europe: Defining a Political Order in Time and Space*. New York and Oxford: Peter Lang.

Peters, A.K. 1987. *Jean Cocteau and His World: An Illustrated Biography*. New York and London: Vendome Press.

Petropoulos, J. 2014. *Artists Under Hitler: Collaboration and Survival in Nazi Germany*. New Haven, CT: Yale University Press.

Phillips, G.D. 1999. *Major Film Directors of the American and British Cinema*. Cranbury, NJ: Associated University Presses.

Phillips, G.D. 2004. *Godfather: The Intimate Francis Ford Coppola*. Lexington: University Press of Kentucky.

Phillips, G.D. and R. Hill, eds. 2004. *Francis Ford Coppola: Interviews*. Jackson: University Press of Mississippi.

Pipolo, T. 2010. *Robert Bresson: A Passion for Film*. Oxford and New York: Oxford University Press.

Pipolo, T. 2013. '*A Man Escaped*: Quintessential Bresson.' *Senses of Cinema*, March 2013. Accessed 1 February 2016. www.criterion.com/current/posts/2628-a-man-escaped-quintessential-bresson

Pirani, S. 2008. *The Russian Revolution in Retreat, 1920–24: Soviet Workers and the New Communist Elite*. London and New York: Routledge.

Portelli, A. 2005. 'The massacre at the Fosse Ardeatine: history, myth, ritual and symbol.' In K. Hodgkin and S. Radstone, eds. *Memory, History, Nation: Contested Pasts*. New Brunswick, NJ: Transaction.

Powrie, P. 2006. *The Cinema of France*. London: Wallflower Press.

Prager, B. 2007. *The Cinema of Werner Herzog: Aesthetic Ecstasy and Truth*. London and New York: Wallflower Press.

Prager, B. 2010. 'Landscape of the Mind: The Indifferent Earth in Werner Herzog's Films.' In G. Harper and J. Rayner, eds. *Cinema and Landscape*. Chicago, IL and Bristol: Intellect.

Pramaggiore, M. and T. Wallis. 2005. *Film: A Critical Introduction*, London: Laurence King.

Prelinger, E., A. Comini and H. Bachert. 1992. *Käthe Kollwitz*. New Haven, CT and London: Yale University Press.

Quandt, J. 2005. '*Au hazard Balthazar*.' The Criterion Collection. Accessed 1 September 2015. www.criterion.com/current/posts/370-au-hasard-balthazar

Reader, K. 2010. *La Regle Du Jeu: French Film Guide*. London and New York: I.B.Tauris.

Reeves, N. 2003. *The Power of Film Propaganda: Myth or Reality?* New York and London: Continuum.

Reimer, R.C. and C.J. Reimer. 2008. *The A to Z of German Cinema*. Lanham, MD: Scarecrow Press.

Renoir, J. 1974. *My Life and My Films*. London: Collins.

Renoir, J. 1989. *Renoir on Renoir: Interviews, Essays and Remarks*. Translated by C. Volk. Cambridge and New York: Cambridge University Press.

Renoir, J. 2004. 'Introduction to La Règle du jeu.' *La Règle du jeu*. DVD. Directed by Jean Renoir (1939). New York: Criterion Collection.

Rheuban, J. 1991. '*The Marriage of Maria Braun*: History, Melodrama, Ideology.' In J. Rheuban, ed. *The Marriage of Maria Braun: Rainer Werner Fassbinder, director*. New Brunswick, NJ: Rutgers University Press.

Robinson, D. 1997. *Das Cabinet Des Dr. Caligari*. London: BFI.

Rose, G. 2007. *Visual Methodologies: An Introduction to the Interpretation of Visual Materials*. London: Sage.

Rosenbaum, J. 2003. 'Abbas Kiarostami.' In M. Saeed-Vafa and J. Rosenbaum, eds. *Abbas Kiarostami*. Urbana and Chicago: University of Illinois Press.

Rosenstone, R., ed. 1995. *Revisioning History: Film and the Construction of a New Past*. Princeton, NJ: Princeton University Press.

Roth, M.S. 1995. 'Hiroshima mon amour: You Must Remember This.' In R. Rosenstone, ed. *Revisioning History: Film and the Construction of a New Past*. Princeton, NJ: Princeton University Press.

Rowell, G. and A. Jackson. 1984. *The Repertory Movement: A History of Regional Theatre in Britain*. Cambridge and New York: Cambridge University Press.

Ruberto, L.E. and K.M. Wilson, eds. 2007. *Italian Neorealism and Global Cinema*. Detroit, MI: Wayne State University Press.

Rueschmann, E. 2000. *Sisters on Screen: Siblings in Contemporary Cinema*. Philadelphia: Temple University Press.

Sadoul, G. 1972. *Dictionary of Films*. Translated by P. Morris. Berkeley and Los Angeles: University of California Press.

Sakwa, R. 1998. *Soviet Politics in Perspective*. 2nd ed. London and New York: Routledge.

Salles Gomes, P.E. 1971. *Jean Vigo*. Berkeley and Los Angeles: University of California Press.

Samuels, C.T. 2009 [1972]. 'Encountering Robert Bresson.' In B. Cardullo, ed. *The Films of Robert Bresson: A Casebook*. London and New York: Anthem Press.

Sanders-Brahms, H. 2005. 'The Lost Face of Germany.' In W. Everett and A. Goodbody, eds. *Revisiting Space: Space and Place in European Cinema*. Bern: Peter Lang.

Sarris, A. 2005 [1962]. 'Auteur Theory and Film Evaluation.' *Film Culture* 27: 1–8. In T. E. Wartenberg and A. Curran, eds. *The Philosophy of Film: Introductory Texts and Readings*. Malden, MA and Oxford: Blackwell.

Sartre, J.-P. 1982 [1948]. *Existentialism and Humanism*. London: Methuen.

Sartre, J.-P. 1992 [1956]. *Being and Nothingness*. New York: Simon & Schuster.

Scheunemann, D., ed. 2003. *Expressionist Film: New Perspectives*. Rochester, NY: Camden House.

Schindler, S.K. and L.P. Koeprick, eds. 2007. *The Cosmopolitan Screen: German Cinema and the Global Imaginary, 1945 to the Present*. Ann Arbor: University of Michigan Press.

Schneckenburger, M. 2000. 'Sculpture.' In K. Ruhrberg, K. Honnef, M. Schneckenburger, C. Fricke and I.F. Walther, eds. *Art of the 20th Century*. Köln and London: Taschen.

Seger, M. 2014. 'Deep Space Compositions in Italian Film: Le Quattro Volte, All at Once.' *The Italianist* 34 (2): 292–297. Accessed 19 February 2016. www.academia.edu/7377714/DEEP_SPACE_COMPOSITIONS_IN_ITALIAN_FILM_Le_quattro_volte_All_at_Once

Sellier, G. 2008. *Masculine Singular: French New Wave Cinema*. Translated by K. Ross. Durham, NC: Duke University Press.

Service, T. 2014. 'Symphony guide: Mahler's Ninth.' *The Guardian*, 29 July 2014. Accessed 17 February 2016. www.theguardian.com/music/tomservice-blog/2014/jul/29/mahlers-ninth-tom-service-symphony-guide

Shiel, M. 2006. *Italian Neorealism: Rebuilding the Cinematic City*. New York: Columbia University Press.

Silberman, M. 1995. *German Cinema: Texts in Context*. Detroit, MI: Wayne State University Press.

Sinyard, N. 2000. *Jack Clayton*. Manchester: Manchester University Press.

Smalls, J. 2013. 'Creating Homoutopia: Féral Benga's Body in the Matrix of Modernism.' In F. Sweeney and K. Marsh, eds. *Afromodernisms: Paris, Harlem and the Avant-Garde*. Edinburgh: Edinburgh University Press.

Smele, J.D. 2015. *Historical Dictionary of the Russian Civil Wars, 1916–1926*. Lanham, MD: Rowman & Littlefield.

Smith, P.J. 2006. 'Spirit of the Beehive: Spanish Lessons.' *The Criterion Collection*. Accessed 5 August 2015. www.criterion.com/current/posts/447-the-spirit-of-the-beehive-spanish-lessons

Solanas, F. and O. Getino. 1997 [1969]. 'Towards a Third Cinema: Notes and Experiences for the Development of a Cinema of Liberation in the Third World.' In M.T. Martin, ed. *New Latin American Cinema, Volume 1, Theory, Practices, and Transcontinental Articulations*. Detroit, MI: Wayne State University Press.

Solomon, S.J. 1972. *The Film Idea*. New York: Harcourt Brace Jovanovich.

Sontag, S. 1983. *A Susan Sontag Reader*. New York: Vintage.

Sorlin, P. 2007. 'Changes in experimental filmmaking between the 1920s and the 1960s: On Luis Buñuel.' In A. Graf and D. Scheunemann, eds. *Avant-garde Film*. New York and Amsterdam: Rodopi.

Staiger, J. 2013. 'Independent of what? Sorting out differences from Hollywood.' In G. King, C. Molloy and Y. Tzioumakis, eds. *American Independent Cinema: Indie, Indiewood, and Beyond*. London and New York: Routledge.

Stam, R. 2000. 'The Birth of the Spectator.' In R. Stam. *Film Theory: An Introduction*. Malden, MA and Oxford: Blackwell.

Stecker, R. 2000. 'Is It Reasonable to Attempt to Define Art?' In N. Carroll, ed. *Theories of Art Today*. Madison: University of Wisconsin Press.

Steene, B. 1970. 'Images and Words in Ingmar Bergman's Films.' *Cinema Journal* 10 (1): 23–33.

Steimatsky, N. 2008. *Italian Locations: Reinhabiting the Past in Postwar Cinema*. Minneapolis: University of Minnesota Press.

Steinberg, J. 2011. *Bismarck: A Life*. Oxford and New York: Oxford University Press.

Stern, J. P. 1980. 'Syberberg's Hitler.' *New York Review of Books*, 29 May 1980: 47.

Sterritt, D. 1998. *Jean-Luc Godard: Interviews*. Jackson: University Press of Mississippi.

Stevenson, J. 2002. *Lars von Trier*. London: BFI.

Stone, C.L. 2005. 'Aguirre Goes to the Movies: Twentieth-Century Visions of Colonial-Era "Relaciones".' *Chasqui: revista de literatura latinoamericana* 34: 24–35.

Stone, I. 2013. 'Para-Formalistic Discourse and Virtual Space in Film.' In D. Harrison, ed. *Digital Media and Technologies for Virtual Artistic Spaces*. Hershey, PA: IGI Global.

Stremmel, K. 2004. *Realism*. Köln: Taschen.

Sultanik, A. 1986. *Film: A Modern Art*. New York, London and Toronto: Cornwall Books.

Sundholm, J., I. Thorsen, L.G. Andersson, O. Hedling, G. Iversen and B.T. Moller. 2012. *Historical Dictionary of Scandinavian Cinema*. Lanham, MD: Scarecrow Press.

Sussex, E. 1969. *Lindsay Anderson*. London: Studio Vista.

Tarkovsky, A. 2005 [1986]. *Sculpting in Time: Reflections on the Cinema*. Translated by K. Hunter-Blair. Austin: University of Texas Press.

Tarkovsky, A. 2013. *Life, Life: Selected Poems*. 3rd ed. Translated by V. Rounding. Maidstone: Crescent Moon Publishing.

Taylor, B.F. 2006. *The British New Wave: A Certain Tendency?* Manchester: Manchester University Press.

Taylor, R. 1988. 'Soviet cinema as popular culture: or, the extraordinary adventures of Mr Nepman in the land of the silver screen.' *Revolutionary Russia* 1 (1): 36–56.

Taylor, R. 2001. *Battleship Potemkin: The Film Companion*. London and New York: I.B.Tauris.

Thompson, K. 1988. *Breaking the Glass Armor: Neoformalist Film Analysis*. Princeton, NJ: Princeton University Press.

Trier, L.V. and T. Vinterberg. 2000 [1995]. 'Dogma 95/The Vow of Chastity.' p.o.v. 10. Accessed 14 March 2016. http://pov.imv.au.dk/Issue_10/section_1/artc1A.html

Tsivian, Y., ed. 2004. *Lines of Resistance: Dziga Vertov and the Twenties*. Bloomington: Indiana University Press.

Tsivian, Y. 2015. 'Montage Theory II (Soviet Avant-Garde).' In E. Branigan and W. Buckland, eds. *The Routledge Encyclopedia of Film Theory*. London and New York: Routledge.

Tudor, A. 2012. 'Genre.' In B.K. Grant, ed. *Film Genre Reader IV*. Austin: University of Texas Press.

Turk, E.B. 1989. *Child of Paradise: Marcel Carné and the Golden Age of French Cinema*. Cambridge, MA: Harvard University Press.

Turner, J. 2013. 'A Girl and a Gun.' *London Review of Books* 35 (19): 35–37.

Turvey, M. 2011. *The Filming of Modern Life: European Avant-Garde Film of the 1920s*. Cambridge, MA: MIT Press.

Tweedie, J. 2013. *The Age of New Waves: Art Cinema and the Staging of Globalization*. Oxford and New York: Oxford University Press.

Uecker, M. 2001. 'A Fatal German Marriage: the National Subtext of Fassbinder's Die Ehe der Maria Braun.' *German Life and Letters* 54 (1): 45–59. Accessed 28 March 2016. http://onlinelibrary.wiley.com/doi/10.1111/1468-0483.00188/abstract

Valcke, J. 2008. 'Rhythmical Images and Visual Music.' In E. Lindley and L. McMahon, eds. 'Rhythms: essays in French literature, thought and culture.' *Modern French Identities* 68: 201–216.

Varon, J. 2004. *Bringing the War Home: the Weather Underground, the Red Army Faction, and Revolutionary Violence in the Sixties and Seventies*. Berkeley and Los Angeles: University of California Press.

Villanueva, D. 1997. *Theories of Literary Realism*. Translated by M.I. Spariosu and S. García-Castañón. Albany: State University of New York Press.

Vincendeau, G. 2002. '*Pépé le Moko*.' In E. Buscombe and R. White, eds. *British Film Institute Film Classics, Volume 1*. London and New York: Routledge.

Wagstaff, C. 2007. *Italian Neorealist Cinema: An Aesthetic Approach*. Toronto: University of Toronto Press.

Waldron, D. 2014. '"Pushing Yourself into Existence": Language, Trauma, Framing in Pat Collins's Silence (2012).' *Nordic Journal of English Studies* 13 (2): 202+. *Academic OneFile*. Accessed 18 February 2016. http://go.galegroup.com/ps/i.do?id=GALE%7CA396323391&v=2.1&u=anglia_itw&it=r&p=AONE&sw=w&asid=ae13c12e1191 1f1a25075eb4dab5d53c

Waller, G.A. 1981. 'Aguirre, Wrath of God: History, Theater, and the Camera.' *South Atlantic Review* 46 (2): 55–69.

Watson, W.S. 1996. *Understanding Rainer Werner Fassbinder: Film as Private and Public Art*. Columbia: University of South Carolina Press.

Wayne, M. 2002. *The Politics of Contemporary European Cinema: Histories, Borders, Diasporas*. Bristol and Portland, OR: Intellect.

Weinberg, R. 1993. *The Revolution of 1905 in Odessa: Blood on the Steps*. Bloomington: Indiana University Press.

Welsh, J.M., G.D. Phillips and R.F. Hill. 2010. *The Francis Ford Coppola Encyclopedia*. Lanham, MD: Scarecrow Press.

Wenders, W. 1997. *The Act of Seeing: Essays and Conversations*. London: Faber & Faber.

West-Leuer, B. 2009. 'Film Essay Colonial Aggression and Collective Aggressor Trauma.' *The International Journal of Psychoanalysis* 90 (5): 1157–1168.

Weston, J. 2003. *The Film Director's Intuition: Script Analysis and Rehearsal Techniques*. Studio City, CA: Michael Wiese Productions.

White, J. 2008. 'Love on the Dole (1943).' In S. Barrow and J. White, eds. Fifty *Key British Films*. London and New York: Routledge.

White, J. 2015. 'À bout de soufflé/Breathless (1959).' In S. Barrow, S. Haenni and J. White, eds. *The Routledge Encyclopedia of Films*. London and New York: Routledge.

Whyte, J. 2013. 'Irish odyssey.' *CineOutsider, beyond the mainstream*, 15 August 2013. Accessed 9 February 2016. www.cineoutsider.com/reviews/films/s/silence.html

Williams, J.S. 2006. *Jean Cocteau*. Manchester and New York: Manchester University Press.

Williams, T. 2014. *Germaine Dulac: A Cinema of Sensations*. Champaign: University of Illinois Press.

Willis, H. 2005. *New Digital Cinema: Reinventing the Moving Image*. London: Wallflower.

Wilson, E. 2001. 'Deforming femininity: Catherine Breillat's Romance.' In L. Mazdon, ed. *France on Film: Reflections on Popular French Cinema*. London: Wallflower.

Wilson, E. 2006. *Alain Resnais*. Manchester: Manchester University Press.

Witt, M. and M. Temple, eds. 2004. *The French Cinema Book*. London: BFI.

Woods, W.F. 2014. *The Medieval Filmscape: Reflections of Fear and Desire in a Cinematic* Mirror. Jefferson, NC: McFarland.

Wymer, R. 2005. *Derek Jarman*. Manchester and New York: Manchester University Press.

Zavattini, C. 2008 [1952]. 'Some Ideas on Cinema.' In A. Gazetas, ed. *An Introduction to World Cinema*. 2nd ed. Jefferson, NC: McFarland.

Ziolkowski, E. 2011. *The Literary Kierkegaard*. Evanston, IL: Northwestern University Press.

SUGGESTIONS FOR FURTHER READING

Andrews, D. 2013. *Theorizing Art Cinemas: Foreign, Cult, Avant-Garde, and Beyond*. Austin: University of Texas Press.

Betz, M. 2009. *Beyond the Subtitle: Remapping European Art Cinema*. Minneapolis: University of Minnesota Press.

Dyer, R. and G. Vincendeau, eds. 1992. *Popular European Cinema*. London and New York: Routledge.

Eleftheriotis, D. 2001. *Popular Cinemas of Europe: Studies of Texts, Contexts and Frameworks*. New York: Continuum.

Elsaesser, T. 2005. *European Cinema: Face to Face with Hollywood*. Amsterdam: Amsterdam University Press.

Everett, W., ed. 2005. *European Identity in Cinema*. 2nd ed. Bristol and Portland, OR: Intellect Books.

Ezra, E. 2004. *European Cinema*. Oxford and New York: Oxford University Press.

Forbes, J., and S. Street, eds. 2000. *European Cinema: An Introduction*. Basingstoke and New York: Palgrave.

Fowler, C., ed. 2002. *The European Cinema Reader*. London and New York: Routledge.

Galt, R. 2006. *The New European Cinema: Redrawing the Map*. New York: Columbia University Press.

Galt, R. and K. Schoonover, eds. 2010. *Global Art Cinema: New Theories and Histories*. Oxford and New York: Oxford University Press.

Kovács, A.B. 2007. *Screening Modernism: European Art Cinema, 1950–1980*. Chicago, IL and London: University of Chicago Press.

INDEX